CW00741025

Treasures Afoot

TREASURES AFOOT

Shoe Stories from the Georgian Era

KIMBERLY S. ALEXANDER

Johns Hopkins University Press | Baltimore

© 2018 Johns Hopkins University Press
All rights reserved. Published 2018
Printed in China
2 4 6 8 9 7 5 3

Johns Hopkins University Press
2715 North Charles Street
Baltimore, Maryland 21218-4363
www.press.jhu.edu

Library of Congress Cataloging-in-Publication Data
Names: Alexander, Kimberly S., 1963–, author.
Title: Treasures afoot : shoe stories from the Georgian era /
Kimberly S. Alexander.
Description: Baltimore : Johns Hopkins University Press, 2018. | Includes
bibliographical references and index.
Identifiers: LCCN 2017046659| ISBN 9781421425849 (hardcover : acid-free paper) |
ISBN 9781421425856 (electronic) |
ISBN 142142584X (hardcover : acid-free paper) |
ISBN 1421425858 (electronic)
Subjects: LCSH: Shoes—United States—History—18th century. |
Shoemakers—Great Britain—History—18th century. |
Clothing and dress—United States—History—18th century. |
Fashion—United States—History—18th century. |
United States—History—Colonial period, ca. 1600–1775. |
United States—Social life and customs—To 1775.
Classification: LCC TS1000 .A376 2018 | DDC 391.4/1309033—dc23
LC record available at https://lccn.loc.gov/2017046659

A catalog record for this book is available from the British Library.

Frontispiece: A composite view of the types of textiles found in eighteenth-century clothing and accessories: brocaded silks, silk damasks, and hand-blocked chintz, among others. Author's collection, photograph by Andrew Davis, February 2017.

*Special discounts are available for bulk purchases of this book. For more information,
please contact Special Sales at specialsales@press.jhu.edu.*

Johns Hopkins University Press uses environmentally friendly
book materials, including recycled text paper that is composed of at least
30 percent post-consumer waste, whenever possible.

Contents

Acknowledgments • vii

INTRODUCTION • 3

ONE • 15
The Cordwainers

TWO • 43
Wedding Shoes

THREE • 81
The Value of a London Label

FOUR • 109
Coveting Calamancos:
From London to Lynn

FIVE • 127
The Cordwainer's Lament
*Benjamin Franklin and John Hose Testify on
the Effects of the Stamp Act*

SIX • 145
"For My Use, Four Pair of Neat Shoes"
*George Washington, Virginia Planter, and
Mr. Didsbury, Boot- and Shoemaker of London*

SEVEN • 159
Boston's Cordwainers Greet President Washington, 1789

CONCLUSION • 171

EPILOGUE • 177

Appendixes • 181   Glossary • 185
Notes • 189   Bibliography • 215   Index • 223

Acknowledgments

Writing this book has been one of the most humbling experiences of my life. The process has filled me with immense appreciation and gratitude for the many scholars, museum professionals, and historical trades practitioners whose work has contributed to this volume both directly and indirectly, as well as for the many new colleagues I have met, whom I have now come to number among my closest friends.

Over the course of nearly eight years, I have visited twenty-nine institutions, examined countless pairs of shoes and textiles, and read hundreds of pages from letters, diaries, account books, and almanacs. Gathering and viewing each piece of information has involved at least one individual to assist me—and usually more. So many souls have generously and unstintingly given of their time and talents: Elizabeth Semmelhack and Suzanne Peterson of the Bata Shoe Museum; Brian Lemay, Nathaniel Sheidley, Tricia Gilrein, and Elizabeth Roscio of the Bostonian Society; Cynthia Walker and Kate Mastrangelo of the Brick Store Museum; Janice Williams of the Buttonwoods Museum; Jan Hiester of the Charleston Museum; Becky Putnam, Nancy Lamb, and the costume committee of the Colonial Dames, Boston; Barbara Ward and Stephanie Rohwer Hewson of the Moffatt-

Ladd House and Gardens, Colonial Dames, Portsmouth; D. A. Saguto, Rob Welch, Valentine Povinelli, and Brett Walker of the Wilson Shoe Shop; Janea Whitaker and Sarah Woodyard of the Margaret Hunter Milliners and Mantuamakers Shop, and curators Linda Baumgarten, Kimberly Ivy, and Neal Hurst, all of the Colonial Williamsburg Foundation; Vanessa DeZorzi and Aimie Westphal of the Currier Museum of Art; Sandra Waxman of the Dedham Historical Society; John Page, Edith Celley, and Mike Marshall of the Haverhill Historical Society; David (Ned) Lazaro of Historic Deer-field; Jane Nylander and Jeanne Gamble of Historic New England; Katherine Chaison of the Ipswich Museum; the staff of the Lynn Museum and the Massachusetts Historical Society; Susan P. Schoelwer and Amanda Isacc of the Mount Vernon Ladies' Association; Malia Ebel of the New Hampshire Historical Society; John Carmichael and the board of the Newmarket Histor-ical Society; Paula Richter of the Peabody Essex Museum / Phillips Library; Richard Candee, Gerald Ward, and Lainey McCartney of the Portsmouth Historical Society / John Paul Jones House; Tom Hardiman and the staff of the Portsmouth Athenæum; Tara Vose Raiselis of the Saco Museum; Emily Murphy of the Salem Maritime National Historic Site; Elizabeth Farrish of the Strawbery Banke Museum; Astrida Schaeffer and Dale Valena of the University of New Hampshire Museum and Special Collections; and Sandra Rux and Jeffrey Hopper of the Warner House.

In 2015, Sandra Rux and I co-curated an exhibition entitled "Cosmopolitan Consumption: New England Shoe Stories, 1750–1850," at the Portsmouth Athenæum, and much of the work that went into the exhibition appears on these pages. In addition to collaborating with Sandra, it was a delight to work with Tom Hardiman, Jeff Hopper, Susan Kress Hamilton, Julia Roberts, Steve Roberts, Elise Danielson, Mary Doering, and the Exhibits Committee of the Portsmouth Athenæum.

An Andrew Oliver Research Fellowship (2016–2017) from the Massachu-setts Historical Society also aided in moving this publication forward, add-ing to the depth of my understanding of pre-1750s textiles and accessories. Working with Anne Bentley, Anna Clutterbuck-Cook, Ondine LaBlanc, Sara Georgini, Elaine Heavey, Sabina Beauchard, Rakashi Chand, Daniel Hinchen, Kate Viens, Conrad Wright, and Chris Worrell made for an excep-tionally satisfying year of both research and collegiality.

As someone with substantial social anxiety, talking about shoes has proved to be a natural conversation icebreaker. And I have talked to dozens of folks about shoes from the past and the present. The stories shared with me have been full of delight—wonderfully rich, and frequently poignant. Informal conversations and correspondence frequently had an impact on my way of thinking about shoes, and for that I thank Stacy Fraser, Joanne Begiato, Jessica Parr, Abby Battis, Liz Covart, Gillian Cusak, Rebecca Mitchell, Meaghan Reddick, J. L. Bell, Trish Allen, Geri Walton, Elaine Chalus, Jane Walton, Lauren Stowell, Abby Cox, Angela Trowbridge Burnley, Sherry Wood, Deborah Kraak, Alden O'Brien, Ben Marsh, Zara Anishanslin, Linzy Brekke-Aloise, Donna Thorland, Bridget Swift, James Garvin, Donna-Belle Garvin, Colin Michael Hose, Linda Pardoe, and Emma Hope.

My colleagues at the University of New Hampshire, especially Eliga Gould, Jan Golinski, and Robert Macieski, have encouraged me along the way, as have Donna Seger and my colleagues at Salem State University. At both institutions, I have benefited from conversations about material culture, architecture, landscapes, and museum studies that often gravitated back to shoes.

Shoe and historic textile and costume historians Tara Vose Raiselis, Nicole Rudolph, Rebecca Shawcross, Linda Baumgarten, Neal Hurst, Althea MacKenzie, Ned Lazaro, June Swann, Paula Richter, Nancy Rexford, Mary Doering, Lynn Zacek Bassett, Edward Meader, and Giorgio Riello have provided assistance at key junctures. I am especially indebted to D. A. Saguto, who has been a constant source of knowledge, which he has shared most generously over the past few years. His insights have greatly improved the volume that you now hold.

My brilliant editor, Elizabeth Demers, at Johns Hopkins University Press believed in the book from the outset, and her keen editorial insight helped revamp the early version of the manuscript. Kathryn Marguy, Meagan Szekely, and Lauren Straley managed the minutia of the process with good spirits and a light touch; Kathleen Capels added her masterstroke in the copy edits, which brought polish to the many rough bits. Juliana McCarthy, Gene Taft, and the entire Johns Hopkins University Press staff have offered support and guidance throughout the process. Their dedication and professionalism is evident at every turn. The photographs of Andrew Davis, Ellen McDermott, and Penny Leveritt added considerably to the visual qualities of the publication.

There are stalwart friends and colleagues who supported and encouraged me along the way and helped me when my energy or confidence flagged. Among them are my sister Amy Alexander, Lynne Francis-Lunn, Karina Corrigan, Tara Raiselis, Jeffrey Hopper, Susan Holloway Scott, Astrida Schaeffer, Kathy Jablonski, Janith Bergeron, Cynthia Chin, and Anne Bentley. Digging well back in time, I offer a special thank-you to my Boston University PhD advisors, Keith N. Morgan and Richard Candee, whose valuable lessons I carry with me to this day in my own research and teaching.

To my family, I owe so much: my grandparents, particularly newsman Grant Angus Salisbury; my extended family of my aunts and uncles and cousins; and especially my sisters Amy, Anne, Megan and my brothers Ben and Bill. A special debt of gratitude belongs to my parents, Suzanne Beckwith and James Alexander, for always encouraging me in every endeavor. In addition, my father and Tom Stocker have helped me visualize the world around me in a variety of ways—as an architect, an artist, and an art historian.

One of the greatest boons to my work is having the advantage of an esteemed historian in the house. To my husband—my professor—Dane Morrison, who saw the potential of this publication long before I did, and without whose encouragement it would still be languishing in a computer dead file—I dedicate the book with hearty and heartfelt love and appreciation. Finally, to live in a household with two professors can be a profound challenge, so, to my daughters Lydia and Abbie, I thank you both for adding brightness and light to my life, and for keeping me from becoming too absorbed in the work—reminding me that there should always be time enough for lemonade.

Treasures Afoot

I.1　*The Shoe Seller,* Martin Engelbrecht, colored engraving, circa 1750. The shoe seller (also referred to as the shoemaker's wife) presents a tempting tray, offering a wide array of colorful footwear: from sturdy boots to beribboned mules (shoes without a back quarter or a heel strap), and from children's shoes to women's metallic-lace buckle shoes. Her wares would have been familiar throughout Europe and in British America. Courtesy of the Bavarian National Museum, Munich, Germany.

INTRODUCTION

*I hate to complain. . . . No one is without difficulties, whether in high or
low life, and every person knows best where their own shoe pinches.*
Abigail Adams to Mary Smith Cranch, 21 March 1790

Abigail Adams (1744–1818) knew shoes. She knew that
a pair of shoes could tell much about their wearer: about a person's struggles and trials, as well as triumphs and successes. She
knew that shoes did not make a woman—or a man—but they
certainly could tell stories. Adams's keen insight connected hu-
man nature with footwear and invoked a question that challenges historians of both fashion and social life. What was it
about shoes that intrigued wearers and observers in the eighteenth century and continues to do so for us today? Shoes have
a creative, often playful expression of style that transforms craft
into art and transports the seemingly mundane into the realm
of the extraordinary. Fashion transforms both how we walk and
our overall carriage. It has the power to influence how we feel
about ourselves and the world we inhabit. It forms the perme-
able boundary between who we are and who we want to be.

Fashion is universal, enabling historians across time, place,
and culture to form an understanding of the people who made

I.2   A portrait of Abigail Adams, pastel on paper, Benjamin Blythe, 1766. Abigail was painted by Blythe
shortly after her 25 October 1764 marriage to John Adams. A companion portrait of Adams was also
completed by this artist. Collection of the Massachusetts Historical Society, artwork 01.026

I.3   Abigail Adams's yellow kidskin shoes, circa the 1790s. Abigail wore these stylish, decorated yellow slippers as the eighteenth century was drawing to a close. They were made in London by the popular shoemaking firm of Hoppe & Heath. Smithsonian Institution National Museum of American History, gift of Susan E. Osgood, negative number 2008-6451l

clothes and those who wore them. But shoes are different. As shoe scholar June Swann opines, "No other garment or accessory maintains the imprint of its wearer—even over long spans of time." A shoe molds to the foot and captures a facet of the physical characteristics of the wearer, as well as, by extension, an element of his or her personal history.[1] We can study how much wear occurred and on what part of the shoe, how a shoe was altered or repaired, why a shoe or a pair of shoes were saved and handed down—and, from this, form an idea of the ordinary lives of the people who wore them.[2]

This book introduces readers to the history of the shoe through seven chapters that reveal how shoes were made, sold, and worn during the "long eighteenth century" (1688–1815). It sets these shoe stories within a cosmopolitan world that carried the elegant fancies of fashionable London to the gentility of provincial British America. In so doing, it recovers lost histories—the journey of the shoe-à-la-mode from the trendiest shops in the days of the Georgian kings (1714–1820) to the striving farms and bustling seaports of Early America; the British and American cordwainers, who crafted these accessories; and the women who wore them to weddings, to church, to market, and for visits.[3]

Through the lives and letters of clever apprentices, skilled cordwainers,

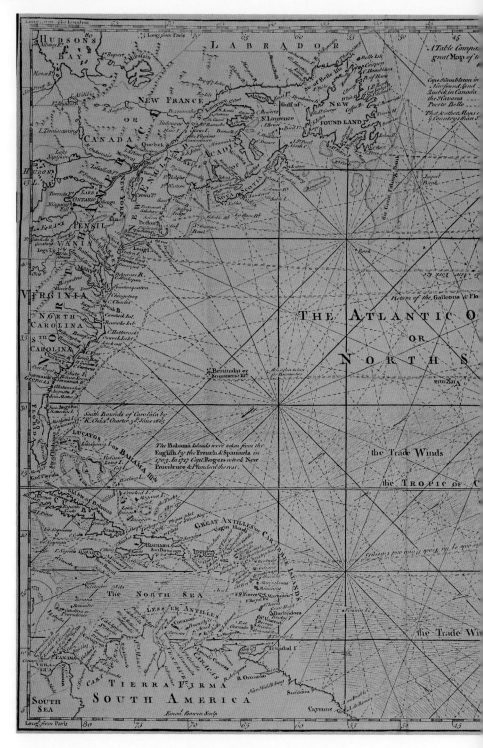

I.4 "A NEW CHART of the Vast ATLANTIC OCEAN: Exhibiting the SEAT OF WAR, both in EUROPE and AMERICA, likewise the Trade Winds & Course of Sailing from one Continent to the other, with the

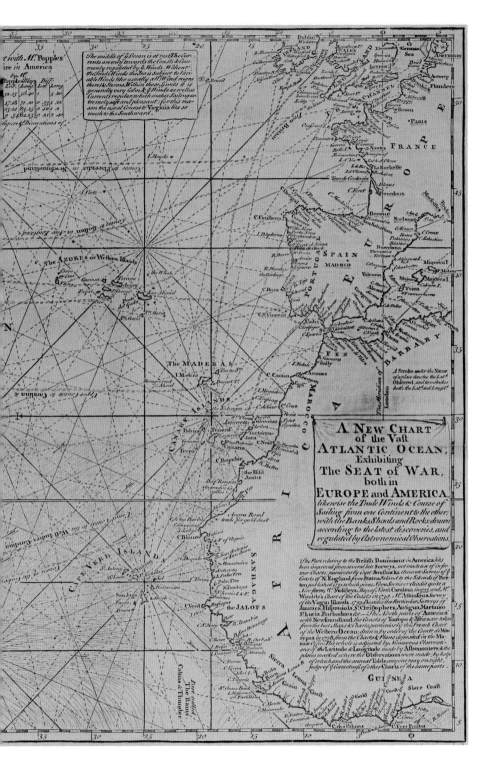

Banks, shoals and Rocks drawn according to the latest discoveries, and regulated by Astronomical Observations," by Emanuel Bowen, 1755. Collection of the Massachusetts Historical Society, Nuview item ID 3174, seq. 1

I.5 "The South part of New England, as it is Planted this yeare, 1639," by William Wood, published in London by John Dawsom, 1639. Courtesy of the Boston Public Library, Norman B. Leventhal Map Center Collection, identifier number 06_01_008627

wealthy merchants, and elegant brides, this volume takes readers on an Atlantic journey through bustling London streets, ships' cargo holds, New England shops, and, ultimately, the stocking-clad feet of eager consumers. It traces the fortunes and misfortunes of wearers as shoes were altered to accommodate poor health, flagging finances, and changing styles. We travel to the rugged Maine frontier in the 1740s, where an aspiring lady promenaded in her London-made silk brocade pumps (shoes with a heel, often attached to the foot with a buckle or ties); sail to London in 1766, where Benjamin Franklin and cordwainer John Hose caution Parliament on the catastrophic effects of British taxes on the shoe trade; journey to Philadelphia in 1775 as John Hancock presides over the Second Continental Congress, while also finding time to select silk and calamanco (glazed wool) shoes for his fiancée just months before their wedding; and arrive in Portsmouth, New Hampshire, in 1789 to peer in on Sally Brewster Gerrish, wearing her silk brocade shoes when riding in George Washington's carriage, on her way to a dance held in his honor during his first presidential tour.

Interweaving biography and material culture, this book raises a number of fresh questions about everyday life in Early America. It addresses how Americans in the Georgian decades used consumer goods—in particular, shoes—in the public sphere to signify who they aspired to be and what they valued, as well as conveying their hopes and dreams. It explores the dispersal of shoes from English manufactories to British American consumers, both bridging and binding an Atlantic community of fashion. It describes how these goods connected cordwainers (also known as shoemakers) in London, merchants in American seaports, and sophisticated gentility in the countryside. Lastly, the volume explains how these artifacts preserve an important part of American history. Many of the women featured in the shoe stories would be little known, if not forgotten, had their shoes not survived, allowing them to emerge from the shadows.

Their stories draw on shoes that are preserved in local, regional, national, and international collections, including the Bata Shoe Museum (Toronto), Bostonian Society's Old State House Museum (Boston), Buttonwoods Museum (Haverhill, Massachusetts), Charleston Museum (South Carolina), Colonial Williamsburg (Virginia), Connecticut Historical Society (Hartford), DAR Museum (Washington, DC), Historic Deerfield (Massachusetts), Historic New England (Haverhill, Massachusetts), Lynn Museum (Massachusetts), Los Angeles County Museum of Art, Massachusetts Historical Society (Boston), Metropolitan Museum (New York City), New Hampshire Historical Society (Concord), Northampton Shoe Museum (United Kingdom), Peabody Essex Museum (Salem, Massachusetts), Portsmouth Historical Society (New Hampshire), Royal Ontario Museum (Toronto), Strawbery Banke Museum (Portsmouth, New Hampshire), and Victoria and Albert Museum (London), among others.

This study traces the significance of shoes in eighteenth-century America, with a particular focus on the elite market. Set during the years predating the consumer revolution of the 1740s and moving into the Federalist Era, and drawing on journals and diaries, newspapers, and financial receipts, accounts, and ledgers—and, particularly, on the shoes themselves—the book fills an important gap in our understanding of consumption in Early America. It demonstrates how goods imported from Britain, and especially London, found a ready market in America, beginning in the early years of provincial life, when both local shoemakers and materials attuned to changing English styles were scarce, through the crisis of the Revolutionary War, and, finally, the creation of the new nation.

We can follow the three phases of a shoe's journey across the Atlantic: from the London shops of renowned master craftsmen such as Thomas Ridout and James Davis in Aldgate and John Hose in Cheapside; to the dressing rooms of genteel consumers who reworked and refurbished beloved family heirlooms; to the banquets, weddings, and dances at which British Americans proudly displayed their luxury footwear. The stories that these shoes tell reveal much about the lives of those who made and wore them.

First, we can trace many of these pairs back to their London shops through the labels that the craftsmen attached to the footbed, identifying the maker, place, and, occasionally, even the intended market (e.g., "for expo"). The shoes fabricated by these skilled artisans were among the earliest to feature labels, illustrating not only the maker's pride in his craft, but also a growing interest in advertising and trade specialization.[4] The abundance of extant shoes that carry the labels of the Hose family, Ridout & Davis, and W. Chamberlain & Sons underscores their importance as luxury commodities in American markets.[5]

Second, the prevalence of manufacturers' labels in American footwear collections helps establish a shoe's provenance and enables us to reconstruct the shoe stories that form the body of this book. Slippers, pumps, flats, and other forms of Early American footwear manufactured by British shoemakers have found their way into public institutions, due to both the high level of craftsmanship they display and their link with significant people and events.

Third, shoes were commonly treasured within families, lovingly reworked or refurbished, and handed down across generations. These shoe stories recover this little-known element of eighteenth-century life. They delve into the conditions surrounding the wearing of shoes by their owners: repairs, refashionings, clues to ailments, signs of aging, and alterations dictated by changing fashions, finances, or health. Many of the clues found in an examination of historic footwear are not present in the traditional historical record and thus serve to augment surviving documentation, especially relating to the lives of women.

The idea that a colonial Bostonian or Philadelphian could choose from a surprisingly wide range of footwear—made of calamanco, leather, silk damask, and brocades; in the form of slippers, pumps, mules (shoes without a back quarter or a heel strap), boots, clogs (also known as pattens, which were wood or leather and intended to protect shoes in inclement weather), and galoshes—reveals that the eighteenth century was indeed an age of consumption. Since colonial shoe wearers also could fashion their own uppers by embroidering them themselves, whether for a wedding or for everyday wear, this indicates a pride in craftsmanship and a parallel sense of economy. There is also

I.6   A pair of brocaded silk buckle shoes with a two-inch French heel, oval toe, and bright polychrome (multicolored) florals, made by London shoemaker John Hose & Son "at the Rose," Cheapside, circa 1770. These brocaded silk shoes signify quality and luxury—not only due to the materials, but also to the perfect matching of the pattern on the toes (and present at the heels), requiring additional use of the expensive textile. Courtesy of Historic New England, gift of Miss Mary C. Wheelwright, accession number 1919.140AB

an irony suggested by how these Americans purchased and used their shoes. They were avid consumers of the latest styles, attuned to the seasons, but they were also careful recyclers of their used goods, imaginatively reinventing them for other purposes and for passage down through the generations. Examples of the reuse of and repairs to shoes are found in the daybooks of many New England cordwainers. Women often brought in textiles or embroidered uppers to be made into shoes. Shoemakers, as well as lesser-skilled cobblers, enlarged shoes to accommodate changes in the wearer's size or weight over time, or dealt with podiatry issues, such as bunions or an uneven pronation. They remade shoes to fit a younger wearer or a toddler in the next generation, or updated an upper, heel, or tongue. Older textiles were cut down to use for new shoes. Men frequently had their shoes resoled or rebound.[6]

    Fourth, these Georgian shoe stories offer some insight into the ongoing debate over the process of anglicization in pre-revolutionary America. Historian John H. Murrin describes the colonies' upper crust, who displayed "a keen desire to recreate British society in America and took pride in the extent

I.7 A woman wearing a silk taffeta *robe à la polonaise*, 1778. This fashionably dressed woman, with her head turned slightly toward the viewer, exposes her leg from foot to just above the knee as she ties on her blue garter. From her bright yellow heeled shoe, to her ensemble adorned with ribbons and bows, to the plumes of her jaunty hat, the ensemble is intended to catch the eye. Engraving from *Galerie des modes et costumes français* (Paris: Esnauts & Rapilly, 1778-1787), plate 37

to which their societies were becoming increasingly Anglicized." T. H. Breen picks up and expands on this theme of anglicization, asserting that a desire to identify with Britain by purchasing imported goods extended through the "middling sorts" (consumers of modest means) and even lower classes. Breen frames this line of reasoning in terms of material goods, positing that a veritable consumer revolution began in the colonies about the 1740s. According to this argument, British merchants dumped vast amounts of goods onto American markets, and British Americans scooped up chests of tea, boxes of porcelains, reams of cloth, pounds of nails, and the like.[7]

Yet what happens if the kaleidoscope is shifted a bit and attention is focused on one specific consumer good? This volume argues that when we turn our gaze to a seemingly mundane, yet indispensable, article of fashion—the shoe—the anglicization interpretation becomes more complicated, more nuanced, and more unanticipated. Shoes tell us stories we might not expect to read about in Early America. British Americans didn't just purchase the shoes that English merchant houses fobbed off on them. They were sophisticated, selective consumers. They favored certain brands, ordering from makers whom they associated with high quality and upscale fashion. Moreover, they changed the shoes they bought according to their own needs and tastes. They engaged in adaptive reuse, modifying their shoes to their own specifications. In effect, they converted their British shoes into British American ones, connoting their own identity. This was literally a process of self-fashioning.

Eighteenth-century Americans, then, were not just consumers of goods foisted on the colonies. Rather, they were active participants in the selection of which goods to purchase, and from whom. This volume describes a long-term process in the consumer revolution, in which the upper class first began to assume agency in the process of selection. By the early republic, the middle class followed suit as this process trickled down to them. It foreshadows what was to come in the nineteenth and twentieth centuries, as even lower-class consumers became active participants in their purchases and imitated middle-class tastes.

1.1 Samuel Lane, almanac page from 1747. Lane kept detailed records of his profits and expenses. In July 1747, he notes that Mr. Bierton was cutting his jacket and breeches, as well as a coat for his younger brother Ebenezer. In August, he states that he has had half a load of English hay brought in from neighbor Ezra Barker. In October, he is having leather breeches made. He also notes making shoes for both Bierton and Barker. The rhythm of the seasons and work with neighbors strongly demarcate the Lane almanacs. New Hampshire Historical Society, Lane Family Papers, file number RS14868

THE CORDWAINERS

The last five years of my Service with my Father, viz,
from 16 to 21 years of my age, I made 1430 pair of Shoes.

Samuel Lane, 1739

Samuel Lane (1718–1806) was a rather ordinary man, a shoemaker by trade and deacon of his church in rural Stratham, New Hampshire. Yet he felt his life was significant enough to leave a record of his sixty-three years of comings and goings. Lane wrote down the highlights and the particulars of his long life: births and deaths, harsh winters and stifling summers, and, not surprisingly, the progress of his success. For if Lane was an ordinary American craftsman, he was also a prosperous one. From his diary we learn much about daily life in Early America and the role that shoes played in it.

In London, another cordwainer, John Hose (c. 1699–1769), also left records that reveal much about the shoe business in Great Britain during the reigns of the Georgian kings (1714–1820), although he left no journal as detailed as Samuel Lane's. The surviving records of London cordwainers such as Hose, Ridout, and Davis, and of the shoemakers' guild—the Worshipful Company of Cordwainers—as well as archives of Lon-

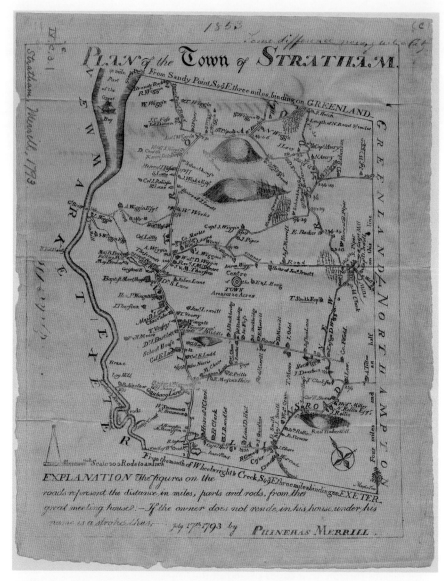

1.2. "PLAN of the Town of STRATHAM," by Phinehas Merrill, 17 July 1793, scale [1:39,600], 200 rods = 1 inch. Samuel Lane moved to Stratham in 1741, as a young man, to take advantage of the location for his business and for his family. He remained in Stratham until his death in 1806. Collection of the Massachusetts Historical Society, maps IV.c.3.1

1.3. Detail of "Cordonnier [Shoemaker]," a plate in Denis Diderot, *Encyclopédie, ou dictionnaire raisonné des sciences, des arts et des métiers*, vol. 3 (Paris: Brisson, 1763), color added. Lanmas/Alamy stock photo, image DG8D1X

don freedmen's papers (signifying the end of an apprenticeship), flesh out the details of a profession that had flourished since the Middle Ages.

LONDON AND THE HOSE FAMILY'S SHOP

A visit to John Hose's shoe shop brought the discriminating Georgian purchaser into the maw of one of Europe's great eighteenth-century metropolises. Skilled shoemakers, such as the well-established Hose family (John and his only son, Thomas), were located first "at the Rose" in Cheapside and later on Lombard Street, "at the boot." (Most likely these were signboards or hanging wooden signs designed to attract customers and identify locations.) Close by, one could easily find his competitors, a former Hose apprentice and journeyman named William Chamberlain, who also occupied a shop in Cheapside,

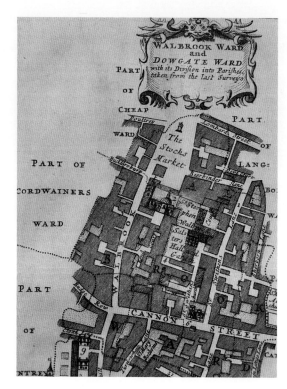

1.4. "Walbrook Ward and Dowgate Ward . . . with part of the Cordwainers Ward," in John Strype, *A Survey of the Cities of London and Westminster* (London: 1720). This survey contains a large number of illustrations, including important post–Great Fire maps, detailing the capital's parishes and wards. Author's collection

while Ridout & Davis hung their sign near Aldgate. They were among the scores of cordwainers who maintained active workshops and stores throughout London. Most were concentrated within the Ward of the Cordwainer, bounded to the north by Cheapside and Poultry, to the south by Cannon Street, to the west by Bread Street, and to the east by Walbrook.[1] D. A. Saguto notes that by 1738, there were "six to seven hundred master shoemakers on the books of the Worshipful Company of Cordwainers in London, but the corps of garrett masters operating off the company's roster were alleged to have inflated the true number of the city's shoemakers to as many as thirty thousand," not including translators (who refashioned "new" shoes from various bits) and cobblers (who repaired shoes). The trade also had large firms that employed up to 160 persons or more. In his testimony before Parliament in 1766, John Hose mentioned his workforce of more than 300, surely making it among the largest. The shops were open long hours, and many stayed busy until midnight.[2]

To reach the well-appointed shops within the Ward of the Cordwainer, the genteel consumer (or an agent) was required to navigate crowded, often

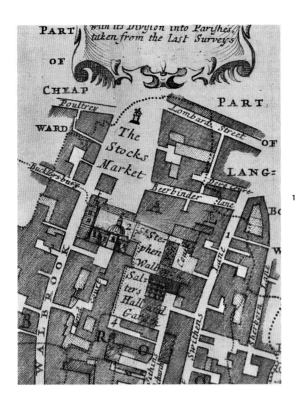

1.5 Detail from "Walbrook Ward and Dowgate Ward . . . with part of the Cordwainers Ward," in John Strype, *A Survey of the Cities of London and Westminster* (London: 1720). The detail shows Lombard Street, just below the cartouche on the upper right. Lombard Street "at the boot" became home to the Hose family's business after the death of patriarch John Hose. Author's collection

noxious, bustling streets. Within the Hose shop, a customer might be greeted by either Hose himself or his son Thomas, both of whom would assist those of sophisticated taste. The picture was more humble and often coarser in the back room of a shop or in the modest homes where craftsmen labored, making a carved wooden heel for women's shoes (or, for men, a stacked leather heel) or cutting and sewing quarters (sides of shoe uppers), vamps (part of the upper), and tongues (a flap at the throat of the vamp, under the lacing or buckles)—whatever was their specialty. An aspiring cordwainer, if fortunate enough to have secured an apprenticeship, spent the seven years of his indenture under the tutelage of a master shoemaker, followed by several years as a journeyman. Ultimately, if he attained a high level of proficiency and could produce a quality practice piece, he could gain admittance into the shoemakers' guild, or livery company: the Worshipful Company of Cordwainers.[3] For many (though not all), the goal was to eventually achieve the status of master and accept apprentices, thus continuing the cycle of the "art and mystery of making shoes."[4] Setting up a shop was expensive, however, and required a significant outlay of cash for space, materials, and tools, making it a difficult goal for many to achieve. Other family members no doubt assisted the Hose enterprise in some capacity, perhaps serving as apprentices.[5] They were probably among the 300 workers that John Hose claimed to represent in his testimony before Parliament. Thus the crafting of elegant shoes did not guarantee a life of comfort or ease.

An overview of the life and career of cordwainer John Hose—a successful purveyor of luxury footwear and patriarch of a flourishing shoemaking family—reveals that even in a major metropolis such as London, and even for those in the upper echelon of their trade, the rewards were mixed.[6] Cordwainers worked long hours. Most shopkeepers opened their doors from about six in the morning until eight in the evening, six days a week. Making shoes frequently required rigorous concentration and a fine hand with tools; the careful husbanding of one's own time and that of dozens, even hundreds, of employees; facility with novel materials and exotic styles; and scrupulous attention to mercurial changes in fashion. In addition, supplies were dear, and delivery was erratic. To craft footwear for London's most fashionable denizens, Hose ordered materials from around the globe, including cordovan (goatskin leather) from Spain and Morocco, and silk and silk thread from China and France.[7]

Complicating the work further, theft and shoplifting were constant concerns.[8] Shoplifter Thomas Waldron, for example, helped himself to a pair of pumps from Hose's Aldgate shop. According to documents preserved in the Old Bailey Gaol, the crime occurred on 28 June 1740. It was a Saturday evening in the congested, dense commercial Cheapside neighborhood, which would have seen many strollers out for the evening. There were dozens of taverns lining the streets where the Hose family ran their shop. It was getting on toward 9:00 p.m., and the bells of St. Mary-le-Bow had probably just rung, when shouts disturbed the master shoemaker's concentration.[9] As Hose testified in the Old Bailey proceedings, "Last Saturday was se'n night, about half an Hour after 8 at Night, I had a Customer or two in my Shop, (I live in Cheapside) and a little Girl cry'd out—Mr. Hose, a Man has got a Pair of Pumps."[10]

The forty-one-year-old Hose was lame and could not give chase, but an alert journeyman raced from the shop to apprehend the would-be thief. The support of one's neighbors—whether employees, clients, or friends—was a common element in the London shopkeeper's business. In the city, residents looked out for one another, pitching in to help when crime or fire or flood threatened the shop. Colonial shoemaker Samuel Lane, in far-distant Stratham, New Hampshire, similarly would assist his neighbors in times of need.

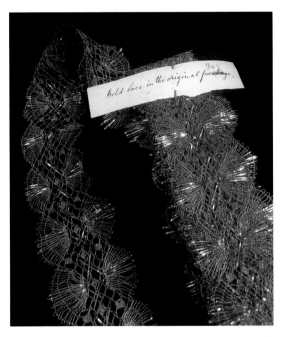

1.6   A length of gold lace, circa the mid-eighteenth century, stored in the original laid paper wrapper, with the price written in iron gall ink. A pencil note on the outer wrap reads: "Gold lace given me with other old-fashioned things by my mother. A.S.U." Lace such as this became trim for just about any type of clothing or accessory for men, women, and children. It was used for bonnets, caps, shoes, waistcoats, gowns, stomachers (a separate piece at the center front of a bodice), and even bodices or stays. Metallic lace was the finishing touch that could add a desired sparkle and shine to eighteenth-century clothing. Collection of the Massachusetts Historical Society, artifact number 1304, removed from the Upham Clark family papers, gift of Hugh Upham Clark, 1978

Despite the overwhelming evidence and abundance of witnesses who supported Hose's account, Waldron was found not guilty and acquitted, leaving the maker with a loss of the invested time and materials. Perhaps Waldron was able to hide the proof—the ill-gotten pumps—in a nearby churchyard, which is where Hose's journeyman caught him.[11] The "turn'd leather pumps" that so tempted the thief were valued at ten pence. At that price, the pumps would have been a modest pair of men's shoes.

John Hose was elected a master of the Worshipful Company of Cordwainers in July 1760. He had a significant amount of property at the time of his death in 1769, as revealed in his probate inventory, and he appears to have been held in esteem by his peers. In February 1766, due to his standing within London's merchant community—both as an employer and as an exporter of valuable luxury items to North America and the West Indies, which generated revenue for the British government—as well as through his business connections with London alderman Barlow Trecothick, Hose was called to give testimony before Parliament regarding the Stamp Act. His son Thomas (c. 1734-1787) and grandson Thomas Jr. (1762-1846) however, were ultimately unable to continue the success of the shop. The precarious nature of a cordwainer's life is indicated by a seemingly mundane document that survives in the Hose family papers.

Thomas Hose finished his apprenticeship with his father and ultimately became a master in the Worshipful Company of Cordwainers himself in 1784. Yet by 1797, the family business suffered major downturns. Thomas's son, Thomas Jr., provided an accounting of his career in a letter of application to the regents of Morden College, Blackheath. He hoped to be accepted into the residential accommodations at the college, which maintained a home for impoverished but hard-working tradespeople and guild members. In his application, Thomas mentioned his past success and noted that he was "engaged in business [at Lombard Street] in exporting goods to America and the British West Indies from the period of 1783-1797." This is a significant quote, because it reveals that the cordwainer was, at least to a certain extent, self-selecting his clientele and certainly had abundant knowledge of the destination of his products.[12] Although Thomas only made reference to his own experience, it is natural to speculate that his father also had a direct role in exporting shoes to America, especially when combined with the evidence supplied by the senior Hose in his surviving shoe labels and advertisements in colonial newspapers.

The Georgian Era brought dramatic changes in fashion and presented daunting challenges in finding the faddish materials that would answer seasonal fancies, even for master shoemakers such as the Hose family. In an increasingly globalized economy, with Western tastes influenced by the fantastical lure of *chinoiserie* and *turquoiserie* styles and the temptations of exotic dyes like cochineal red from Mexico, the Hose establishment needed to craft quantities of footwear that would dazzle the eye of the most cosmopolitan consumer. Success required an efficient business strategy that would expedite the design challenges. To this end, they arranged for financing with established merchant houses to procure the high-quality materials that made a Hose shoe a sought-after luxury item. Anticipating or, hopefully, influencing the upcoming season's styles, they ordered the softest leathers from Cordoba; gold and silver lace from Italy, France, and Spain; richly woven brocades from

1.7 Brocaded silk buckle shoes with a leather sole and carved wooden heel, London-made by John Hose & Son, circa 1760. These shoes are believed to be the wedding shoes of Elizabeth Lord, born in 1735 in Lyme, Connecticut, and married in 1760, at the age of twenty-five, to Jared Eliot in nearby Killingworth, Connecticut. Note the excellent pattern matching at the toes. Daughters of the American Revolution Museum, Washington, DC, accession number 3629.A-B

Spitalfields in England; bright, glazed wool calamanco from Norwich; and silk from China. Creating shine and luster were of tantamount importance.

The cordwainer or his assignees purchased or commissioned several portions of the shoe—the upper, vamp, and heels—from pieceworkers: men, women, and children scattered around the city and paid by the number of pieces, or shoe parts, they produced. Once a pair of Hose shoes were finished in the shop or workrooms, this footwear still faced a number of obstacles on the journey to distant markets. Even before the shoes left a London warehouse, they drew the attention of thieves and pilferers. On the westward voyage, fierce Atlantic gales whipped up waves that could deluge a ship's hold, tingeing a cargo with mold or mildew. Moreover, on the eve of the American

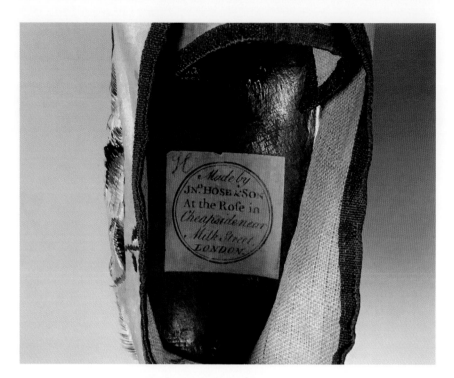

1.8   Detail, brocaded silk buckle shoes with a leather sole and carved wooden heel, London-made by John Hose & Son, circa 1760, showing the John Hose & Son label. Daughters of the American Revolution Museum, Washington, DC, accession number 3629.A-B

Revolution, shoes and other imported luxuries would be targeted for "non-intercourse" (i.e., non-importation) via the boycotts staged by Patriot leaders, such as John Hancock, in the cities of Portsmouth, Boston, Charleston, Williamsburg, Norfolk, and Philadelphia.

SAMUEL LANE'S WORLD

To follow the journey of a pair of Hose shoes, we must leave London and turn to the rural haunts of the colonial American countryside, far from the New World's fashionable seaports.[13] Shoemaking in eighteenth-century rural New England was a challenging enterprise, although it allowed a family to supplement its income from farming, lumbering, and husbandry. A suitable living in this world of small markets and primitive roads required every member of a family to contribute to the household, whether through agriculture, trades, or services. This was different from the world of Britain's urban shoemakers, who largely specialized in a single trade.

Shoemaking was essential to the colonial economy. Indeed, without a rudimentary shoemaking industry, the colonies would not have survived. We might take them for granted today, but "sensible shoes" were essential for the American colonists in the seventeenth and early eighteenth centuries. Captain John Smith, in his *Generall Historie of Virginia* (1624), emphasized the importance of good shoes to the colonial enterprise, stating that "for want of Shooes among the Oyster Banks wee tore our hatts and Clothes and those being worne, wee tied the Barkes of trees about our Feete to keepe them from being Cutt by the shelles amongst which we must goe or starve, yett how many thousand of Shooes hath been transported to these plantations."[14] Smith could not have trekked through a "howling wilderness" of forest trails and soggy swamps without rugged footwear. Likewise, horses were rare for later families of settlers, and good shoes eased the discomforts of travel along rough paths, primitive roads, and even the few pocked and muddied lanes that served as streets in the colonies.

John Smith's Jamestown settlement seems to have recruited cordwainers as early as 1609. By 1616, a domestic shoe trade was thriving in Virginia. The Massachusetts Bay Colony made similar efforts to foster a homegrown shoe industry. Soon after its founding, William Wood offered advice to would-be immigrants in his 1634 guide, *New England Prospect*, noting that "every man likewise must carry over good store of Apparrell . . . Hats, Bootes, Shooes, good Irish stockings, which if they be good, are much more service-able than knit-ones . . . [from England]."[15] Consequently, New England drew tradesmen who could practice the shoemaker's craft and accept the rigor of Puritan regulations. By 1635, shoemakers Henry Elwell and Philip Kirkland settled in Lynn, Massachusetts, and established the trade for which the "shoe city" would become renowned. Given the activity in shoemaking and tanning in the northern colonies, it is not surprising that the first American guild was that of the "Shoomakers of Boston." Its charter of incorporation was granted by the "Colony of the Massachusetts Bay" on 18 October 1648.

The Lanes, in Stratham and Hampton, New Hampshire, probably are the best-documented New England shoemakers, due to Samuel Lane's daybooks, or "almanacks," which provide a glimpse into the world of the colonial cordwainer. These daybooks, covering a sixty-year period, follow his life from his time as an apprentice to his father to his own old age. As a young man, Lane wrote, "The last five years of my Service with my Father viz from 16 to 21 years

1.9 "Jacob Sheafe, of Portsmouth, Esq. to Sam Lane," Samuel Lane invoice spanning April 1777 through June 1779. The itemized bill to Jacob Sheafe underscores the versatility of Samuel Lane and many American cordwainers. Lane supplied shoes and mending for Mr. and Mrs. Sheafe, their daughter (such as a "black girls shoes made on a man's last"), and a maid, in differing materials, sizes, and quality. He also mentions "7 barrels of Syder" sent by his son Joshua. Of interest in regard to payment and the bartering of goods for services, the final line of the document reads, "Ballanced this Acco[un]t as Equal as we could by Setting one thing against another." New Hampshire Historical Society, Lane family papers, 1727-1924, file number RS14277

of my age, I made 1430 pair of Shoes." This averages out to 286 pairs a year, crafted while still an apprentice. Yet only one pair of this family's large output of shoes are known to exist, despite contemporary accounts revealing that Lane-made shoes were a popular purchase in Portsmouth on market days.[16] Lane served all sectors of society: from the wealthy Portsmouth merchant Jacob Sheafe's family and their household servants and children, to hardworking fishing families on the Isles of Shoals, to his own farming and church neighbors in Stratham, Greenland, and Exeter.

Luxury British shoes were highly desirable among elite consumers in eigh-

1.10 The Smith Shoe Shop in Reading, Massachusetts, a typical ten-footer shoe workshop. The small out-building, placed on the National Register of Historic Places in 1985, is one of a few surviving remnants of the local home-shop shoemaking industry that prospered during the last years of the eighteenth century and up to the mid-nineteenth century. Similar extant examples are scattered throughout New England. Creative Commons CC-BY-SA 3.0 license, https://creativecommons.org, photograph by John Phelan

teenth-century British America. Yet much of the colonial American market was satisfied by local shoemakers: not only Samuel Lane of Stratham but also Colonel Joseph Welch of Plaistow, New Hampshire, and, in Massachusetts, Eleazar Pope of Salem, Moses Perkins or the Putnam family of Danvers, the Hewes of Lynnfield, and Francis Pingree of Rowley. The early factories in Lynn, Massachusetts, produced large quantities of ladies' shoes by the middle of the century (see chapter 5). Materials were costly and thus were purchased in judicious amounts. Colonel Welch, for example, bought only a single ounce of "endego" [*sic*] in 1768.[17] Most New England cordwainers could be found at work alone or with a single journeyman and one or two apprentices—and occasionally a slave—in a modest shop, known as a "ten-footer," surrounded by lasts and tools, or in a small space adjoining the house, such as a kitchen.[18]

A small shoe shop, such as those in New England, could not compete with

1.11   Interior view of the "Lye Shoe Shop, Essex St. previously on Mall St." Shops like this one were used for part of the shoemaking process in the central- or home-shop phase of shoemaking. It is possible to discern some elements of traditional shoemaking: a leather apron on the back wall, stools, and workbenches with tools and lasts scattered about. A cast iron stove was the heat source for the shoemakers, journeymen, and apprentices. Courtesy of the Lynn Public Library, via Digital Commonwealth

the production of most larger London shops, nor could it finance the purchase of exotic raw materials, especially quality leathers, that were required to make shoes in quantity. Instead, both British and British American shoemakers hired additional hands to supply the various components of shoes, such as carved heels for women's shoes and stacked leather pieces for men's shoes, as well as to cut uppers or embroider vamps. This piecework could be completed by several members of a family, either to supplement their income or to barter for services. In New England, a network of neighbors often supplied these various parts of a shoe, completing the work during the winter months, when they were not involved in agricultural or other seasonal endeavors. This home-shop system was found throughout New England. It would ultimately lend itself to larger production numbers, in combination with mechanization, in the decades after the American Revolution.

Notations such as the one found in the daybook of Colonel Joseph Welch (1734–1829) for April/June 1762, "by making Sarah cloth shoes with my sole," amplify the range of work completed by shoemakers. In this case, the client worked on or purchased the textile for the shoe upper—it could have been specially dyed fabric or an embroidered piece—for her own shoes, which he then completed with his leather sole.[19] The cost, calculated in Welch's own idiosyncratic system, was 4 shillings, comparable to the purchase of a new pair of workaday shoes.[20]

A colonial shoemaker possessed staggeringly versatile skills. All manner of footwear production, as well as the mending of shoes, composed the menu of offerings for cordwainers such as Samuel Lane or Joseph Welch. Many shoemakers made both plain and fancy women's, men's, and children's shoes. Slippers, boots (for walking, fishing, and riding), pumps, "golashes," and even "spatterdashes" were available for purchase from one's local shoemaker. He (or family members or neighbors) cut out vamps, built leather soles, or carved women's wooden heels. He could also resole, rebind, or alter shoes, and mend tears. Many New England shoemakers cured and tanned hides for their own shoes and sold their excess leather to others in the trade. They also produced additional leather goods, such as letter cases, saddlery, and equine equipage. Customers could order shoes made of hog-, sheep-, and calfskin, as well as horsehide. There is even an occasional mention of dog leather. This may refer to a very thin leather that was often used for gloves but was not substantial enough for shoes, as noted by George Washington in his correspondence with shoe- and bootmaker John Didsbury.[21] D. A. Saguto, master boot- and shoe-maker (emeritus), Colonial Williamsburg Foundation, and consulting curator for archaeological footwear, Historic Jamestowne, has yet to find an example of American-made shoes that used dog leather.[22]

Under the terms of his apprenticeship with his father, Samuel Lane could not compete with him in the production of footwear. He was, however, permitted to undertake the production of horsewhips, which became a specialty for him and formed a good source of income. Although none of his horse-whips have survived, once he had concluded his apprenticeship and struck out on his own, Lane did craft a letter case and a portfolio for himself, which are now held by the New Hampshire Historical Society. Lane's youngest son Jabez continued in his father's cordwaining footsteps and created leather wallets, such as a patriotic example from circa 1775, with "liberty" emblazoned on the front and the word "unity" found on the inside roundels. It is a very special survival. According to a number of day- and account books, rural shoemakers

The Lane family's home and outbuildings, Stratham, New Hampshire. In 1741, Samuel Lane began work, developing his business and his home from this site. Many successive generations of the Lane family lived on the property, adding to it and changing it as their needs required. Photograph by the author, January 2017

such as Lane also operated as semi-itinerant artisans: delivering completed footwear to customers, taking measurements at a customer's home (sometimes for the entire family), and subsequently making shoes for them in the shop.

Samuel Lane was representative of Yankee cordwainers across the northern British provinces, and he was an especially successful one. A combination of diversification (farming, carting, hiring out, producing textiles) and specialization (shoemaking) was key to increasing one's property and providing for one's family. Given the rather primitive network of roads that linked rural Stratham to the seaport of Portsmouth (roughly eighteen miles away)—marked by foot-deep sludge in the spring thaw, or mud season, and ice-clogged trenches in deep winter—Lane faced a market that was too geographically dispersed to permit him to specialize, as John Hose could in crowded London. Similar to the bulk of American cordwainers, the Lane family devoted much of their calendar year to farming, livestock-raising, and related pursuits. In his almanac, Lane gives us a sense of the centrality of farming for colonial families, even those who pursued a trade as their livelihood. An entry for summer 1775,

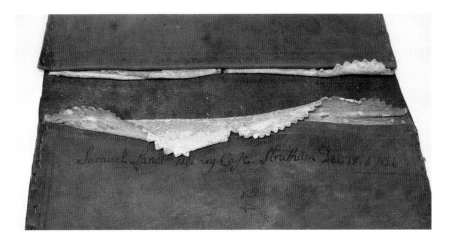

1.13   A leather money case, made by Samuel Lane, Stratham, New Hampshire, 18 December 1746. New Hampshire Historical Society, Lane Family Collection, file number 1994.510.03_4

amid the swirling events of the American Revolution, records that "we have had a verry Moderate Winter the year past a verry Short crop of English Corn & Hay; many Cattle were oblig'd to be Kill'd tho' but thin Beaf: but we had a good Crop of Indian Corn tho' almost all Seem'd likely to be cut off by an Early Distressing Drought." To make the fullest use of his time, Lane even apprenticed in a second trade, learning the art of surveying. This was an important skill in eighteenth-century New Hampshire, as he and his neighbors opened new lands, not only to provide for their families and children, but also for speculation and investment. Over the ensuing decades, Lane became quite adept in the business of charting new lands, making claims, and exchanging real estate. As a respected member of the Stratham community, who maintained various enterprises, he acquired significant legal knowledge, confirmed by the contents of his extensive library of just over three hundred books. These were primarily religious writings, however, which he gave as gifts to his family and friends.[23]

Being a shoemaker was a worthy profession in the British colonies, and many successful men—including Roger Sherman of Connecticut, a delegate to the 1787 Constitutional Convention—proudly announced this trade affiliation. John Jones—Benjamin Franklin's Junto, or Leather Apron Club, colleague—was a cordwainer, as were Colonel Joseph Welch and Captain Winthrop Gray. In urban workshops, a trained shoemaker might employ, and instruct, several apprentices and journeymen. While cordwainers' experiences certainly varied, some elements were common to most. An indentured apprenticeship of approximately seven years, under the direction of a master cordwainer, was followed by a stint as a journeyman. Ultimately, if one attained a high level of proficiency, a shoemaker became known as a master once he had hired a journeyman or took on an apprentice.[24] He was thus able to impart the "art and mystery of making shoes" to a new crop of apprentices. This system of shoe manufacture was imported from Britain and became especially strong in seaport cities, such as Boston, Charleston, and Philadelphia.

Lane was born in Hampton, when New Hampshire was still part of the Massachusetts Bay Colony. As he grew into adulthood, he became an important member of the Stratham community, marrying, raising a family, and serving as a deacon of the Congregationalist First Church there. Although Lane's apprenticeship document with his father has yet to be found, the apprenticeship agreement between Daniel Putnam of Danvers and Joseph Verry shows how the process worked:

The indenture of JOSEPH VERRY, *apprentice*
to DANIEL PUTNAM, *Danvers, Massachusetts, shoemaker*
March 16, 1804

This indenture witnesseth that I, Daniel Verry of Danvers, in the County of Essex, Yeoman, Do put my son Joseph Verry, an apprentice to Daniel Putnam of said Danvers, Yeoman, to learn of his art or mystery of making shoes, and with him to serve after the manner of an apprentice from the day of the date hereof, for the term of five years and three months next ensuing: — During all which time the said apprentice is to serve the said Daniel faithfully, and obey all his lawful commands, he shall do no damage to his said master nor see any by others without giving him notice thereof. He shall not waste any of the said Putnams goods, nor lend them unlawfully to any person; he shall not play at cards, dice or any other unlawful game, whereby the said Putnam may be damaged; he shall not absent himself unreasonable time from his said masters service, neither by day or night; nor stay long at Ale-houses or Taverns; but in all things behave himself as a faithful and honest apprentice in the trade or mystery he now followeth. And I, the said Daniel Putnam, do on my part Covenant to and with the said Daniel Verry, that I will procure and provide for the said apprentice, sufficient meat and drink, apparil, lodging, washing and mending, and other necessary things that he may want during said term. And when he, the said Joseph, has completed his apprenticeship, I, the said Daniel, do hereby agree to furnish him with a suit of Clothes that shall be worth thirty dollars, or give him that sum of money, whichever he may choose. And it is further mutually agreed that the said Joseph is to work half the said term at farming work.

And I, the said Daniel, do agree that the said Joseph shall have two months to go to school each of the next two winters; and if that should not prove sufficient to give him good learning, he is to have one month schooling the third winter; and I agree to pay him fifty dollars more besides the $30.00 above mentioned, after he has completed his apprenticeship. And for the true and faithfull performance of the said Covenant and agreement, we the said parties bind our selves each to the other firmly by these presents. In witness whereof we have hereunto set our hands and seals this sixteenth day of March, in the year of our Lord, one thousand eight hundred and four. DANIEL VERRY. (Seal) And I, the said Joseph Verry above named, do hereby consent to the condition of foregoing indenture, and have hereunto subscribed my name. JOSEPH VERRY. [Seal] Signed, sealed and delivered in presence of us.[25]

What makes this indenture different from those in more urban areas is the understanding that half of Verry's term with Putnam would be spent engaged in farm work. Even as an apprentice, the young man would be learning the significance of building and diversifying his talents to ready him for possible life as a New England rural shoemaker and farmer. Also of note is the focus on education. Young Verry was to spend some time during the winter at school, so he could acquire "good learning."

The year 1741 was a significant one for Lane. His journal records that the twenty-five-year-old man traveled to "the Banke" (Strawbery Banke was the original name for Portsmouth, sited along the banks of the Piscataqua River) and "bought cloth for my wedding cloathes" on 19 December. Lane recorded 24 December in his journal simply as "the day of our marriage." He concluded the year with a full accounting of his blessings: "We have had this year a wonderful time of health. this year hes been a verry remarkable year with me. I have this year (by the help of a kind Providence) bought Land to Settle upon convenient for my business; this year I removed from my native Town to another: this year I built me a house to dwell in: this year I rais'd my Barkhouse [tannery]. This year I married a wife: & this year I have been comfortably

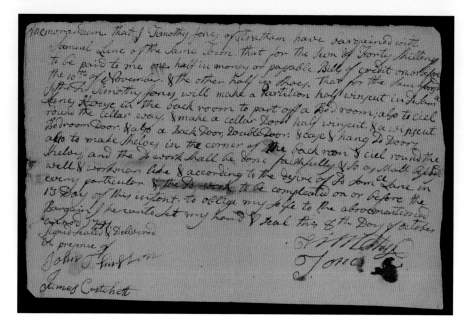

1.14. An agreement between Timothy Jones and Samuel Lane, October 1741. Lane's receipts reveal that he frequently used his shoes as payment for services rendered. In October 1741, he has a written agreement with Timothy Jones to make alterations to his house, including the addition of interior finishes, such as partitions and doors. Lane agreed to pay Jones the sum of 40 shillings, half of which was to be in money or a "payable Bill of Credit," and "the other half in shoes." New Hampshire Historical Society, Lane Family Collection, file number RS14115

carried through many changes & difficultys and having obtained help from God I am yet a living (though most unworthy) [signature] Samuel Lane."[26]

In addition to his marriage, 1741 was also the year in which Lane moved from his childhood home in Hampton to a new homestead in Stratham, a site more "convenient for my business." He traveled frequently to "the Banke" to buy and barter for supplies, as well as to bring shoes to his customers, such as the wealthy Sheafe family. Lane's receipts reveal that he frequently used his shoes as payment for services rendered. In October 1741, he signed a written agreement with Timothy Jones for the latter to make alterations to Lane's house, including the addition of interior finishes, such as partitions and doors. Lane agreed to pay Jones the sum of 40 shillings, half of which was to be in money or a payable bill of credit, and "the other half in shoes."[27]

A decade later, Lane sold thirty-nine pounds of sole leather, valued in Massachusetts' "old tenor" paper currency at £15 and 12 shillings, to Davis Mason.

Lane's terms were that he was to be paid in hides and in labor. He also required Mason to make several pairs of shoes of differing qualities for him, when requested.[28] This suggests that Lane was extending his business outside the family to meet a heavy demand for his shoes. In today's world, Mason would have been a subcontractor.

Eventually, Lane would visit Portsmouth to sell not only his shoes, but also the homespun produced by his wife and daughters. In time, Lane traded for the items necessary for his daughters "to go to housekeeping." He was a regular in adjacent Newmarket, along the Lamprey River, and in Exeter, along the Squamscott. His Stratham property, in addition to its accessibility to customers and suppliers in neighboring towns, permitted him to erect a barkhouse to aid in the tanning process. Although it would take several seasons for this leather, tanned on site, to be ready, it nonetheless enabled him to consolidate his business, keeping more money within the household. Furthermore, the barkhouse enabled Lane to provide tanning services for other shoemakers and saddlers. Therefore, it is not surprising when he observes, with a sense of satisfaction, that he "rais'd my Barkhouse." Lane's homestead, with both its land and a shop (possibly a ten-footer), was well situated on a primary thoroughfare, the post road through Greenland and into Portsmouth. He had indeed positioned himself well for his multiple trades.

Shoemaking was in his blood. His father had been a shoemaker, and his brother Ebenezer was also one. Samuel's three sons would also follow in the trade. While John Hose was dealing with theft and competition, Lane's cordwaining business, as well as his work as a surveyor, were frequently delayed, due to long spells of bad winter weather. Winters were incredibly long during that period, which was known as the Little Ice Age,[29] and winter 1748 was particularly daunting. A few extracts from Lane's diary vividly capture a sense of life on those snowy days. His description of a fierce storm from February of that year makes this challenge abundantly clear. While 19 February was a "pleasant day," 20 February brought "a great storm of snow I believe near a foot deep." By the following day, it was "pretty cold no Meeting the ways are now Block'd up So as the like was hardly ever known; and there's hardly any passing except on SnowShoes the roads are full higher than ye tops of the fences." By 23 February, an additional three or four inches of snow lay on the ground. Yet "on the 24th very pleasant people broke the ways from greenland to Exeter with 30 or 40 oxen and 20 or 30 men." It would now be possible to once again travel on the main road by horse and possibly by wagon, rather than having to take to the open fields on snowshoes. Trade resumed, and, as importantly, one could escape the house and greet neighbors. Lane estimated the snowfall depth that winter to have been more than three feet.[30]

Lane's almanac calls Martha Ballard (1735–1812) to mind. She kept a diary for more than thirty years, describing her life as a midwife in rural Maine. In it she reveals cycles of movement and stasis, rhythms of energy and inertia, year in and year out, so regular that we can describe them as the rituals of the colonial calendar.[31] The challenges that nature brought with each new season make it clear that a colonial family could never have functioned as a separate, self-sufficient household, despite common, pervasive mythology. The rigors of living in a "howling wilderness" made day-to-day existence a precarious endeavor. A colonial family such as the Lanes supported itself through connections with neighbors, who supplied necessities and were also customers who purchased the family's household productions. Consequently, a family survived by diversifying its economic activities. The women produced textiles, such as homespun and woolens, while the children gathered firewood and water, fed livestock, and prepared flax for spinning. Sometimes a man hired out himself, or even his children, for wages, as did the young shoemaker who planned to "let himself for 6 or 8 months" to Abigail Adams in February 1794.[32]

The letters between John and Abigail Adams reveal much about the details of everyday life in Early America. John's father, like Samuel Lane, was both a cordwainer and a deacon of his church, and he plied several trades to support his children. From mid-March to autumn, his plot of fifty acres in Braintree, Massachusetts, occupied the bulk of his attention. "When the lowering fall skies signaled an end to the growing season, he turned to making shoes working at a low bench in a tiny room off the kitchen," historian John Ferling reports.[33]

Lane, however, made and repaired shoes, perhaps in a ten-footer, another outbuilding, or a space inside the main house where he kept his workbench, tools, and materials. Records indicate that he generally had one to three apprentices, frequently family members, working with him. He also took on a young man who may have been an orphan or who suffered from a disability. In this particular case, the apprenticeship documents consist of a contract between Lane and the town officials in Stratham, rather than the young man's parents.

Ten-footers were once ubiquitous throughout the New England countryside, vernacular (characteristic) architectural symbols of Yankee enterprise and ingenuity. It is difficult to calculate how many of these simple wooden structures once peppered rural landscapes between 1750 and 1850. It is also hard to discern how many examples of ten-footers survive today, as one will frequently find them repurposed as outbuildings on the original site or moved to a new location. Two examples of relocated ten-footers on New England museum sites are on view at the Lynn Museum in Lynn, Massachusetts, and on the campus of the Peabody Essex Museum in Salem, Massachusetts. The Lynn Museum has had a ten-footer in its collection since 1923. It was owned by Hiram N. Breed, Lynn's ninth mayor and a descendant of a long line of Lynn shoemakers.[34] One of the advantages of the ten-footer was that it could easily be moved. For instance, the Lye-Tapley Shoe Shop (c. 1832) was moved several times before coming to rest in the Federal Garden area of the Peabody Exeter Museum. Other extant New England ten-footers, such as the one located at the Ipswich Museum, are used for a variety of interpretive purposes. In home-steads from Massachusetts to Maine, a shop was often tucked away in a barn or an ell, and the only surviving evidence is through archaeology, since owners have reworked structures, repaired foundations, and so on. The mechanization of the shoe industry would ultimately render these ten-footers obsolete.[35]

Like other young men of this rising generation, Samuel Lane was touched by the spirit of the Enlightenment. It is not clear if he read the works of another aspiring tradesman, printer Benjamin Franklin of Philadelphia, but Lane certainly emulated men like him.[36] He would have found Franklin's 1757 essay, "The Way to Wealth," appealing. Franklin's guide to fortune was not the kind of self-help tract that one might find in the business section of a popular bookstore today. Instead, Franklin advised young men on the make in colonial America to strengthen their character through the four virtues that brought success: industry, frugality, responsibility, and charity. As young as age seventeen, Samuel Lane committed himself to his trades and to two hours of daily reading. He apparently followed this regimen of reading through the remainder of his long life. Over time, he acquired a reputation for knowledge and sobriety, and he became a church deacon on 4 July 1765.[37]

Samuel Lane's almanac reveals his thoughts on the larger issues occurring in his world—events that would change his life and that of his neighbors. In 1775, in an entry filled with uncharacteristic detail and emotion, he wrote, "But the Most Remarkable Occurrences of this year is, the most Unnatural Civil War Between great Britain & America; which begun on the Memorable 19th of April 1775 in a Battle at Lexington; and increased and Continued by Raising Large Armies and fortifications Against Each other; Battle at Bunkers Hill, Burning Charlestown in 1 Day and Casco Bay &c &c &c which Cannot so much as be Enumerated in this Leafe: in Short the Continent are in the Utmost Distress & Confusion & know not what to do."[38]

The business of producing and distributing shoes would expand dramatically in the years immediately following the Revolutionary War. The modest beginnings of this industry in America had started in the early eighteenth century, gained momentum after the revolution, and ultimately rendered regions, such as New England, into production powerhouses.[39]

TWO CONTRASTING PAIRS OF SHOES

Within the collection of the New Hampshire Historical Society, in the state capital of Concord, are a pair of modest leather shoes crafted in the mid-eighteenth century. On the surface, these unpretentious shoes are not eye catching, but they tell a story about everyday life in the British Empire and, in particular, of the struggles of a family of cordwainers. They are a pair of simple, black leather child's shoes—the kind of sturdy, no-nonsense, workaday footwear that British Americans wore in the eighteenth century. The very basic appearance and hard use of shoes such as these have made them scare in museum collections.

Although we do not know for certain who made them, these shoes are attributed to cordwainer Ebenezer Lane of Stratham, New Hampshire. Lane hailed from an extended family of provincial leatherworkers that included his father, Joshua (1696–1766), and his older brother, Samuel. Most likely Ebenezer crafted the shoes for his four-year-old daughter, Huldah, around 1759. According to journeyman shoemaker Brett Walker of Colonial Williamsburg, Huldah's shoes exhibit construction techniques associated with an earlier generation.[40] This is not surprising. We know that Ebenezer apprenticed with his older brother Samuel, and that Samuel apprenticed with his father. Diaries, account books, probate inventories, and even a list of the volumes in Samuel Lane's library survive, as do many related Lane family papers.[41]

A very different type of shoe from that period can be found elsewhere. Approximately fifty miles below Concord, New Hampshire, sits the historic village of Deerfield, Massachusetts, perched along the Connecticut River and nestled in a wide, field-filled plain beneath the rolling Pocumtuck hills. Here, in a colonial settlement (today part of the Historic Deerfield outdoor museum), visitors can wander past the homes of Ebenezer and Anna Williams (1730), the Allen family (1734), Asa Stebbins (1799), and others, featuring distinctively carved doorways and furniture, and explore the paths along which a French and Indian raiding party attacked the village and made off with fifty captives in 1704. Here, too, the modern and meticulously maintained Flynt Center of Early New England Life in Historic Deerfield holds carefully

1.15 A child's leather shoe, probably made by Ebenezer Lane for his daughter Huldah, circa 1759. Despite the substantial shoe production by the Lane family and its popularity in the seacoast region of New Hampshire, this is currently the only known survivor of their decades of shoemaking. New Hampshire Historical Society, Lane Family Collection, file number 1986.036.01_2

preserved examples of Georgian-era footwear. One pair stands out because the shoes seem to be at variance with the mythology of colonial Americans as homespun-clad pioneers struggling in a wilderness and surviving through simple self-sufficiency. The provenance of these ornately styled, polychrome (multicolored), wool brocade shoes, with their carved French heels, has been lost, yet they feature a label, original to the shoes, that identifies their point of origin: "made by John Hose, London."

Although fabricated at roughly the same time as Huldah Lane's simple leather child's shoes, the Hose luxury pumps found at Deerfield seem worlds apart. Caught up in a consumer revolution, British Americans craved, purchased, and promenaded in shoes of the latest fashion, imported from England "in the last ships," as merchants' advertisements gleefully announced, and produced in bulk by specialists such as John Hose. They also donned more-humble leather footwear that was turned out by neighbors and part-time cordwainers, such as Ebenezer and Samuel Lane. Similar to consumers today, British Americans purchased and wore both luxury and everyday shoes, contingent on matters such as the occasions for which they were needed, availability, and family finances.

1.16 Women's polychrome brocaded wool buckle shoes, London-made by John Hose & Son, mid-eighteenth century. This is an excellent representative example of what might have been imported into the British American colonies during the 1740s–1760. Historic Deerfield, gift of Mr. and Mrs. Kendall Bancroft, object number 76.095.1, photograph by Penny Leveritt

WILLS AND WAYS

The spheres of John Hose and Samuel Lane never touched, yet their lives and careers moved along parallel paths. We get a sense of their worlds, and how each man had made his way in them, in the wills they made out as they neared their final days. Their testaments reveal the hopes and fears that formed the common concerns of Georgian cordwainers in the Atlantic world.

Hose departed this life as "Citizen and Cordwainer of London," on the eve of a revolution that would decimate his trade. As a widower, his primary concern was for the future of his adult daughter and son. To that end, in his will, dated 20 February 1769, he directed that two close Cheapside friends, John Clements and William Burford, invest his funds in stocks and government bonds for the benefit of his daughter, Anne Woolley, and her son. It was a considerable sum—£1,700—attesting to the success of his long and renowned career. Clements, a trunkmaker, and Burford, a hosier, were probably friends and business associates who ate at the same clubs and moved in the same circles. Anne would also receive "all my Household goods plate Linen and furniture whatsoever." Although Hose allocated £100 for Anne's husband, there is a hint here that he fretted about his daughter's support, and provisions for her maintenance formed the bulk of the will. Bypassing the conventional idea that a woman's property became her husband's upon marriage, Hose stipulated that Anne's "receipts alone and without her said husband shall be good acquittances to my said Trustees from time to time for the same notwithstanding her Coveture." Hose's "dear and only son" Thomas would inherit the "residue" of his father's Milk Street property, home, and business. He would carry on the family name, and his father's shoemaking business, from a new site: on Lombard Street "at the Sign of the Boot."[42]

Samuel Lane wrote at least three wills, since his life extended longer than he expected it to. As was common at that time, he begins each fresh version of his testament with a prayer: "In the name of God, amen. I Samuel Lane of Stratham in the County of Rockingham, in the state of New Hampshire, Esq., being in health of body and of a sound disposing mind knowing that it is appointed for all men once to die: do make an[d] ordain this my last will and testament: that is to say principally and first of all, I recommend my soul into the hands of God that gave it; and my body I recommend to the Earth to be decently buried."[43]

Lane's next concern was his large family. In his first will, dated 20 May 1789, twenty years after Hose's, he accounted for the distribution of his worldly estate. His "Beloved Wife" Rachel (Lane's second wife) had come into the marriage with lands in neighboring Newmarket, household goods and money, and a slave named Dinah. Lane instructed that all of these be returned to Rachel upon his death. Many colonial wills allowed a wife to receive a "widow's third" (or dower portion) of a family's house and domestic goods, but the Lanes retained title to Rachel's Newmarket property when she moved into the Stratham home after her marriage to Samuel. Samuel's youngest son, Jabez, raised his own family on the Stratham homestead. To eldest son Samuel Jr., Lane left a one-third right to his pews in the Stratham meeting house, "besides what I have given him by Deed." Joshua, his second son, would receive sizable allotments of land in neighboring towns and a similar right to pews in Stratham. The patriarch set aside 30 shillings for his five daughters, having given all of them domestic goods both at the time of each one's marriage and periodically throughout their lives. Jabez would receive "all the Remainder of my Estate, both Real & Personal." This would include the Stratham homestead, with its barkhouse and associated outbuildings, its workbenches and tools, and its leather and other materials. Jabez, along with his brothers (who had relocated to neighboring towns), would carry on the family business.[44]

2.1 *The Wedding of Stephen Beckingham and Mary Cox*, by William Hogarth, oil on canvas, 1729. American weddings were held in a number of settings—among family or friends, or in houses of worship—depending on a variety of factors. In many communities, the posting of banns or the writing of the marriage contract between the parents of the soon-to-be-wed couple was more significant than a ceremony. The wedding depicted by Hogarth is probably not unlike that of Bostonian Elizabeth Bull to Anglican Reverend Roger Price in April 1735. Courtesy of the Metropolitan Museum of Art, Marquand Fund, 1936, accession number 36.111

WEDDING SHOES

I retain an unalterable affection for you which
neither time or distance can change.

George Washington to Martha Washington, 23 June 1775

Weddings are powerful events, infused with joy, ritual, and tradition. In eighteenth-century America, as now, weddings were an occasion in which to look one's best. Brides or grooms purchased the finest clothing that their households could afford. Preferably, this would be the latest fashion from London. If their budgets did not allow for the extravagance of clothing worn only on that sole occasion, the couple donned their best clothes, or repaired or refurbished what they had—perhaps a gown handed down from a grandmother to mother, or a pair of shoe buckles from a favorite aunt. For instance, in the 1742 novel *Pamela; or, Virtue Rewarded*, the father of the bride does not have appropriate footwear for the wedding, but her groom "was then pleased to give him the silver buckles out of his own shoes."[1]

Whether one measured one's station in society in pounds sterling or in shillings, the clothing of the bride and groom would have been their finest. In colonial America, whatever one's current status, a betrothed couple hoped to move up the economic ladder. Dressing for the future in clothing that revealed how people hoped others would perceive them is a phenomenon called "self-fashioning." An examination of wedding shoes emphasizes the highly personal choices made by the betrothed couple, as well as their intentional self-fashioning.[2]

During the eighteenth century, baroque and then rococo styles dominated European art, architecture, and fashion, introducing a taste for dramatic, theatrical movement and the interplay of light and shadow. As global trade expanded, new materials and ideas from foreign ports became less expensive and more accessible. Designers and artisans experimented with bold palettes, active patterns, undulating lines, and S curves. The naturalistic motifs found in rich brocades and silks were not limited to interior furnishings and textiles, but permeated all aspects of elite dress. Shoes were no exception. Cordwainers could draw upon Chinese, English, and French silks, metallic threads and trim (then known as lace), and the softest of Spanish and Moroccan leathers.

In keeping with the aesthetics of the era, it was possible to produce a dramatic effect through a woman's hair, dress, and accessories, particularly for special occasions. The goal was to create a sense of movement and a play of light by employing shining silk damask and brocade shoes, clocked stockings (with decorative detail, extending up the outer side of the leg) worked with metallic threads, and glittering silver buckles with paste stones—some even featuring real gems, such as diamonds and sapphires.[3] A silk brocaded with metallic threads or a silk with metallic lace would have displayed shine and luster, which, in combination with glittering buckles, epitomized popular Georgian-style footwear. Vivid polychrome palettes or rich gemlike hues were featured in floral motifs that coordinated with the colorways (arrangements of colors) or matched the textile of a bride's gown, as in Rebecca Tailer's 1747 wedding ensemble.[4] At times their choices were economic, or fashion or market driven, or proud examples of the skill and handwork of the bride or groom. Sometimes—as in the years leading up to the American Revolution—they could be imbued with politics.[5]

A wide variety of shoes were available to the American bride (and the occasional groom) for this significant event: silk damasks and brocades; wool calamancos; supple leathers; hand embroidered materials; and even reused textiles. In the following selection of ten brides—some well known, others obscure—we are privy to small vignettes of each one's wedding day, as seen through their footwear. Included are shoes embroidered by the bride who wore them, as well as imported shoes of green damask, red silk, cala-

2.2   Detail of *Stages of Man*, probably American, watercolor and ink on woven paper, most likely circa 1815-1835. This charming early nineteenth-century wedding vignette nonetheless depicts the participants in clothing typical of the eighteenth century. The bride and her female companion appear to be wearing open robes featuring a petticoat and a stomacher. The wedding party is intimate, with the imposing figure of the minister, in his robes, standing on a riser, or elevated platform. Courtesy of the Colonial Williamsburg Foundation, gift of Abby Aldrich Rockefeller, accession number 1939.301.3

2.3   Shoe buckles set with paste stones, French or English (no discernible hallmark), mid-eighteenth century. Shoe buckles were used to attach both men's and women's shoes and could range from a simple plated variety to those set with paste stones or even gems. On 22 January 1660, famed London diarist Samuel Pepys noted, "This day I began to put on buckles to my shoes." Author's collection, photograph by Andrew Davis, February 2017

manco, purple and ivory satin, and leather.[6] The weddings, held in Massachusetts, Connecticut, Pennsylvania, and Virginia, generally featured brides from elite families, but several were "middling sorts." Most were Patriots, but at least one bride married a staunch Loyalist. The political leanings of others are unknown.

Given the nature of such a special occasion, it is not surprising to find numerous examples of eighteenth-century wedding shoes in museums and related institutions. The notion of saving one's wedding attire or some aspect of a bridal trousseau is familiar to us today. The amount of space taken up by a pair of wedding shoes has a much smaller "footprint" in storage than an entire bridal ensemble. Therefore, many collections are skewed toward a larger number of wedding shoes, rather than other types of shoes or wedding raiment. Several significant pre-1760s American weddings reveal much about the links to Britain. In a time when a young woman of privilege received an education that had much to do with drawing-room skills, such as dance, music, and foreign languages, accomplishments in needlework were paramount. They were a testimony to her abilities and her family's wealth.[7] As a reflection of that learning, young women in the colonies created samplers, small domestic items, linens, and white work (embroidery where the stitching is the same color as the foundation textile), a number of which have survived and are among the many and varied examples preserved in museum collections. For example, the importance of displaying one's skill in embroidery appears in two pre-1750s examples: Elizabeth Bull's wedding dress and Hannah Edwards's wedding shoes.

ELIZABETH BULL PRICE'S EMBROIDERED
BOSTON WEDDING DRESS, 1731–1735 • Worn in Boston, 1735;
Collection of the Bostonian Society, Old State House Museum

Walking past the Old State House (1713), now the home of the Bostonian Society and its museum, and along Boston's Freedom Trail, visitors can retrace the footsteps of John Hancock, Samuel Adams, and the men who threw tea into Boston Harbor in 1773. Within the brick walls of the Old State House is the recently restored Governor's Council Chamber, where Governor Francis Bernard planned the province's strategy for the French and Indian War (1754–1763) and sent young men to the frontier, and Thomas Hutchinson debated with his councilors the disturbances that led to the American Revolution. Beneath its balcony, five protestors died in the Boston Massacre (5 March 1770). Among the textile treasures housed in this building are Governor John

Hancock's crimson coat, Dorothy Hancock's wedding shoes, and silk embroidery from Susanna Rowson's Female Academy in Boston. A rare survival was recently conserved and put on exhibit: a 1731–1735 wedding dress, embroidered by Elizabeth Bull and worn for her nuptials in 1735. Her dress is a striking example of a garment ornamented by the wearer herself, embroidered in rich detail with Jacobean designs. The maker, wearer, date and place the dress was worn, and its provenance are all known. But the dress leaves us with mystery, a kind of Cinderella story. Where are her shoes?

This wedding dress is a particularly notable example from the first decades of the eighteenth century. It appears that Elizabeth Bull (1717–1780), the only daughter from a wealthy Boston merchant family, received every opportunity accorded to a young, privileged woman living on the periphery of the British Empire. Much of her embroidery survives, despite alterations by family members in the later eighteenth century, the 1830s, and possibly later. Her distinctive embroidery style and choice of colors are particularly noteworthy in the petticoat, which saw fewer alterations. It was hidden—or actually sewn up inside the dress by nineteenth-century alterations—and, thus protected, appears virtually new. Elizabeth's dress and matching petticoat, an embroidered silk flower garden blooming with roses, chrysanthemums, and tulips, would certainly been have been fashionable in the rococo style of the day. The silk of the dress was originally a celadon green, now faded to cream. The impressive expanse of silk was imported from China, and the embroidery was completed with silk threads.[8]

Like other genteel young ladies, Elizabeth Bull was expected to develop the skills and deportment that marked her station as the daughter of a well-to-do merchant in British America.[9] For birthdays and other special occasions, parents and relations would have presented her with the popular books of the day for young readers. She may have read Richard Allestree's *The Ladies' Calling* (first published in 1673 and available in later editions) or Richard Brathwaite's *The English Gentlewoman* (appearing in 1631 and similarly republished in later editions). Perhaps she received a copy of *A Lady's New-Years Book; or, Advice to a Daughter*, first published in 1688. She might have studied *The School of Good Manners*, by Boston schoolmaster Eliezer Moody, the first British American writer on manners. Moody's guide to gentility appeared in Boston in 1715, just a few years before Elizabeth was born, and included such pearls as "gnaw not bones at the table, but clean them with a knife," advice apparently copied from Erasmus. Also available was *Ornaments for the Daughters of Zion*, by Boston minister Cotton Mather, originally published in 1692. Handbooks such as

2.4   (*opposite*) The wedding dress of Elizabeth Bull Price, polychromatic floral design, hand embroidered in silk threads on celadon green silk. It was worn by the maker in 1735, with alterations undertaken in the eighteenth and nineteenth centuries. When Elizabeth, at age nineteen, married the Reverend Roger Price on a cool, damp April day in 1735, she wore a wedding dress that was not yet completed. She started the embroidery for her dress about four years earlier, circa 1731. Due to the many later alterations, it is not certain what the style of the original was, but by the 1730s, an open robe with a petticoat was beginning to replace a mantua (originally a loose-fitting gown) for some formal occasions. Despite the numerous alterations in the late eighteenth and nineteenth centuries, the survival of large intact portions (such as the petticoat) of this North American garment is indeed special. Today the dress features a bell-shaped skirt, short puffed sleeves, and a V-shaped neck. Courtesy of the Bostonian Society, object number 1910.0050.035

2.5   Petticoat detail of the wedding dress of Elizabeth Bull Price, polychromatic floral design, hand embroidered in silk threads on celadon green silk. Elizabeth Bull's skilled silk-thread embroidery remains vibrant. Courtesy of the Bostonian Society, object number 1910.0050.035

these filled the bookshelves of "the quality" in colonial Virginia and Massachusetts and would have been found in the libraries of Chesapeake planters like Thomas Jefferson and George Washington, as well as in those of New England merchants such as Thomas Hancock. In these books on proper comportment, imitation was the key to learning how to fit into society and engage with a company of like individuals.[10]

From her home near Summer Street in Boston, Elizabeth would have passed by the province's headquarters, situated in the center of the tadpole-shaped peninsula that housed the town of nearly 15,000, on her way to mass at King's Chapel. She was a teenager, probably about fifteen years old, when she began to embroider the dress that she would ultimately wear for her marriage to the Reverend Roger Price. She most likely had not met, and was certainly not yet betrothed to, her future groom.[11] The *Annals of King's Chapel* notes: "Tradition in the family states that Reverend Price attended divine worship at Trinity Church, and there saw, for the first time, Miss Elizabeth Bull. He was so much pleased with her beauty that he gave up his intention of returning to England, sought her acquaintance, and during the year 1735 she became his wife."[12]

While family documents record her "high heeled wedding shoes" as included in the initial gift to the Bostonian Society in 1911, unfortunately their current whereabouts are unknown. There were certainly many types of footwear Elizabeth could have donned for her marriage to Reverend Price. She may have worn silk damask or brocade shoes from London, or embellished mules from France. Given her penchant for, and obvious skill with, fine needlework, possibly she worked the uppers herself, and a cordwainer made them into her wedding shoes. Perhaps some day, the mystery shoes will resurface.

THE EDWARDS SISTERS WORK A PAIR
OF WEDDING SHOES, CONNECTICUT, 1742 •
Worn in East Windsor (or Middletown), Connecticut, 1742;
Collection of the Connecticut Historical Society

Hannah Edwards's wedding shoes are another rare survival. Hannah (1713–1773) and her sister Mary (1701–1776), also called Molly, created these hand-sewn, embroidered, American-made shoes for Hannah's 1742 wedding to Judge Seth Wetmore (1700–1788).[13] Although historians such as T. H. Breen see the 1740s as the beginning of a consumer revolution in Early America, this pair of shoes illustrate an alternative to a British import—the handmade, embroidered uppers that most likely would have been completed by a local

2.6 Woman's shoes, hand-stitched and embroidered with silk and metallic threads on silk and linen, leather, and wood, made by Hannah Edwards, circa 1746. Courtesy of the Connecticut Historical Society, gift of Hannah Whittlesey, accession number 1840.7.1a,b

shoemaker.[14] As the daughter of an elite family, she certainly could have worn shoes imported from Great Britain, as Rebecca Tailer did for her Boston wedding five years later, yet Hannah made a different choice. By opting for her hand-embroidered footwear, she made a significant statement about her values, as well as those of her family and husband-to-be.

Practicing such "gentle arts" was part of a select woman's education. With access to a library, contact with intellectual as well as social elites, and an advanced level of instruction, which included being proficient in skilled needlework, the daughters of the Reverend Timothy Edwards of East Windsor, Connecticut, led lives of privilege that were out of reach for those of the "middling sort" of British Americans. In addition to the shoes, other examples of the sisters' needlework have survived, including a finely stitched, crewel-on-linen dress fragment (most likely a dress robing) from 1742.[15] A larger Edwards family grouping of textiles, which includes the work of Hannah and Mary, has been identified by curator Susan Schoelwer, who has also observed the connection between women in clerical families and the role of female education. As she notes: "The families were willing to incur these costs, [which] urges a reconsideration of the cultural significance and meaning of female accomplishments—needlework chief among them. Far from being mere useless frivolities castigated by critics, needlework performed important cultural work. Like other genteel accouterments—symmetrical Georgian-style houses, elegantly written letters, correct posture—decorative needlework signaled refinement."[16] The connection with genteel learning within elite circles firmly rooted the Edwards family within an English system. The education the two sisters received, being tutored alongside their noted theologian brother, Rev. Jonathan Edwards (1703–1751), was among the best in New England.[17]

Hannah's rococo-style shoes were hand stitched with the most expensive materials available. The uppers feature embroidered silk and metallic threads on silk and linen, covered with naturalistic floral motifs. There are hints that her sister Mary helped her with the shoes, perhaps to ensure that they were completed before the nuptials. The hand-embroidered uppers most likely would have been affixed to the leather sole by a local shoemaker. According to the Connecticut Historical Society: "The silk embroidery is worked through the plain-woven linen lining. The stitches include long-and-short, outline, couching, and French knots. Each toe is worked with a thistle, from which emanates a stylized iris flower with a green frond curving over it. Other flowers include carnations and less identifiable species. Colors include pink, blue, red, and green in the silk, and gold metallic thread."[18] The style, types of flowers, and colors are similar to those found in Elizabeth Bull's dress and commonly used in rococo designs.

In 1746, about four years after her marriage, Hannah moved into a grand Georgian home on a hill in Middleton, Connecticut. The house, built by an unknown master housewright under direction of her husband, still exists, though elements of the splendid parlor, including the paneling, were removed and reinstalled at the Wadsworth Atheneum in Hartford, Connecticut.[19] It features the elaborate "broken scroll" motif associated with Connecticut River Valley doorways. The influential and well-connected Wetmores received visits from the leading personalities of the day, including Aaron Burr, Timothy Dwight, the Marquis de Lafayette, and, of course, Hannah's brother, theologian Jonathan Edwards.

In 1770, several years before Hannah's death, the Wetmores' "house was broke open." The thieves took a number of costly items from their home, including "one black double Sattin Cloak, a full Suit of black Paduasoy (Women's Cloaths, large), a black Taffety Quilt and Apron, a light-coloured Chintz gown, four Yards of double-folded white Holland, six Yards of whitened Tow-Cloth, three or four Pocket Handkerchiefs, not made up, a Woman's shift, and sundry other things."[20]

Her husband offered a reward for the return of these possessions, declaring that "whoever shall secure the aforesaid goods or the greater Part of them and confine the Felons, so they may be brought to justice shall over and above said Fifteen Dollars from the Goaler, have Six Dollars Reward, and cost of taking, paid by me." Subsequent newspaper notices described the miscreants, who were escaped convicts, and their appearance, as well as documented the attempts to capture them. It is not known if Hannah's belongings were ever recovered, or if the culprits finally came to justice.[21]

REBECCA TAILER BYLES'S GREEN SILK DAMASK WEDDING DRESS AND MATCHING SHOES, A RARE SURVIVAL • Married in Boston, 1747; Collection of the Massachusetts Historical Society

This rich, heavy, and luxurious emerald-green silk damask wedding dress was worn by Rebecca Tailer (d. 1773) for her marriage to Rev. Mather Byles (1707-1788) on 11 June 1747 at Boston's Old South Meeting House, the Reverend Sewall officiating.[22] The bride, who was Byles's second wife, hailed from a wealthy Boston family. Her father, William Tailer (1675/76-1731/32), served as the lieutenant governor of the Province of Massachusetts Bay on several occasions.[23]

The family was connected with members of Boston's merchant elite, such as the Stoughtons. That both a wedding dress and matching shoes from this early date in North America have survived is unusual. Although the bodice of the dress has been altered and appears to retain little of its original construction, the yards of textile in the skirt offer an excellent example of the high quality of silk available in the colonies in 1747 — for a price. The silk was most likely woven at Spitalfields in London.[24] In addition to the weight of the silk damask, the repeated design in the large-scale pattern was also associated with expensive textiles at that time. Even today, in the careful care of the Massachusetts Historical Society, the textile is in incredibly good condition, belying its 250-plus years.

2.7 Detail of Lieutenant Governor William Tailer's (Rebecca Tailer's father) silk waistcoat, with silk- and metallic-thread embroidery and spangles (sequins), made in England or France, circa 1732. The detail illustrates the rich embellishment that was a hallmark of elite Bostonians' clothing, as well as a demonstration of their access to foreign markets. Collection of the Massachusetts Historical Society, artifact number 1113

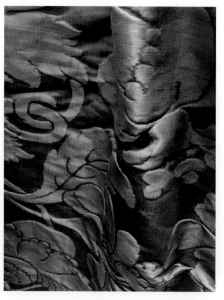

2.8 Detail of a deep green silk damask wedding dress, worn by Rebecca Tailer for her marriage to Rev. Mather Byles on 11 June 1747. This rich green color was popular during much of the eighteenth century. The large-patterned damask was probably woven at Spitalfields in London. The bodice of the wedding dress was altered—most likely for fancy dress in the nineteenth century—but the skirt retains its original luster and heft. Collection of the Massachusetts Historical Society, artifact number 1110

2.9 Green silk damask shoes worn by Rebecca Tailer for her Boston wedding to Rev. Mather Byles, 1747. These London-made shoes feature pattern-matched toes and heels, stiffener in the pointed toes, a white rand (a strip of leather between the sole and the upper) in the sole seam, and carved wooden heels. Collection of the Massachusetts Historical Society, artifact number 1111.01-02

2.10 View of a single shoe from the pair of Rebecca Tailer Byles's wedding shoes, circa 1747, made in London, worn in Boston. Collection of the Massachusetts Historical Society, artifact number 1111.01-02

2.11 View of silk-covered wooden heels from the pair of Rebecca Tailer Byles's wedding shoes, circa 1747, made in London, worn in Boston. Note the shape of the French heel, often called a "Louis heel" today. Collection of the Massachusetts Historical Society, artifact number 1111.01-02

Rebecca's shoes were made of matching emerald-green silk damask, with well-aligned floral textile patterns on the toes and an elegant French heel, just over two inches high, that features a contrasting white rand (a structural strip of leather included in the sole seam, placed between the sole and the upper). This gemlike green seems to have been the "it" color of the mid-eighteenth century. The dying process for creating such a deep, colorfast green was probably very costly, adding to the expense of her wedding raiment. The shoes are similar to several other pairs in American and European museum collections. Indeed, there are a plethora of surviving dresses and shoes made from variations on this green textile.[25] Rebecca clearly had access to the latest fashions from London. The ensemble reveals the choices a bride had for her wedding attire and accessories, here opting for what was most likely a pair of shoes made by London cordwainer Robert Dasson (or perhaps Basson—the name is difficult to decipher), rather than employing work from her own needle, as Hannah Edwards Wetmore had done a few years earlier. Unlike Hannah or Elizabeth Bull Price, there is no direct evidence that Rebecca Tailer Byles had a family tradition of, or especial interest in, sewing, embroidery, or lace-making.[26]

Of particular note, the cordwainer stenciled or stamped his name in the leather on the side, or quarter, of one of the shoes. While paper labels pasted onto the footbed would become popular by midcentury, this is a less common and earlier method of labeling.[27] Without this surviving mark, we would have no indication of who made the shoe, though certainly the style and characteristics—such as small, even stitching; a white rand; a well-fashioned heel, and pattern-matched silk—indicate an English, most likely London, origin.[28]

Although there are indications that the Byles's marriage was not a particularly happy one, historic events and her husband's politics make Rebecca's story even more clouded.[29] As anti-tax sentiment was building in Boston in the 1760s, Reverend Byles proclaimed himself loyal to the king and a staunch Tory. This unpopular stance eroded the family's friendships and undermined his position as minster at Hollis Street Congregational Church. According to biographical sources, he stood virtually alone in his commitment to the British Crown, as parishioners, neighbors, and erstwhile friends deserted the family. Apparently, young Boston minister John Eliot publicly repeated the gossip "the women all proclaimed," that Mather Byles's ostracism from church and community was God's punishment for his mistreatment of both his wives. With the evacuation of Boston by General Howe's troops in March 1776, the reverend faced two years of house arrest. Rebecca may have been spared the worst of the shunning, as she predeceased her husband on 23 July 1773.[30] His son from his first marriage, Mather Byles Jr., who was also a Loyalist, departed for Canada. Reverend Byles died on 5 July 1788. Rebecca and Mather's two daughters, Mary and Catherine, remained in the house on Tremont Street in Boston until their deaths in 1832 and 1837, respectively. It is not known if the shoes stayed in Canada for some period with the son or remained in Boston with the daughters before wending their way to a family member in Brussels, who sold them to the Massachusetts Historical Society.[31]

We have begun our march to the Ohio. A courier is starting for Williamsburg, and I embrace the opportunity to send a few words to one whose life is now inseparable from mine. Since that happy hour when we made our pledges to each other, my thoughts have been continually going to you as to another Self. That All-powerful Providence may keep us both in safety is the prayer of your faithful and ever affectionate friend,

——— G. Washington.[32]

So much has been written on America's initial first couple that the bibliography on the Washingtons is intimidating. Yet their clothing selections, even their shoes, reveal a daily life in which shopping and purchasing goods played a complicated and often unexpected role.

Martha Dandridge (1731–1802) first met Daniel Parke Custis (1711–1757) when he was thirty-seven and she but sixteen years old. Custis was a wealthy planter from a socially prominent Virginia family. After a two-year courtship, they married in 1750. Together they had four children. Custis's death in 1757 (most likely of a heart attack) left Martha a wealthy twenty-five-year-old widow. She assumed substantial new responsibilities for managing not only the domestic aspects of her household (including the care of her young children), but also the administration of the entire estate. This included her late husband's extensive commercial operations. Her business savvy and diplomatic acumen certainly stood her in good stead in her future life as President George Washington's wife and partner. As befitted a woman of position and responsibility, she dressed appropriately but stylishly. Therefore, in addition to negotiating commodity sales, such as tobacco, she ordered the most fashionable silks, jewelry, footwear, and adornments from England. The records at Mount Vernon tell us that she continued to use Robert Cary & Company of London, the factors, or agents, favored by her first husband.[33]

After a very brief courtship, George Washington (1731/32–1799) and Martha Custis married on 6 January 1759. In a letter to Lady Frances Shelbourne in London, attributed to Charlotte Chamberlain of New Kent County, Virginia, Charlotte penned observations on the nuptials:

2.12 Martha Custis Washington's wedding shoes of silk, linen, leather, metallic lace and sequins, and a carved wood heel, worn for her marriage to George Washington on 6 January 1759. 'Her purple silk shoes are richly embellished with sterling silver spangles and couching (a type of embroidered stitch), which create a design of flowers and trailing abstract vines. They feature a white rand, elegant carved heels, a kidskin lining, and a strip of silk brocade across the inside of the tongue, hidden from view for all but her intimates. Although the maker is unknown, these highly fashionable shoes were fabricated in London, most likely to her detailed specifications. Courtesy of the Mount Vernon Ladies' Association, object number W-2667/A-B

The greatest social event that has ever taken place in our colony, occurred some three months ago, being the wedding of our mutual friend Mrs. Dandridge's daughter, Mrs. Martha Custis to Colonel George Washington. The wedding was a splendid affair, conducted after the old English style that prevailed among wealthy planters. Military and civil officers with their wives graced the occasion. Ladies appeared in the costliest brocades, laces, and jewels which the old world could provide. The bride was arrayed in the height of English fashion, her wealth of charms a fit accompaniment to the manly beauty of the bridegroom, who stood six feet three inches in his shoes. The tallest and handsomest man of the Old Dominion. . . . I know you have heard his name often mentioned in England, and will be interested in him so [I] will tell you more particularly of the life of this young man to whom we give a kind of hero worship.[34]

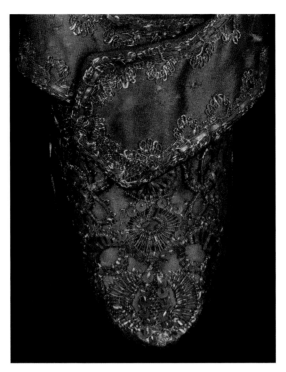

2.13 Detail of Martha Custis Washington's wedding shoes, worn on her marriage to George Washington on 6 January 1759. The detail shows the shoes' sterling silver spangles and couching. The tiny holes in the straps may have been left by her buckles. Courtesy of the Mount Vernon Ladies' Association, object number W-2667/A-B

Martha would have appeared on her wedding day much as she does in the 1757 portrait by John Wollaston in the Lee Chapel and Museum at Washington and Lee University. Her wedding dress was fashioned of gold damask (some have called it a yellow brocade), trimmed with lace.[35] Beneath her gown she wore a white silk petticoat stitched with silver threads. Observers reported that Martha also wore pearls in her hair for the occasion.

Her London-made shoes featured dramatic purple satin uppers, encrusted in silver metallic lace and the spangles (known today as sequins) that were popular at the time. A French heel, a white rand, and a strip of silk brocade lining the underside of the tongue accentuated Martha's footwear. As D. A. Saguto has observed, Martha Washington wore "the largest [size] 4s or smallest 5s." Based on her extant wedding shoes, they correspond to a US size 7.[36] No doubt these shoes were a much more vibrant shade of purple when she

2.14 Purple silk shoes, embroidered with metallic silk threads, European, 1760s. Pre–nineteenth century purples were particularly susceptible to fading, given the nature of the dyestuffs. These shoes have dulled to a purplish brown, and they are not dissimilar to Martha Washington's wedding shoes in that regard (figures 2.12 and 2.13). Few examples of eighteenth-century purple-hued shoes appear to survive in North American collections, though the color of many may be identified as brown, due to fading. Courtesy of the Colonial Williamsburg Foundation, museum purchase, accession number 1954-280-1

wore them for her nuptials, but purple is very prone to fading when exposed to light. Even in Martha's time, the color purple was known to be difficult to keep fresh. Eliza Pinckney, in her circa 1756 receipt book, included a treatment for this problem: "To make a Water to Recover faded purple. Take an ounce of Salt of Tartar & put it in a pint of Spring water and Shake it well together; 'tis fit for use emediately."[37]

While Martha's shoes are not labeled (nor recorded specifically in her accounts with Cary & Company), there is enough evidence to support the speculation that the shoemaker may have been John Gresham, John Didsbury, or, possibly, James Davis—all London cordwainers with long lists of clients "of quality" on both sides of the Atlantic. John Gresham (d. 1787) had provided shoes for Martha prior to her marriage to George Washington. Gresham, like Didsbury, had elite clients in both Britain and North America.[38] In addition to a pair of extant Gresham shoes in the collection at Colonial Williamsburg, a pair of elegant court shoes attributed to Gresham survive at the Northampton Shoe Museum in England.[39] Gresham affixed labels to the footbed of his shoes, while it may be that Didsbury did not, making examples from his shop difficult to locate. We do know that Martha engaged Gresham for her shoe needs, and his name appears in advertisements and collections throughout the Chesapeake region and the southern colonies. Similar to Didsbury, Gresham's work seems to have been a favorite with southern planters, but references to his work are currently unknown in New England. A rare survival is a draft of a 1738 printed trade card for Gresham. While Didsbury supplied both men's and women's shoes, Gresham's trade card reveals that his target clientele was predominately female, with him specializing in women's shoes.[40]

Didsbury supplied shoes to George Washington for the entire family, including Martha, for more than a dozen years, beginning at the time of the couple's marriage. Didsbury appears in Williamsburg newspaper advertisements for ladies' shoes as well as those for gentlemen.[41] Unfortunately, Didsbury's probate (he died in 1803) listed few references to his life or material goods.[42]

Cordwainer James Davis furnished Martha Washington with several pairs of shoes in 1771. While the surviving invoice is dated more than a decade later

2.15 (*opposite*) Shoes from England, circa 1750-1760. The blue silk satin shoe with metallic silver lace and leather (*third row from top, left*) offers a useful comparison with Martha Washington's wedding shoes (figures 2.12 and 2.13). Note the silver lace–encrusted surfaces and the placement and style of the embellishments. Courtesy of the Colonial Williamsburg Foundation, museum purchase. The blue silk satin shoe, accession number 1954-905-1, is included in a group of shoes, accession numbers 1954-1025,2; 1953-983,2; 1954-905,2; 1964-476,2; 1977-265,2; 1964-393,2; 1953-106,1; 1954-1026,2; 1954-1024,1; and 1957-148,1.

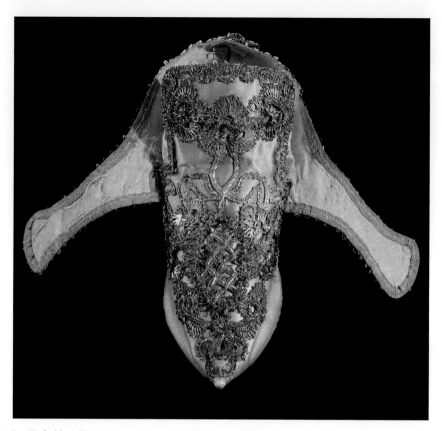

2.16 Detail of a blue silk satin shoe with metallic silver lace and leather, English, circa 1750-1760. The lace in this image compares well with similar detailing found on Martha Washington's wedding shoes (figure 2.13). Courtesy of the Colonial Williamsburg Foundation, museum purchase, accession number 1954-905-1

than her wedding, it may indicate that a relationship was already in place. Davis and his frequent partner, Thomas Ridout, appear to have labeled their shoes before the 1750s, although the practice may not have been universal, or perhaps labels were not included for some clients.

No matter who the shoemaker was, Martha's wedding shoes were an expensive and uncommon purchase, due to the use of purple satin.[43] There are very few eighteenth-century purple shoes that appear to have survived and made their way into museum collections. Given the issue with fading, there may be shoes that were originally purple but now appear to be lavender or brown. In the 1750s, however, it is difficult to find a pair of extant shoes of similar color and embellishments to Martha's. Colonial Williamsburg holds a pair of silk satin purple shoes, embroidered with metallic silver threads, from the 1760s, as well as a pair of blue silk satin shoes, also with metallic silver lace, circa 1750–1760.

In this second pair, the embellishment is much more akin to the style found on Martha's shoes. Given her shopping and fashion savvy, it becomes clear that the closest parallels to her shoes are court shoes, such as a pair from the Victoria and Albert Museum.[44]

For his part, the groom donned a blue suit with a white satin waistcoat (often associated with eighteenth-century men's wedding garb), and blue buckles on his shoes, according to historian Ruth Ashby.[45] With Martha at about five feet tall (although reaching to at least five feet two inches in her heels) and George at six feet—as he repeatedly told his tailors—the pair must have been striking indeed: her gold dress and his blue suit; her white petticoat and his white satin waistcoat, her sparkly spangled shoes and his bright buckles.[46] Small wonder that the Washingtons' nuptials were considered the "greatest social event that has ever taken place in our colony."

After spending their honeymoon in Williamsburg, Virginia, the newly-weds soon parted company, with George returning to his duties. Some years later, in 1775, Washington remained extremely pleased with his bride and their relationship when he penned, "I retain an unalterable affection for you which neither time or distance can change."[47]

2.17 Blue silk shoes with rich silver lace and braid embellishments, English, circa the 1750s. A one-centimeter thick, white kid platform separates the leather sole from the silk and silver-lace upper. Although the maker is unknown, these high-style Georgian shoes (probably intended to be worn at Court or for similar events) provide a valuable comparison with Martha Washington's wedding shoes (figures 2.12 and 2.13), underscoring her knowledge of current London fashions.
Courtesy of the Victoria and Albert Museum, accession number T.70+A-1947

According to Ipswich Museum files, the silk brocade shoes belonging to Mary Wise (1741–1792) were worn at her wedding to Nathaniel Farley (1731–1809) in 1764 or early 1765 (their intention to marry was dated 17 November 1764). She was in her early twenties. This was her first marriage, while it was Nathaniel's second.[48] Mary was born and died in Chebacco (Ipswich, Essex County, Massachusetts). Her first child was a son named Daniel, born on 26 September 1765. Her husband had a son, also named Nathaniel, by his first wife, Elizabeth Cogswell. Mary's shoes were passed down through the family and are now in the care of the Ipswich Museum.[49]

On first glance, it is clear these shoes are unusual. One shoe has been built up at the sole and heel to accommodate the difference in the length of the bride's legs. The height of one of the heels is 1.25 inches and the other is

2.18   Mary Wise Farley's brocaded silk wedding shoes, circa 1764. These custom-made wedding shoes were designed to accommodate the bride's lameness. One shoe has been built up at the sole and heel to accommodate the difference in the length of her legs. The height of one of the heels is 1.25 inches and the other is 2.75 inches. This was accomplished by the addition of a special wooden "platform," or superstructure, on one shoe. Courtesy of the Ipswich Museum, gift of Mrs. William C. West, 364 Essex Street, Salem, Massachusetts, 13 June 1900, accession number 1900.023.001a-b

2.75 inches, indicating that the bride probably was lame. A special wood and leather platform was added to one shoe. Using the same-quality materials that constitute the shoes' textile, special care was employed to match the front portion of the addition. It is neatly, meticulously sewn.

This pair reveal a style similar to the slap-sole construction of the seventeenth and early eighteenth centuries, when a flat sole was attached to the shoe, connected at the toe and ball of the foot but not the heel, thereby creating a "slap" as the sole hit the floor. This type of sole, originally intended to keep heels from sinking into mud and muck, became fashionable as a status symbol for wealthy women in Britain. More study, however, is needed regarding the construction of Mary Wise Farley's shoes, including their wood and leather superstructure, its method of construction and attachment, and interior details. The style, quality of material, and work indicate a London manufacturer, a special order, or an especially highly skilled colonial American cordwainer. These shoes were not meant to be hidden. Mary, who was from comfortable circumstances but not part of "the quality," nonetheless celebrated her wedding in the elegant style of the times. The silk of her brocade shoes would have caught glints of light as she walked, as would the glittering buckles.

A MOTHER'S DRESS, A DAUGHTER'S SHOES—
DEBORAH THAXTER TODD, 1773 • Wedding in Hingham, Massachusetts;
Collection of the Maine Historical Society

Textiles held their value long after a given style had ceased to be popular. Again and again, brocades, damasks, and woolens were cut down and remade into smaller items: a child's dress sewn from a mother's gown; a woman's bodice fashioned from a man's coat or an earlier dress; a quilted petticoat transformed into a bedspread and textiles, or made into shoes, sewing cases, and any number of smaller belongings. The Maine Historical Society features an excellent example of this colonial-era recycling: silk brocade from a 1739 wedding dress refashioned into wedding shoes in 1773. This reused textile, turned into footwear, is consistent with the idea of a wedding as a family ritual, naturally imbued with traditions shared across generations.

The Thaxters appear to have been a family steeped in tradition. Deborah Thaxter (1752–1832) could trace her roots back to the founding of Hingham, Massachusetts. Her wedding celebrated not only her betrothal, but also her family's heritage. When twenty-one-year-old Deborah married Captain James Todd (1751–1831) on 10 September 1772, her beloved mother had died

2.19 Deborah Thaxter Todd's brocaded silk wedding shoes, circa 1772. Deborah Thaxter, of Hingham, Massachusetts, married Captain James Todd, also of Hingham, on 10 September 1772. According to records associated with the shoes, they were made from the silk brocade of her mother's wedding dress. Collection of the Maine Historical Society, item number 48254

several years earlier. According to the Maine Historical Society, the young bride wore these silk brocade shoes, made from the fabric of her mother's wedding dress.[50]

The early years of Deborah's married life were punctuated by uncertainty. Her husband was captured by the British while en route from Havana to Boston shortly after their marriage. The couple's first child was born on 4 May 1774, but their next child was not born until 1788. Todd, held prisoner for nearly nine years, was released in June 1784. He remained a sea captain until 1804.

The survival of these remade or repurposed shoes most likely held a personal significance and meanings lost from the written family record. While the silk brocade from the 1830s features a rosy, peach-colored floral motif (at the toes of the shoes) and bold plant forms associated with rococo textiles, the shape of the 1770s shoe is in keeping with the changes found later in the eighteenth century, featuring a longer shoe with a pointed toe and a much smaller and narrower heel. The silk brocade would have been taken to a shoemaker, who would have attached it to his leather. It is likely that the decision to employ a more than thirty-year-old fabric was the bride's choice.

John Hancock (1737/36-1793) married the wealthy, polished, beautiful Dorothy Quincy (1747-1830) on 28 August 1775 at the Thaddeus Burr estate in Fairfield, Connecticut, shortly after the start of the American Revolution. According to family tradition, and based on the style of her footwear, it is possible that "Dolly," as she was known to friends, wore on this occasion the shoes that are now in the Bostonian Society's collection. Their wedding took place while John was on recess from the Second Continental Congress, where, as its president, he oversaw the colonies' military effort against Britain. It may seem surprising that Dorothy had donned products made by English cordwainers, but it was not uncommon—even for those who were deeply committed to the American Revolution—to wear goods manufactured in Britain.

John Hancock and Dorothy Quincy were joined in marriage in a style befitting their family situations. By the time they were wed in 1775, their courtship had extended over a five-year time span. Most likely they met at the home of her father, Edmund Quincy, in nearby Braintree, Massachusetts. Justice Quincy was known as a staunch Patriot, and the Quincy home was, no doubt, bustling with activity. Dorothy's upbringing, as the youngest of ten, was in contrast to John's, who was sent to live with his uncle, Thomas Hancock, after his father died when he was seven years old.

While we do not know what gown Dolly wore for her nuptials, we can certainly surmise that her outfit was elegant and refined, stylish but not excessive, based on her portraits by John Singleton Copley and Edward Savage, the small number of clothing items of hers that have survived, her position as John Hancock's wife, and on a few scattered references to items John sent her during their courtship. A dress fragment in the collection of Historic Deerfield, in Deerfield, Massachusetts, may be from her wedding dress.[51] Two pairs of shoes, associated with the Hancock family and said to be Dorothy's, survive at the Bostonian Society. One pair are purported to be her wedding shoes. Of delicate cream silk, with a low heel and pointed toes, they certainly would have been appropriate for such an occasion. Both pairs have a paper label, attributing their manufacture to the London cordwainers Bragg & Luckin. Also of interest is the statement "for expo. [export] only" on the labels.

The letters between John and Dolly show a couple struggling to balance the ordinary concerns of a young family against the extraordinary developments of a country in revolution. One of the main themes of the Hancocks' early years of marriage are frequent dislocations: picking up a household, transporting goods from town to town, and setting down roots in a new place. A second aspect was the success of the American Revolution and John's burgeoning influence, which stood in stark contrast to tragedy at home. John's beloved aunt (and surrogate mother to both John and Dolly), Lydia Henchman Hancock, died in 1776. The following year was marked by the death of a baby daughter, also named Lydia Henchman Hancock (1777), just a few months after she had reached her first birthday. Ten years later, the couple again mourned, this time for the loss of their adored nine-year-old son, John George Washington Hancock (1778-1787), known as Johnny. A promising youth of "the rising generation," he died from a head injury sustained when he fell while ice skating. There are suggestions in the evidence that his father bore a burden of guilt for this, having purchased ice skates for his son a few weeks earlier. To make matters worse, constant, painful gout eroded Hancock's health and aged him prematurely. At moments of great political import, he was all but crippled by this disease.

Through frequent upheavals, Dolly oversaw the packing of trunks and made arrangements on her own for their transportation, as well as for that of her children, household staff, material goods, and foodstuffs. Throughout the first few years of their marriage, John would instruct his wife to "ransack" the house, have the light wagon loaded, and meet him in various locations. They moved from Boston to Philadelphia to Fairfield, Connecticut, to Baltimore. They were even robbed in Baltimore, yet through all this, Dolly managed either to save her shoes or to have someone safeguard them for her.

As a delegate to the Continental Congress, meeting in Philadelphia, John Hancock had important matters of tremendous consequence on his mind. Each day brought news, gossip, rumors, and lies that had to be evaluated and addressed. Yet, despite the chaos and turmoil, the high tensions and emotion, he found time to correspond with his beloved Dorothy and even shop for her in the bustling streets of Philadelphia. John appears to have been a trifle obsessed with shopping. Much of his surviving correspondence with Dolly concerns finding the latest fashions and luxury goods for her and the children. A letter from June 1775, just one month before their wedding, reveals much

2.20 Dorothy Quincy Hancock's purported wedding shoes of ivory silk satin. London cord-wainer John Gresham's label is pasted into one shoe. Gresham had many wealthy customers, including Martha Washington. Courtesy of the Bostonian Society, object number 0064.1887.002

about his state of mind regarding his bride-to-be, showing his concerns for her affections toward him and his efforts in securing items for her, long the province of the betrothed. He confided:

> MY DEAR DOLLY: I am almost prevail'd on to think that my letters to my Aunt & you are not read, for I cannot obtain a reply, I have ask'd million questions & not an answer to one, I beg' d you to let me know what things my Aunt wanted & you and many other matters I wanted to know but not one word in answer. I Really Take it extreme unkind, pray, my dear, use not so much Ceremony & Reservedness, why can't you use freedom in writing, be not afraid of me, I want long Letters. I am glad the little things I sent you were agreeable. Why did you not write me of the top of the Umbrella. I am sorry it was spoiled, but I will send you another by my Express which will go in a few days. How did my Aunt like her gown, & let me know if

the Stockings suited her; she had better send a pattern shoe & stocking, I warrant I will suit her. . . . I Beg, my dear Dolly, you will write me often and long Letters, I will forgive the past if you will mend in future. Do ask my Aunt to make me up and send me a Watch String, and do you make up another and send me, I wear them out fast. I want some little thing of your doing. Remember me to all my Friends with you, as if named. I am Call'd upon and must obey.

I have sent you by Doctor Church in a paper Box Directed to you, the following things, for your acceptance, & which I do insist You wear, if you do not I shall think the Donor is the objection:

2 pair white silk	}	which stockings
4 pair white thread	}	I think will fit you
1 pair black satin	}	Shoes, the other,
1 pair Calem Co.	}	Shall be sent when done.
1 very pretty light hat		
1 neat airy summer Cloak		
2 caps		
1 Fann		

I wish these may please you, I shall be gratified if they do, pray write me, I will attend to all your Commands.

Adieu, my dear Girl. and believe me with great Esteem & affection,

Yours without reserve,

JOHN HANCOCK[52]

Anxiety over separation and a longing to please are repeated themes in John's letters to Dolly. Under the dateline Philadelphia, 10 March 1777, John bemoaned: "I shall make out as well as I can, but I assure you, my Dear Soul, I long to have you here, & I know you will be as expeditious as you can in coming. When I part from you again it must be a very extraordinary occasion." He then continued: "I have sent everywhere to get a gold or silver rattle for the child with a coral to send, but cannot get one. I will have one if possible on your coming. I have sent a sash for her & two little papers of pins for you. If you do not want them you can give them away. . . . May every blessing of an Indulgent Providence attend you. I most sincerely wish you a good journey & hope I shall soon have the happiness of seeing you with the utmost affection and Love. My dear Dolly, I am yours forever, JOHN HANCOCK."[53]

John Hancock died in 1793, at the age of fifty-six, leaving Dolly, ten years younger, with a considerable estate and the esteem of the country. In time she remarried, wedding Hancock's long-trusted former ship captain, James Scott, and moving to Portsmouth, New Hampshire. When Captain Scott died in 1809, Dorothy returned to Boston. She died in 1830 at the age of eighty-three, remembered by generations of Bostonians as a kind, generous, and engaging hostess.

RED WEDDING SHOES

As the *Tatler* once reported, "A sincere heart has not made half so many conquests as an open waistcoat and I should be glad to see an able head make so good a figure in a woman's company as a Pair of Red Heels."[54] To our contemporary minds, red shoes may seem an odd choice for wedding footwear. Given our culture's association with white for weddings, red seems less than suitable for such attire. Despite the survival of numerous white wedding dresses from the eighteenth century, white as a color motif for weddings is indelibly associated with Queen Victoria (1819–1901). Her marriage in 1840 to Prince Albert was a social extravaganza, but it was also a political statement. To bolster the decimated British lace industry, she donned a white gown that was extensively adorned with fine, British-made Honiton lace. Her shoes, too, were a decidedly British product. The venerable shoe- and bootmakers Cundry & Sons crafted a pair of elegant shoes, made of white satin, featuring white ribbon ties that wrapped at the ankle to hold them in place. From then on, white has been the go-to color for weddings.

It was not always this way. A profusion of blues, greens, and floral patterns decorated wedding gowns and shoes worn in mid-eighteenth-century America. Red, however, appears to have been a particularly coveted color for a woman's wedding shoes. Before the advent of inexpensive chemical aniline dyes in the mid-nineteenth century, red was an especially exotic and costly color to produce. In an age when dyes were derived primarily from plant, animal, and insect sources, merchants searched far and wide for the rare dyes that could bring a hefty profit. To produce the rich, intense effect of deep red—"a color like no other"—European merchants went to Spanish Mexico. There, indigenous peoples had discovered a method for securing the desirable dye from cochineal: the crushed, dried shells of a tiny female insect native to the region. While there were other methods for attaining a desired red or reddish hue, it was carmine, a pigment made from these cochineal insects, that produced the most effective red dye.[55]

A delightful bit of satire from the pen of Bernard Mandeville reveals something of the efforts required to attain such a desirable color. In "The Vanity of Men and Women," an essay for the *Tatler*, a favorite magazine for genteel readers during the British Enlightenment, Mandeville lampooned efforts to acquire this dye: "Crimson cloth can be produced, what Multiplicity of Trades and Artificers must be employ'd! Not only such as are obvious as Wool-combers, Spinners, the Weaver, the Cloth-worker, the Scourer, the Dyer, the Setter, the Drawer and the Packer but others that are more remote. What a Bustle is there to be made in several Parts of the World before a fine scarlet."[56]

The author went on to recount the excessive time, hardships, and dangers required to scour the world to secure items such as cochineal. If a chemist from that period could provide the latest fashionable colors and high-quality dyes, then he would be assured of a profitable livelihood. In an advertisement from Boston, for example, an experienced dyer, James Vincent, promoted his business to the wealthy in 1729. Vincent placed various ads during the 1720s, but there is evidence that skilled dyers were already at work in this colonial city. His ads made much of the fact that he was from London and thus had access to the "best and newest manor, at reasonable rates for ready money." Among his specialties, he noted that he "dyes and scours all sorts of women's wearing apparel, tabbies, mohairs, rich damasks, fine brocade . . . new dips Scarlet Cloth and Camblets, dyes cherry and grain colours, and Blews and Greens in silks."[57] For betrothed women who could afford the finest that the Atlantic world's economy offered, such as Elizabeth Bull (m. 1735), Rebecca Tailer (m. 1747), or Catherine Dexter (m.1756), one could have ready access to the sought-after "it" colors of the season.

An August 1771 advertisement speaks to the value of red shoes in British America. It seems that a pair of a pair of women's "red stuff shoes with red heels and sharp toes" were stolen from the house of Isaac Lawrence in the rural Pennsylvania town of Chichester, in Chester County. For the return of the shoes and several other valuable textiles, Lawrence generously offered "20 shillings reward or 10 shillings for the goods only."[58]

John and Abigail Adams confirm the importance and desirability of red textiles. Writing to Abigail in October 1782 from Paris, where he served as an American ambassador to France, John recorded: "I have Sent you an whole Piece of most excellent and beautiful Scarlet Cloth—it is very Saucy. 9 florins almost a Guinea a Dutch ell, much less than an English Yard. I have sent some blue too very good. Give your Boys a suit of Cloths if you will or keep enough for it some years hence and yourself and Daughter a Ridinghood in honour of the Manufactures of Haerlem. The Scarlet is 'croise' as they call it. You never saw such a Cloth."[59]

That the three American brides discussed below, all from different regions, selected red for their wedding shoes illustrates its popularity. While these particular shoes date from the 1740s through the 1760s, there are no doubt many more which have no known provenance to connect them with a bride and her wedding.

MAGDALENA DOUW, PAINTED IN RED SHOES •
Married in 1740; Collection of the Winterthur Museum

Magdalena Douw (1718–1796), a contemporary of Elizabeth Bull Price, grew up in Albany, New York, at Wolvenhook, the family home. The Douws were a leading family in the area during the eighteenth century. In 1740, Magdalena married merchant Harman Gansevoort (1712–1801). They had nine children, all baptized at the Albany Dutch Church.

A striking portrait by limner John Heaton was probably painted about the time of her wedding.[60] Although we do not have the actual shoes that were depicted, the portrait of Magdalena, in her stylish green silk damask dress (similar to that of Rebecca Tailer Byles's Spitalfields silk damask wedding dress), wearing vibrant red shoes (most likely her wedding shoes, given their style and the date of the wedding), is vividly captured. Her portrait is placed within an interior setting, and the viewer's eye is immediately drawn to Magdalena, standing framed between two arched windows that look out onto a landscape. She gazes directly at the viewer, as if an interloper has just walked into her space and interrupted her activity and her thoughts. The skillful application of red begins in the ribbon of her cap and continues to her stomacher, largely hidden behind bows on the bodice of her gown. She holds a red covered book in one hand and a bunch of ripe cherries in the other. The viewer's focus is drawn to her emerald-green, silk damask sack- (or saque-) back gown, dominated by a large foliate rococo pattern, before resting on her vibrant red shoes.

Her shoes feature French heels, high but stout and weighty, with pointed, upturned toes. The painter included her shoe buckles, and although there appears to be a strip of white down the front of the shoes, it was probably meant to indicate an expensive swath of either metallic lace or braid from toe to tongue, which certainly would have been appropriate for that time period.

2.22 Red wool (broadcloth) buckle shoes, English, circa 1750-1760. Note the wide band of natural-colored woven silk lace, running from the toe to just below the tongue, and the flared heel, covered in cream kidskin. Copyright © 2017, Bata Shoe Museum, Toronto, accession number P87.0032.AB, photograph by Tanya Higgins and Fiona Rutka

Although the type of fabric is difficult to ascertain from the painting, given Magdalena's ensemble and the addition of the metallic lace, we may conjecture that they are silk shoes, though they could easily have been made from wool or cloth, as is found in a pair of red broadcloth shoes, with wide silk lace extending up the vamp, in the collection at the Bata Shoe Museum.[61] We will get a closer look at this treatment in examining Catherine Dexter Haven's shoes.

CATHERINE DEXTER HAVEN'S CHERRY RED

WEDDING SHOES • Married in Dedham, Massachusetts, 1756;

Collection of the Bata Shoe Museum

Catherine Dexter was born on 21 November 1737 to Reverend Samuel Dexter and Catherina Mears. Her husband Jason, born on 2 March 1733, was the youngest son of Moses Haven of Framingham, Massachusetts. Jason graduated from Harvard College in 1754 and was ordained as pastor of the First Church in Dedham on 5 February 1756, the same year in which he and Catherine married. Jason was also a delegate to the convention that framed and

2.21 (opposite) A portrait of Magdalena Douw (Mrs. Harman Gansevoor), by John Heaten, oil on linen, 1740. Magdalena Douw, a contemporary of Elizabeth Bull, grew up in Albany, New York. In 1740, Magdalena married merchant Harman Gansevoort. This striking portrait was probably painted about the time of her wedding. Although the actual shoes are not known to survive, the portrait vividly captures Magdalena in her stylish green silk damask dress and vibrant red shoes. The shoes feature French heels—high, but stout and weighty—and pointed, upturned toes. The painter included her shoe buckles, and, although there appears to be a strip of white down the front of the shoes, it was probably meant to indicate an expensive swath of metallic lace or braid, extending from toe to tongue, which certainly would have been appropriate for the time and similar to the shoes in figure 2.22. Courtesy of the Winterthur Museum, gift of Henry Francis du Pont, object ID 1963.0852A

adopted the Constitution of Massachusetts in 1780. Catherine Dexter was the daughter of his immediate predecessor at First Church, Rev. Samuel Dexter. The couple had five children, although the first three all died before reaching adulthood. Jason died on 17 May 1803. Catherine died on 2 September 1814, at the age of seventy-seven.[62]

For her nuptials on 12 October 1756, Catherine selected bright cherry red, ribbed silk shoes, with luxurious metallic braid running up the vamp and heels. This pair of treasures remain in excellent condition and are housed in the collection of the Bata Shoe Museum.[63] The shoes appear to have experienced very little wear. Indeed, one wonders if they were only worn on that special day.

Catherine was making a statement when she flashed her stylish, vibrant red silk shoes at her wedding to the Dedham minister. They exhibited the latest London fashion: a thick French heel, clad in matching silk, featuring a contrasting white rand. In a rather bold manner (though consistent with the style of the day), a wide strip of a metallic lace dominated the vamp and also ran up the back of the shoe. The toe was rounded, in the style of that year, as noted in advertisements such as that of Boston merchant Edward Green. His ad in the *Boston Gazette and Country Journal* for June 1756 read, in part, "russell and callimanco shoes, clogs, light blue and black satten shoes with round toes."[64]

In addition to the obvious high quality of the calamanco shoes discussed in

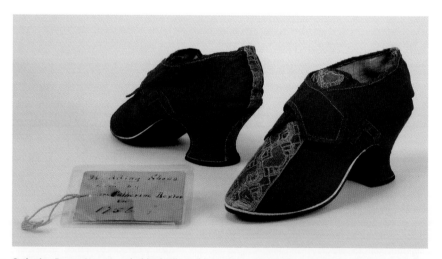

2.23 Catherine Dexter Haven's red ribbed-silk wedding shoes, worn in Massachusetts, October 1756. Her silk buckle shoes feature a wide metallic-lace band from toe to tongue, with a narrow band on the back seam and heel, a contrasting white rand, and fine stitching. Copyright © 2017, Bata Shoe Museum, Toronto, accession number P99.0085.A-C, photograph by Tanya Higgins and Fiona Rutka

2.24 Mary Flint Spoffard's rosy red calamanco wedding shoes, English, circa 1765. The buckles are not original to the shoes. Mary Flint married Deacon Elezar Spoffard in South Danvers, Massachusetts, in January 1765. More modest than Catherine Dexter Haven's footwear (figure 2.23), these are examples of a shoe type that was widely popular in British America—calendered (smoothed and coated) wool, known as calamanco, with its glazed, glossy surface. The patterns of wear on the shoes indicate that she continued to use them after her marriage. They were most likely purchased in England. Historic Deerfield, Museum Collections Fund purchase, with funds donated by James Ciaschini in memory of his mother, Eva Ferioli, object number HD 2004.26, photograph by Penny Leveritt

this chapter, they also reveal much about the wealth and social position held by the three women wearing them, all of whom espoused clerics: Elizabeth Bull, who married Rev. Roger Price, an Anglican; Rebecca Tailer, who married Rev. Mather Byles, a Congregationalist and minster of the Hollis Street Church, Boston; and Catherine Dexter, who married Rev. Jason Haven, of the First Church in Dedham.

MARY FLINT SPOFFARD'S ROSY RED CALAMANCOS •
Married in South Danvers, Massachusetts, 1765;
Collection of Historic Deerfield

Mary Flint was from Danvers, Massachusetts, a town that, seventy years earlier, was known as Salem Village, the epicenter of the infamous witch trials in 1692. She was the daughter of Elisha and Mirriam Putnam Flint. According to family lore, Mary wore red calamanco shoes for her wedding, and the patterns of wear on these shoes indicate that she used them for less formal occasions after her marriage. More modest than Catherine Dexter Haven's footwear, they are examples of a shoe type that was widely popular in British America— calendered (smoothed and coated) wool calamanco, with its glossy surface.

The calamancos, recently conserved, are in the care of Historic Deerfield. They were most likely purchased in England and donned by Mary for her marriage to Deacon Eleazer Spofford in South Danvers, Massachusetts, on 24 January 1765, the year of the infamous Stamp Act. Vital records, as well as the shoes themselves, leave a trail that tells more about this rather ordinary, little-known couple. They were both in their twenties when they married. According to the family's and town histories, Eleazar, who was born in nearby Rowley, "built a valuable set of mills on the Contoocook River, at the site of the present factories in East Jaffrey [New Hampshire]; was an ingenious mechanic, an upright, godly man, and a good citizen, being especially interested in the construction of turnpike roads, the great public improvement of that day. He was for many years a deacon of the First Church in Jaffrey. Late in life they removed to East Bradford [now Groveland], Massachusetts, where he died in 1828. Mary returned to Jaffrey and died [on] October 28, 1832, aged 92."[65]

The couple had ten children, at least eight of whom lived to adulthood. A tragedy struck the family in 1788, with the death of one young son in a house fire. His grave marker in the Old Burying Ground in Jaffrey, New Hampshire, poignantly recorded, "Oh say grim death here is entered the last remains of Isaac Spofford, son of deacon Eleazar and Mrs. Mary Spofford, a brand plucked from the ashes of Reverend Laban Ainsworth House, 13th of February 1788; age 8 years."

The evidence for the shoes' provenance comes from a family tradition — often the only link in the attribution of material culture — arising from a label attached to the sole of one shoe. The handwritten note shows that these shoes were handed down through the generations, perhaps as treasured remnants brought out for public celebrations, holiday jubilees, or family gatherings. In addition, the collection label tells us something about these shoes as curatorial objects: "Pair of women's shoes in reddish-pink, glazed wool with buckles, which according to family tradition were worn for the 24 January 1765 wedding of Mary Flint (1742–1832) to Eleazer Spofford (1739–1828) in South Danvers, Massachusetts. Paper labels are attached to both shoes [and are] inscribed in ink: 'Made for or brought from England for Mrs. Mary Flint-Spofford — wife of Dea. Eleazer Spofford of Bradford Mass., about 1760. Suppose to be the wedding shoes.'"[66]

The paper labels cannot, however, share more about the design and making of the shoes, aside from the simple beauty of the calamanco uppers themselves, and they say nothing about the woman who treasured them. Perhaps these shoes complemented Mary's wedding dress, which could have been made

2.25 Red shoes of wool, leather, silver, linen, silk, and wood, probably made in New England, circa 1750. These charming vernacular wool shoes, characteristic of the period, feature a wide strip of metallic braid and an interior lined with blue-and-white checked linen. Courtesy of the Colonial Williamsburg Foundation, museum purchase, the Antique Collectors' Guild, in memory of Jim Bilderback, Barbara Driscoll, Richard Kent, Arthur Kimball, Tom Wood, and Phil Young, accession number 2016-198, 1-2

2.26 Red wool buckle shoes, lined with coarse-weave gray linen, with a carved wooden heel clad in wool, a white rand, and upturned toes. Made in British America, possibly New England, circa 1735-1750. These vernacular red wool shoes feature self-covered seams and no top binding. The stitching, somewhat awkward heel, and overall finish work probably indicate that the maker did not have access to the training and tools of his British counterparts. Not pictured are the matching clogs. Copyright © 2017 Bata Shoe Museum, Toronto, accession number P89.0270.A-F, photograph by Tanya Higgins and Fiona Rutka

of the same fabric or exhibited the same colorways. There is evidence from other calamancos that the wool yarn used in their manufacture was sometimes dyed to match a dress, allowing an opportunity to select similarly colored knit stockings for the ensemble as well.

Mary apparently wore her wedding shoes on other occasions. They are well worn and a bit stretched at the toes and sides. Clearly the shoes had some "give" and relaxed over time and with wear. They have the look of comfortable footwear, cradling her feet. Perhaps her purchase of the calamancos was based on practical concerns for their future use, which one would anticipate from a person of the "middling sort."

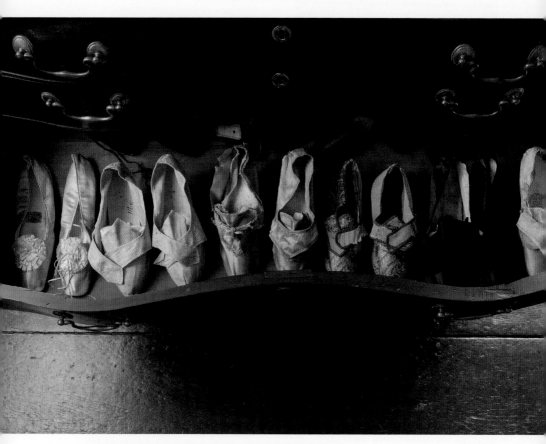

3.1   A collection of eighteenth- and nineteenth-century shoes. Courtesy of the Warner House, accession numbers WH1968.8.5-6, WH1949.1, WH1968.8.3-4, WH1949.2.A-B, WH1968.8.7-8, and WH1968.8.9-10, photographed on site at the Warner House, Portsmouth, New Hampshire, by Andrew Davis, May 2016

THE VALUE OF A LONDON LABEL

In 1786, Sophie von La Roche, a minor German aristocrat, traveler, and writer who was then touring England, turned her thoughts to the temptations of London window-shopping. The baroness mused: "Now large shoe and slipper shops for anything from adults down to dolls can be seen. . . . Behind great glass windows absolutely everything one can think of is neatly, attractively displayed, and in such abundance of choice as almost to make one greedy."[1] We might wonder how the fascinations of a consumer's gaze translated from the busy streets of the great metropolis to the seaport shoe shops to the market-square days in county seats, the rustic ten-footer cordwainer sheds that dotted the New England countryside, and the wares peddled by itinerant shoemakers throughout British America.[2]

Historians of material culture have generally maintained that American imports from Britain conveyed an inherent message

3.2   "The Shoemaker," by Abraham Bosse, etching, from the series/portfolio *Les Métiers* [Trades] (Paris: Jean I. Leblond, 1632–1633). The well-dressed seated customer appears to be trying on a pair of elaborately embellished high-heeled shoes, or "slap shoes." One of her low-heeled mules is seen on the floor. Courtesy of the Metropolitan Museum of Art, Harris Brisbane Dick Fund, 1926, accession number 26.49.58

of local cultural inferiority. Colonists, these scholars assert, bought British goods, especially luxury fashions, in order to imitate the stylish trends in the metropolis, which they perceived as the being center of sophistication, and indeed of civilization generally—a phenomenon referred to as anglicization. The shoe stories told here reveal a rather different conclusion, which suggests questions arising from a fresh point of view. Is it not more likely that colonists viewed these items as markers of their status as a provincial people, living on the edge of empire, but no less capable of gentility and civility than their transatlantic counterparts? Rather than mindless imitation, these shoes and their stories suggest a process of creative re-adaption that drew upon English ideals of sophistication but modified them to fit an American environment and a Yankee culture.[3]

The Georgian London that Sophie von La Roche roamed in 1786 was one of the world's great entrepôts. She encountered bustling streets in which vendors and shopkeepers sold their wares to sophisticated consumers who sought the ultimate in fashion. In the Ward of the Cordwainer, scores of skilled shoemakers kept hours much like those in our own big box stores, opening their shops from early morning until late at night. John Hose of Milk Street employed around 300 workers, filling trunks with shoes that he dispatched to merchants in British America.[4] It was fortunate for colonial shoemakers, such as Samuel Lane in New Hampshire, that they did not have to compete head-to-head with Hose and his British counterparts, for the scale and quality of a London shoe surpassed almost any footwear produced in America before the Revolutionary War. Conditions would change with the rise of mechanization in the early to mid-nineteenth century, as manufacturing centers (such as Lynn, Massachusetts) spewed out millions of pieces of footwear each year. But that would be in the future.

ACROSS THE ATLANTIC

Tracing the dispersal of luxury shoes from London's shops, across the shipping lanes of the Atlantic Ocean, to the wharves and warehouses of Boston, Richmond, and Charleston is complicated. The trail lies in the archives of the British Library and the Peabody Essex Museum, the National Archives and the Massachusetts Historical Society, and dozens of other sites where one can decipher ships' manifests and cargo lists, customshouse records, and store advertisements. What is evident is that ladies shoes' were in high demand in the colonies, exported by British and American merchants in substantial numbers. For instance, in a ship's manifest kept by Captain Hubbakuk Bowditch, eighty pairs of ladies' shoes arrived in Salem, Massachusetts, in 1772. The sloop *Exeter Packet*, owned by James Bott, also of Salem, sailed from London with thirty-three pairs of women's shoes on 5 January 1775, most likely bound for New England. Like the *Exeter Packet*, hundreds of ships departed from London, Plymouth, and Bristol for the colonies, carrying manifests that listed women's shoes separately from other items in their cargoes. There are also scattered references of shoes being shipped regionally from one American port to another, providing evidence of pre-revolutionary colonial trading practices.

For example, a customshouse record notes outbound merchandise from Salem to Philadelphia, loaded on the forty-five ton sloop *Joanna*, master and owner William Bartlitt, which cleared customs on 14 October 1762. Along with potatoes and rum, her cargo included "a trunk of women's shoes here made."[5] Whether Philadelphia was the final destination is unknown.

TO AMERICA

On the other side of the Atlantic, we find a cornucopia of advertisements in the *Boston Post-Boy*, *Charleston Gazette*, and *Independent Chronicle* that document the demand and availability—at a premium—of ladies' shoes to the "foot-trade" via their sale in high-end shops in various seaport towns. "Lately arrived from London," these ads boasted gleefully to shoppers in New York, Portsmouth, and Philadelphia.[6] All of these advertisements reflected a sense of Georgian gentility, and the goods that were sold contributed to the imperial and, after independence, national economy.

British Americans read multiple meanings into a pair of London-made shoes. A purchase or a gift of fashionable pumps "just arrived from London" allowed the provinces' cultural elites to stay connected with the manners, mores, and styles of British high society, reinforcing their sense of cultural identity, despite living on the peripheries of the empire. British Americans considered themselves to be Americans by geography, but British by nationality.

The time between the manufacture of a shoe in a London shop to its purchase in America was a matter of months (or less), enabling merchants to advertise the "latest from London" and well-to-do colonial consumers to display their sophistication. Moreover, the opportunity to show off one's refined taste was not confined to the upper classes. A large market for older, secondhand textiles and shoes served the "middling sorts" in the provinces, so they could also participate in the same rituals of conspicuous consumption and imperial identification. Advertisements by New England auction houses connected with this trade—such as those run by Samuel Larkin and William Lang in Portsmouth, New Hampshire, or John Gerrish in Boston—frequently listed secondhand clothing, sold for cash.[7] This was a flourishing business, though it is difficult to glean its impact, since there was only a sporadic paper trail regarding the exact numbers of sales, the overall volume of the transactions, and those involved in the trade: from the salesman in London to the translator who refashioned shoes from various bits. Because the tradition of recycling clothing was such an accepted practice, the actual business of buying or selling such clothing had no reason to come under the scrutiny of local, regional, or national officials. It was such a part of everyday life in the eighteenth century that the trade in secondhand garments, textiles, and accessories was commonplace, even for those of more elite status.

In spring 1770, a London salesman, John Matthews, advertised in *Jackson's Oxford Journal* that he "buys Ladies and Gentleman's cast-off cloaths, either laced, embroidered, or brocaded, full-trimmed or not, of every Colour and sort, and will give the most Money for any: As I can deal for London, the Country, and Abroad." Prior to the American Revolution, used footwear cost less to export than new shoes, as the tariffs were much lower.[8]

Another's misfortune could be a boon to the savvy shopper.[9] One such sad case is that of Henrietta Maria East Caine. The enterprising Henrietta, a Londoner, arrived in the colonies at the crest of the consumer revolution. She came to Boston well stocked with the latest in fashionable London textiles, garments, and accessories, including a range of shoes. Several years later, in 1747, she wed Hugh Caine, also from London, who turned out to be quite a cad. It appears that he was already married, with a wife living in London. He soon abandoned Henrietta, after helping himself to her earnings, and returned home. Merchants and customers in Boston no longer would undertake business with her, because of her connection with a bigamist. Addressing the courts, in an effort to dissolve her marriage, also proved to be unsuccessful. On 18 September 1754, Henrietta was forced to sell off her entire stock of goods at auction, to cover her debts.[10] Although the financial result of that sale is not known, no doubt many were only too happy to purchase her very fashionable goods at less than retail prices. The sale was held in her home (above her shop), at the Sign of the Fann in Marlborough Street. There were approximately 283 lots (many with multiple items), including extensive yardages of fabrics, a staggering variety of clothing-related materials, and even some of her household cooking vessels from London and France.

A brief mention in the Willing family papers, at the Historical Society of Pennsylvania in Philadelphia, indicates the importance of keeping one's shoes in top condition—at least for those who could afford to. Writing from London to "my dear Nancy" on 30 June 1755, Colonel Thomas Willing informs her that "I have delivered to Captain Ritchie the six pairs of black shoes you sent for and the silks you sent over last fall to be cleaned."[11] While dispatching her shoes to London to be refreshed was undeniably a luxury, it also reveals

3.3 Apprentice shoemaker Rob Welch, in the shoe shop at Colonial Williamsburg in Virginia. The shoemaker's shop represents that of George Wilson, who moved to Williamsburg from Norfolk, Virginia, in the late 1760s. Photograph by the author, March 2017

3.4 Interior of the Colonial Williamsburg shoe shop. Photograph by the author, March 2017

the value of the purchase to her. In addition, if all of them belonged to her, they provide a benchmark for how many pairs of shoes a wealthy woman might own.

Imported "stuff" (worsted wool uppers), as well as silk and calamanco shoes, were particularly popular with British American consumers, as is apparent from shopkeepers' inventories and household accounts. Large quantities of Lynn-made ladies' shoes, for example, were available for purchase in most urban areas along the eastern seaboard, and they showed up frequently in shopkeepers' advertisements by the 1760s. The shopping patterns of rural southern planters and their wives, such as Martha Washington and her peers, were frequently different from those found in New England. The former relied on the sale of tobacco and other crops to purchase British calamancos, satin pumps, and leather shoes directly from London, through a factor or a broker. Nonetheless, there were certainly opportunities to shop in colonial towns, such as Williamsburg.

Whether it was because of the initial investment in such goods or the intervening Revolutionary War—or perhaps a combination of both—one finds a great number of British women's shoes available in the colonies up to the years 1770–1775, after which the supply slows dramatically. Women kept their shoes, updating and repairing them as needed. In Boston, Philadelphia, and New York, revolutionary Committees of Safety imposed various nonintercourse acts, beginning as early as 1764 and culminating with the closing of Boston Harbor in 1774. A gap follows until about 1784. With the return of peace, London merchants attempted to glut the hungry American market with excess stock. While there continued to be an abundance of London- and British-made shoes in post-revolutionary America, consumers began to have more and more choices. Certainly by the late 1780s, French shoes and slippers begin to make inroads into the American footwear market. Moreover, the work of American cordwainers had already begun to gain acceptance, even before the Revolutionary War. Fashions in footwear were constantly changing, and a new, easily identifiable style emerged as low-heeled, delicate, neoclassical French slippers and shoes pervaded American shores.

3.5   **A view of shoe heels.** *Left to right:* A pair of shoes, gift of Mrs. Albert Remick, object number 593; single center shoe, gift of Samuel Gerrish, object number 847, these three shoes courtesy of the Portsmouth Historical Society; and a pair of shoes, author's collection, photographed on site at the John Paul Jones House, Portsmouth, New Hampshire, by Andrew Davis, February 2017

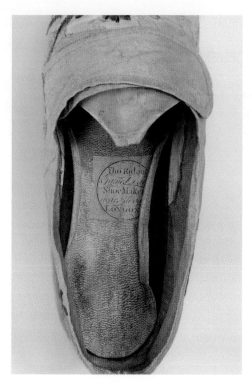

3.6 A paper label, "Thomas Ridout & James Davis ShoeMakers near Aldgate LONDON." Courtesy of the Brooklyn Museum Costume Collection at the Metropolitan Museum of Art, gift of Charles Blaney, 1926, and gift of the Brooklyn Museum, 2009, accession number 2009.300.1406a,b

LABELS

By the 1750s, John Hose had begun to differentiate his luxury shoes from others by prominently attaching labels in the footbed, an innovation in marketing that was just taking off among London's fashionable cordwainers. The shoes fabricated by these skilled artisans and displayed in the posh Aldgate shops were among the earliest to carry labels. These generally were a one-inch square or round, featuring the name of the shoemaker and the location of his shop. Mary Simpkins Rand's 1773 wedding shoes (see chapter 5) carried the identification "made by Jno. Hose & Son At the Rose in Cheapside, near Milk Street, London." The label gave Mary the certitude of a shoe proper to her station. London's shoemakers, pioneering an early form of product branding, signaled an important moment in how shoe manufacturers thought about consumption. The labels illustrated not only a man's pride in his craft, but also a growing sophistication in the arts of advertising and trade specialization.

In the world of the shoe trade in Georgian London, the survival of dozens of labeled ladies' shoes in North American collections provides a unique opportunity for costume historians. According to several authorities on English shoes, such as Lucy Johnston and Linda Woolley, the earliest London labels first appeared in the 1750s. Examination of an abundance of labeled shoes, ranging from the 1740s through the 1810s, in North American collections has made it possible to identify many production details for two well-established London cordwainers—John Hose & Son and Ridout & Davis—not only because of the luxury and high quality of their goods, but also through an examination of the simple square, rectangular, or circular labels—affixed to the insole, or footbed, of their shoes—that gave the cordwainer's name and place of business.[12] With just this bit of information, it is possible to locate archival records relating to the shoemaker, such as apprenticeship records and probate inventories. Changes in partnerships may also be identified through labels. For example, John Hose added "& Son" to his labels after Thomas completed his apprenticeship. When John died, his son continued the business as Thomas Hose, though he moved to a new location on Lombard Street. Ridout & Davis sometimes worked together and, at other times, independently, information brought to light by the labels on their shoes.

In their shop under the shadow of London's eastern-most medieval gateway, Aldgate, in the Ward of the Cordwainer, Thomas Ridout & James Davis created Georgian footwear that was no doubt the envy of many. Their collaboration appears to have spanned several decades, from the 1740s through the 1770s. It is only because they labeled their footwear that it is possible to gather a collection of their shoes, and even some of their customers, into an easily discernable whole. It was a single Ridout & Davis shoe, held in the collection of the Strawbery Banke Museum, in Portsmouth, New Hampshire, that first caught my attention in 2010.[13]

While little is known about this shoe—it was given to the museum by a generous donor, who does not appear to have a direct family connection with or provenance for it—a few things can be inferred with some level of certainty. The makers were well-known London cordwainers. As often occurs in museum collections, only one shoe has survived. This most likely indicates that the pair were divided between two family members, so each could have a memento. It is undeniably much easier to divide a pair of shoes than a wedding dress. Though made in London, the shoes were most likely worn in the colonies, based on the donor record. The remaining shoe is accompanied by a single clog (an overshoe, also referred to as a patten, that kept the shoe above the dirt and muck of the street), which probably was not part of the original pair.[14] On 24 January 1660, the famous London diarist Samuel Pepys comments that he "then called on

3.8 A single brocaded silk shoe, with polychrome florals and a silk-clad carved wooden heel, made in London by Ridout & Davis, circa the 1740s–1750s. Courtesy of the Strawbery Banke Museum, gift of Anna D. Souter, accession number 1987.1034, photograph by Ellen McDermott

my wife and took her to Mr. Pierces, she in the way being exceedingly troubled with a pair of new pattens and I vexed to go so slow, it being late."

Tracking down other surviving examples of Ridout & Davis's work has yielded many results. In addition to the Strawbery Banke Museum, their shoes are found in collections at Colonial Williamsburg, the Connecticut Historical Society, the Metropolitan Museum of Art, the Peabody Essex Museum, the Royal Ontario Museum, and the Warner House in Portsmouth, New Hampshire, among others, revealing that certain makers' shoes found favor with American women. Some cordwainers secured semi-exclusive means to export their shoes from London to the colonies.[15] Both Ridout and Davis were contemporaries of John Hose and his son, Thomas. The senior member of the partnership appears to have been Thomas Ridout, who was elected master of the Worshipful Company of Cordwainers in July 1720. His son, also named Thomas, continued the work, and, like his father, was elected master of the Worshipful Company of Cordwainers in 1751.[16] Working both independently

3.7 (*opposite*) A shoe label from Boston shoemaker P. Gull, in a silk satin shoe with embroidery at the toe, circa 1785-1790s. Also see the John Hose & Son label in figure 1.8. Author's collection, photograph by Andrew Davis, February 2017

3.9 A blue-green silk shoe and matching patten, maker unknown, circa 1760, possibly worn by Dorothy Sherburne of Portsmouth, New Hampshire. A patten (also known as a clog) served to slightly elevate the shoe from dirty or muddy paths. The silk patten for this shoe most likely was attached to the shoe with leather ties or ribbons. Courtesy of the Warner House, accession number WH1968.8.3-4, photographed on site at the Warner House, Portsmouth, New Hampshire, by Andrew Davis, May 2016

3.10 A blue-green silk shoe and matching patten, maker unknown, circa 1760, possibly worn by Dorothy Sherburne of Portsmouth, New Hampshire. The image illustrates how a shoe and patten are worn. Courtesy of the Warner House, accession number WH1968.8.3-4>, photographed on site at the Warner House, Portsmouth, New Hampshire, by Andrew Davis, May 2016

and in partnership, Thomas Ridout and James Davis had begun to affix labels to their footwear by the mid-eighteenth century. Stylistically, the labels are round or feature a shield set within the roundel. The border is simple, although, in the example of Mehitable Rindge Rogers' shoe (c. 1760–1770) in the Warner House collection, made by Davis alone, the treatment has a more baroque flourish.[17]

The very existence of labeled work attests to the makers' professionalization, and their desire for recognition. It was also a form of advertising. Further, since many of these shoes seem to have been destined for the export trade, the existence of a label may have been a distinguishing factor for tariff payments on British goods, as ladies' shoes are frequently listed separately on ships' manifests, cargo lists, and customshouse records in seaport cities such as Salem and Portsmouth.[18]

A pair of silk brocade or damask shoes imported from England bore the mark of gentility and civility for the wearer. One particular pair of silk brocade shoes, also by Ridout & Davis, were discovered in a home in Maine, a region that then was part of the Massachusetts Bay Colony. These elegant shoes, made in London circa the 1740s by the Ridout & Davis partnership, were among the finest of their era. Their vibrant yellow-gold ground and covered wooden French heels represented the epitome of rococo fashion footwear. They most likely were cherished by their owner, a woman who lived on the frontier of provincial America. It is not clear, however, if these shoes were custom-made or elegant ready-mades.

The name of their wearer is unknown, yet these shoes provide a glimpse of the elite fashions found along the eastern seaboard before the American Revolution. Now in the collection of Colonial Williamsburg, they are in fine condition and exemplify the height of shoe styles at that time.[19] The label on the shoe, dated to the 1740s–1750s, may be one of the earliest examples of this practice, indicating that the Ridout & Davis firm was at the front end of this nascent marketing trend.

Another pair of Ridout & Davis shoes, from the 1760s, are housed in the collection of the Peabody Essex Museum in Salem, Massachusetts. They are in fine condition and also feature the brilliant yellow ground that was popular at the time. A splendid example of rococo style, they are a vibrant gold-yellow silk brocade, with wooden heels clad in the same fabric. The pattern is matched on the heels and toes. A teasing strip of striped ombré silk, lining the underside of the top of the tongue, adds even more flourish to these eye-catching beauties.[20]

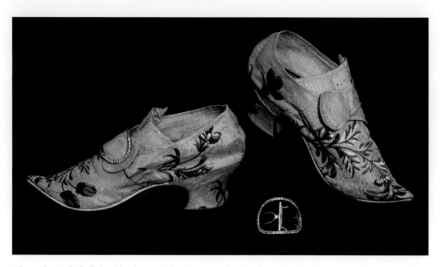

3.11 Vibrant brocaded silk buckle shoes, with silk-covered, carved wooden heels and a white rand, made in London by Ridout & Davis, circa the 1740s. The shoes were worn in America, probably in Maine. Courtesy of the Colonial Williamsburg Foundation, purchase partially funded by Margie and Harold Gill, Kimberly Ivey, Linda Baumgarten and John Watson, and Liza and Wallace Gusler in memory of Mildred Lanier, accession number 2008-139,1&2

James Davis could boast of one particularly esteemed provincial client—Martha Washington, who purchased no fewer than thirteen pairs of shoes from him in 1771 alone. Her order was found among correspondence with the Washingtons' factor, Robert Cary & Company. The invoice was dated 3 December 1771 and included "8 pair Women's neat rich black calamancos lined; 2 pair neat leather pumps; 2 pair ditto shoes, 1 pair rich black satin lined."[21] Unfortunately, none of Martha's Davis-made shoes seem to have survived. For comparison, however, a pair of red leather shoes by Davis, circa 1770, however, in the collection of the Connecticut Historical Society, can serve as a comparable example, given the closeness in date and the description of "neat leather pumps." even though a color is not specified in the Washingtons' order.

ELIZA LUCAS PINCKNEY'S VERY SPECIAL
LONDON SHOES, 1760S–1770S

After John Hose died in 1769, his son Thomas inherited his father's business on Milk Street, Cheapside, "at the Rose." Shortly thereafter, Thomas relocated it to Lombard Street, "at the boot." Numerous pairs of Thomas Hose shoes have survived, and he apparently made use of the colonial contacts his father had fostered. One of his customers was Eliza Pinckney (1722–1793), best known for her experiments, in colonial South Carolina's Low Country, in sericulture (raising silkworms to produce raw silk) and with plants used to make indigo dye. Through her innovation and perseverance with the development of indigo, she ultimately transformed a nonnative species into one of the colony's staple, and most lucrative, crops. With astute business acumen, she developed indigo in an effort to edge out the French market.[22]

Eliza—a daughter of one of the colony's most respectable families and the wife of Charles Pinckney, a lawyer, judge, and member of the House of Commons—had particular access to some of the most luxurious goods to be found in the world at that time, including the elegant pumps and slippers produced by London shoemakers. She had attended school in London as a teenager and was accustomed to British goods. Eliza would later spend time in London with her husband and children.

Only a few garments and textiles associated with her have survived, among them a pair of diminutive silk shoes (6.75 inches in length, with a heel a smidgen more than 2 inches high), made in London by Thomas Hose. Thomas's

3.12 Woman's wedding shoes, hand-stitched leather, wood, and linen, made in London by James Davis, circa 1770. James Davis's shoes were popular in British America, and they appear in numerous museum and historical society collections. He frequently worked in partnership with Thomas Ridout. Martha Washington ordered thirteen pairs of shoes from him in 1771. Her order was found among the correspondence with the Washingtons' agent, or factor, Robert Cary & Company. The invoice, dated 3 December 1771, included eight pairs of calamanco shoes and two pairs of neat leather pumps, probably not unlike the leather shoes shown here. Courtesy of the Connecticut Historical Society, gift of Rosamond Danielson, accession number 1955.6.0a,b

3.13 A salmon silk robe à la française and petticoat—also known as a sack-back gown—1760s–1770s, belonging to Eliza Lucas Pinckney. In addition to the luxurious textile, the dress features extensive ruching (a gathered strip of fabric) that trims the open front, as well as the elegant tiered sleeves. This significant gown was conserved in 2017, and the photo captures the post-treatment sheen of the silk. Courtesy of the Charleston Museum, accession number HT 604

3.14   Pale blue silk buckle shoes, heavily embellished with metallic braid or lace, laid on a geometric pattern, English, 1760s–1770s, belonging to Eliza Lucas Pinckney. The paper label affixed to the footbed credits Thomas Hose (son of John Hose) as the shoemaker, located at 3 Lombard Street, "the Sign of the Boot." Courtesy of the Charleston Museum, accession number HT 4033

label was similar to that used by his father, but it noted his new address. Eliza's elegant, well-appointed shoes feature an intriguing profusion of costly metallic braid, also known as lace. This treatment alone might encourage us to situate the shoes several decades earlier, but the shape of their heels suggest a revolutionary-era provenance, probably in the 1760s-1770s.[23] These light blue, silk satin shoes are distinctive, in part, because of who their original owner was, which places them into the category of rare and significant clothing survivals. Hose's design is beautiful. He crafted the taper of the French heel to make it appear even more slender, through the placement of the metallic braid. This careful positioning also created a well-articulated geometrical pattern. This is especially striking in the outline of the heel and culminates in a stylized floral motif at the vamp.[24]

Offering further evidence that the shoes were costly, much of the interior was lined with two separate versions of striped silk, one of salmon pink and white, and the other of olive and tan. Silk also lines the underside of the tongue, a detail that appears often in high-end shoes of that time. It frequently goes unnoticed, however, due to damage in this delicate area. The

3.15 Silk satin shoes, made in London by Chamberlain & Son, circa the 1780s, worn in New Hampshire. See figure 3.5 for a view of the heels of these shoes. *Left to right*: A pair of shoes probably belonging to Martha (Patty) Rogers; a single shoe owned by Sally Brewster Gerrish, worn in Portsmouth, New Hampshire; late eighteenth–century shoes made in Boston, wearer unknown. The pink (now much faded) pair of shoes on the left are a fine example of Chamberlain & Son's footwear and would have been worn with buckles. For another pair of Chamberlain shoes worn in New England, see figure 3.17. *Left to right*: A pair of shoes, gift of Mrs. Albert Remick object number 593; single center shoe, gift of Samuel Gerrish object number 847, these three shoes courtesy of the Portsmouth Historical Society; a pair of shoes, author's collection, photographed on site at the John Paul Jones House, Portsmouth, New Hampshire, by Andrew Davis, February 2017

treatment of the inside of Eliza's shoes offers an instant visual pop, although only she (and perhaps one or two intimates, such as her husband or her maid) would notice this detailing. It was a small, but luxurious, special addition, appreciated by the owner.

These were almost certainly custom-made shoes, designed especially for Eliza. One suspects that perhaps the pale blue silk was a nod to her indigo crop—although that is merely speculation, as no dye or fiber analysis of the shoes has been undertaken. Eliza spent five years in England, from 1753 through 1758, to educate her children (just as she had been educated in London), while her husband served as a colonial agent. These shoes may well have been bought during that time, when she was in her thirties and enjoying London's social whirl.[25] On the other hand, given the likely date range for the shoes and her departure from London in 1758, they could just as easily be purchases she made after her return.

Another pair of shoes that reveal a transatlantic connection are in the collection of the Portsmouth Historical Society in New Hampshire. They are silk satin shoes, which stylistically belong to the 1780s. The label "Chamberlain & Sons, London" offers a clue to their provenance and their journey to America. William Chamberlain was apprenticed to John Hose, and the survival of many pairs of his shoes, with their high level of craftsmanship, provides an opportunity to observe Hose's influence as a master cordwainer. Chamberlain, by this time a cordwainer in his own right, most likely was competing for the same clients as John Hose's son, Thomas.

The delicate pair of shoes (figure 3.15, far left) probably belonged to Martha (Patty) Rogers (1762–1840), youngest daughter of the Reverend Daniel Rogers of Exeter, New Hampshire. They are a fine example of Chamberlain &

3.16   Eighteenth-century silk wallets, maker unknown. The blue-green and salmon silk damask wallet was probably fashioned from a small bit of an older textile. It may have belonged to the wearer of the shoes on the left in figure 3.15, for tucked inside the wallet was a note asking Miss Rogers to dance at a soirée in Exeter, New Hampshire. Curator Emerita Sandra Rux discovered the small, folded missive when cataloging the collection. The second wallet is a blue silk brocade. Courtesy of the Portsmouth Historical Society, gift of Mrs. Albert Remick, object numbers 2005.039 and 2005.040, photograph by Andrew Davis, February 2017

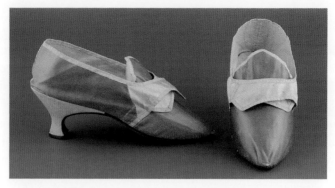

3.17 A pair of pink satin buckle shoes with satin-covered heels and a pointed tongue and toe, made by London cordwainer William Chamberlain, apprenticed to John Hose, circa the 1780s. These shoes are a good example of Chamberlain's output and were popular with American customers. They also illustrate the transition to a lighter color palette and less-complex patterns, as well as the use of materials associated with the neoclassical period. Courtesy of Historic New England, gift of Albert C. Frothingham, accession number 1961.12AB

3.18 A paper label, Chamberlain & Sons, shoemakers in Cheapside, London, circa the 1780s. Courtesy of the Portsmouth Historical Society, gift of Mrs. Albert Remick, object number 593, photograph by Andrew Davis, February 2017

Sons footwear and would have been worn with buckles to attach them to the foot. Although now faded, it is possible to observe the original pink hue beneath the straps for the buckle. A small green-and-pink brocaded wallet, with a pale pink salmon-hued interior, may have been made to match these shoes. The original textile is circa the 1750s,[26] and the wallet was probably fashioned from remnants of earlier garments. Recently, a carefully folded message, resembling an origami tulip—a love fold—was found tucked into the wallet. Although not dated, the note is probably from the mid-1780s, contemporary with the shoes. It says: "—— Parkers compliments to Miss Rogers Would be glad to wait on her this evening to dance at Capt True Gilman's Friday 10 Oclock." Captain Trueworthy Gilman (b. 1738) lived in Exeter, and Nathaniel Parker (1760–1812) was the likely author. Parker later married Catherine Tilton, while Miss Rogers never wed.[27]

SHOES OF EXCEPTIONAL QUALITY • Winthrop Gray and John Gonsolve

Sometimes it was not just the shoe that crossed the Atlantic, but an idea or image of gentility and fashion, to be transformed by American tradesmen who were born and trained in the colonies. An example of the latter is housed in the collection of Historic New England: a pair of silk brocade women's shoes, completed by 1775 or 1776. They are made of steel gray silk, richly brocaded with large stylized flowers in silver and gold metallic threads on a geometric-patterned ground. They also feature a white rand, an oval toe, and a square tongue. The tiny stitching (noticeable along the heel and the instep) is associated with top-end British shoes.[28] The heel measures 2.5 inches, a height often found in the shoes of colonial women.[29]

The label verifies that these shoes did not originate in Aldgate, nor did they come from the workbenches of Thomas Hose or William Chamberlain. Rather, they were fabricated in Boston, in the shop of cordwainer Winthrop Gray, and are an excellent example of elegant shoes made in the colonies on the eve of the American Revolution. That Gray used a label to identify his work is significant, demonstrating that Yankee shoemakers had begun to implement English marketing techniques.

Another key element in his shoe label is the notation that Gray's shop was located "near the cornfields" in Boston. The Cornfields (not to be confused with Cornhill) was close to today's Union Oyster House restaurant. In 1742, before the building became a restaurant, it housed the shop of successful im-

3.19 A brocaded silk buckle shoe with silver and gold metallic threads, a floral motif, an oval toe, and a 2.5-inch heel, made by Boston cordwainer Winthrop Gray, by 1775. Captain Winthrop Gray enlisted by 1775-1776 and does not appear to have continued shoemaking after the American Revolution. Courtesy of Historic New England, accession number 1949.130AB

porter Hopestill Capen. Capen's "fancy" textile goods business was known colorfully as "at the Sign of the Cornfields." With the Boston waterfront literally at the back door of the establishment—at that time, high tide from the harbor came right up to the building—it would have been convenient for ships to deliver their cloth and goods from Europe, and a cordwainer like Gray would have had ready access to the finest materials for his shoes, including high-quality, woven silk brocade. In an additional clue about the maker, the label features a compass, which is a Masonic symbol. It would not be uncommon for Winthrop to be a Freemason, as were many of his contemporaries.[30] What is unusual is the inclusion of a masonic symbol on his shoe label.

Winthrop Gray did not learn his trade in Europe or in Britain. He apprenticed in a Lynn-based workshop, honing his skills as the member of a shoemaking family. After his training, he set up shop in Boston sometime before the Revolutionary War. Whether his shop catered to a local clientele—elites or "middling sorts"—is unknown. The surviving shoes, however, are an example of a luxury purchase, as the brocaded silk features both gold and silver metallic threads. They were most likely made between 1765 and 1775, since by May 1776 he had received his commission in the Continental Army.[31] Fortu-

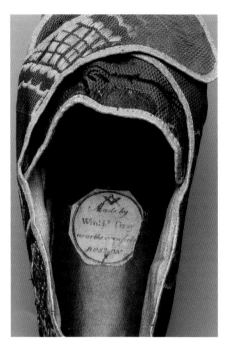

3.20 The interior of a Winthrop Gray shoe, with a paper label that reads "Made by Winthrop Gray near the cornfields BOSTON." It features a Masonic compass symbol. Courtesy of Historic New England, accession number 1949.130AB

nately, the label allows us to identify an outstanding artifact by an American shoemaker just prior to the outbreak of the revolution. The quality of the shoes—the materials, the stitching, and the finish work—rivals the work of many a British cordwainer. By the time Gray placed his label in the insole of the shoe, shoemakers from Lynn had been making ladies' silk, wool, and cloth shoes for several decades.

The Gray family of Lynn and Salem traced its roots back to William Gray.[32] He, his brothers, and his father's father were all cordwainers in Lynn. Winthrop Gray was most likely born in Lynn, but he removed to Boston at an unknown date as a young man.[33] He was commissioned on 10 May 1776, and became a captain in the Fifth Company Colonel Crafts Artillery Regiment on 9 October 1776. Continental Army accounts reveal that he served from 1 January 1777 through 26 February 1779, when he tendered his resignation. According to several sources, in 1779 he had a disagreement with Paul Revere concerning the reorganization of various regiments.[34] He may well have come into a family inheritance in 1780–1781, for by 1781 he appears in city directories as an innholder at the American Exchange Tavern on State Street in Boston. He died a year later, in Boston, on 3 June 1782, at age forty-two. Gray is buried in the King's Chapel burying ground. He was survived by his wife Mary (who was also a first cousin).[35]

John Gonsolve of Providence, Rhode Island, is another cordwainer who, prior to the outbreak of the Revolutionary War, made shoes that could rival those of London cordwainers. He was one of several Italian and Portuguese shoemakers who set up shop in Rhode Island prior to the revolution.[36] A pair of charming silk damask shoes, bearing Gonsolve's label, were sold by Augusta Auctions on 14 November 2012 in New York City. Looking past the abraded surfaces, it is possible to glimpse the original silk sheen of the rich sage green and mocha hues. These shoes, lined with linen, feature an Italian-style heel and a white rand. Gonsolve branded his shoes with a simple rectangular label. A hand-inked date of 1767 was written on the label at some unknown time. This was the year that the wearer of the shoes, Phebe Wardell (1748–1840), married James Smith of Bristol, Rhode Island, who would later take part in the notorious Gaspee Affair on 9 June 1772.[37] They may well be her wedding shoes, worn in December of that year.

Phebe and her young children removed to Dighton, Massachusetts, for the duration of the revolutionary conflict. The couple had six children. Phebe died on 23 September 1840 at age ninety-two, handing her shoes down to her daughter, Fanny Smith, who in turn passed them on to her son. This impeccable provenance—knowing who the original owner of this pair of damask shoes was, when they were made, and who made them—is an especial find indeed. The small label in these shoes served as an advertisement or calling card for John Gonsolve and his business, located near the Mill Bridge. Gonsolve clearly was successful in his trade as a shoemaker. In 1785, he posted a notice seeking "any Gentlemen of the Craft, duly qualified . . . and wanting a Seat in my shop, near the Mill Bridge . . . may have constant Employ, and good Wages."[38]

Winthrop Gray and John Gonsolve provide an opportunity to rethink the way shoes have been examined in the past, which was primarily through the lens of footwear exported from Great Britain. The survival of shoes by Gray and Gonsolve (and no doubt countless others currently unknown and unnamed) gives considerable credibility to the abilities of colonial tradesmen in New England and elsewhere. The pair made by Winthrop Gray are an example of the type of shoe that could have been produced not only in Lynn, but in any number of bastions of local or regional shoemaking. While there are many mentions of shoes from Lynn in the historical record, there are very few Lynn-made examples with labels prior to the 1790s, despite the fact that it was a training ground for the next generation of cordwainers, who then went on to Boston, Newburyport, or Philadelphia. A smattering of examples of pre-revolutionary labeled shoes survive in New York, New Jersey, and Massachusetts collections.[39]

In some respects, the surviving pair of shoes by Winthrop Gray can be considered a Rosetta Stone for understanding the work being carried out in the colonies. In Lynn, on the eve of the American Revolution, cordwainers such as Gray were turning out calamanco or silk or russell (a finely corded fabric) or Moroccan leather shoes and slippers. The quality was very high and would have been perfectly acceptable to most clients, who would have ranged from the "middling sorts" to the elite. By the mid-1760s, and especially with the implementation of the Stamp Act, where clothing was produced and from whom it was purchased took on a new meaning, one that was of political import for many consumers. As clothing became more closely connected with politics, Lynn-made footwear was a suitable alternative to a British import if one was interested in making a statement about buying locally, from one's "neighbor," versus buying imported British goods whose sale would line the monarchy's treasury.

There remains much to learn about shoemaking in eighteenth-century towns and villages, including how one obtained shoes in rural areas. An example is found in the 1793 account book of General John Montgomery of Haverhill, New Hampshire.[40] Shoemakers in this northern region could purchase raw materials from Montgomery's store to use in fabricating shoes at home or in an outbuilding. The shoe—or its component parts—were returned to his store for sale or for custom orders. Montgomery's daybook indicates that shoes generally cost 4 to 6 shillings. Partially premade or made-to-order shoes were sometimes combined with needlework. This helps explain the many references to leather, sole leather, soles, sole nails, heels, and binding found in Montgomery's daybook. It mentions a local woman, Phebe Ladd, who bought fabrics and silk thread at the store, which may well have been for her use in crafting uppers. She came from a family of tanners and leatherworkers whose business site was just across the Oliverian Brook from Montgomery's home and store. Furthermore, with the prevalence of home embroidery in the town, it is highly likely that local women brought their own work to the Ladd family, Phineas Swan, and others, in order to incorporate these vamps or uppers with leather soles. Montgomery's daybook frequently mentions shoe buckles, which would have been a way of updating older shoes to current styles.

In addition, the presence of itinerant ironworkers and tailors, who would set up shop at Montgomery's store for a few days, could easily indicate the

3.21 A single silk shoe, made in London by shoemaker James Davis, circa the 1760s, worn in Portsmouth, New Hampshire. The shoe shown here, possibly a wedding shoe, was worn by Mehitable Rindge Rogers, who married the Honorable Daniel Rogers, ten years her senior, of His Majesty's Council for New Hampshire. The couple were both raised in Portsmouth and are buried in the Proprietor's Cemetery. Courtesy of the Warner House, accession number WH1968.8.9-10, photographed on site at the Warner House, Portsmouth, New Hampshire, by Andrew Davis, May 2016

3.22 View of the heel of Mehitable Rindge Rogers's shoe (figure 3.21). The three-inch heel is higher than is usually seen in New England shoe collections. The taller, courtly heel may indicate special-occasion wear. Perhaps they were her wedding shoes, or, due to her husband's position as a member of the King's Council in New Hampshire, they may have been necessary accessories for her position in society. The stitching of the back seam is noticeable, though badly abraded. Note the graceful nipped-in waist of the heel, which then flares out again at its base. Courtesy of the Warner House, accession number WH1968.8.9-1, photographed on site at the Warner House, Portsmouth, New Hampshire, by Andrew Davis, May 2016

existence of traveling shoemakers and cobblers, something that the guilds in Boston and Philadelphia were anxious to extinguish. Smaller communities, such as Haverhill, had access to the latest materials and textiles that were available in Boston and Hartford, as well as residents who possessed the skills to produce shoes on a small, as-needed scale. The Ladds had a strong corner on the local shoe and leather trade, with several brothers, sisters, and sisters-in-law as workers. More importantly, they had a tannery and several other businesses along Oliverian Brook.

Whether English- or American-made, women's heeled shoes were frequently criticized or satirized as examples of their undue interest in fashion. Among the detractors of this female penchant for high heels was a Dutchman, Dr. Petrus Camper (1722–1789), who railed against the dangers they posed. For example, in the mid-1700s, Camper, in his "On the Best Form of Shoe," opined that elite women had been "misled by ridiculous vanity." He criticized the fashion that directed women to "cram their feet into smaller than required sized shoes that are tight fitting with high and slender heels." In contrast, he commended those of the "middling sort" for selecting shoes that promoted stable soles for walking.[41]

Calamanco shoes, discussed in the next chapter, provide a case study in the changing relationship between making patriotic purchases or supporting the Crown and Parliament. The purchase of calamanco shoes, however—whether from London or from Lynn—is equally a question of status. Chapter 5 explores the burgeoning resistance to the Stamp Act, largely through the colonial newspapers and the testimonies before Parliament by Benjamin Franklin and cordwainer John Hose.

3.23 A James Davis label, pasted into the footbed of Mehitable Rindge Rogers's silk satin shoe (figure 3.21). Note also the strip of pink satin that lines the inside of the top of the tongue, adding a bit of extra splash visible only by the wearer and her intimates. Courtesy of the Warner House, accession number WH1968.8.9-10, photographed on site at the Warner House, Portsmouth, New Hampshire, by Andrew Davis, May 2016

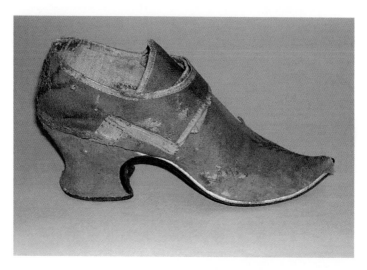

4.1 Pink wool buckle shoes, English, maker unknown, circa the 1740s. Despite being well worn, a bit of surface sheen is still discernible, indicating that the wool was glazed, or calendered—hence a calamanco shoe. Courtesy of the Metropolitan Museum of Art, gift of Mrs. Moseley Taylor, 1944, accession number C.I.44.79

COVETING CALAMANCOS

• From London to Lynn •

There the young ladies were taught dancing and music, for which,
as well as for their frocks and "pink calamanco shoes," their fathers paid
enormous sums in depreciated Continental currency.

Theodore Roosevelt, *The Winning of the West*

One special item, fancied by women from both the high and low ends of society throughout the British American provinces, was popularly known as calamanco.[1] It was among the most common materials used for shoe uppers through the third quarter of the eighteenth century.[2] Martha Washington asked her husband George to purchase hers in London. Dorothy Quincy received a pair as a gift from her fiancé, John Hancock, while he was in Philadelphia on business with the Continental Congress. Abigail Adams wistfully mentioned to her husband in a letter on 16 July 1775 that, despite the scarcity of supplies, she wished she had two yards of it to make shoes.[3]

Some sources attribute the word to a modification of the Spanish word *calamaco*, derived from the Latin *calamaucus*, referring to a felt cap or skullcap. Historians trace the earliest usage of the term back to the late sixteenth century. Calamanco is a worsted wool, finished with a glazed surface.[4] To create this glossy, calendered finish, the textile was forced through hot roll-

4.2 A calamanco quilt, made in New England, maker unknown, circa 1775-1800. Courtesy of the Metropolitan Museum of Art, museum purchase, gift of Joan G. Hancock in memory of Frances Burrall Henry, received by exchange, 1998, accession number 1998.105

ers. The sheen that resulted from this treatment was highly desirable, as shine, or luster, was a key element in the visual language of the eighteenth century, from clothing to furniture to decorative arts. Consumers used calamanco for a variety of household textiles, such as bed coverings, as well as for clothing, including petticoats, waistcoats, and shoes.

Calamanco came to American shores in a variety of weaves: plain, damasked, and brocaded. The wool held dyes well and was also frequently associated with bright colors, such as the vibrant reds and yellows fancied in the early part of the century, and the elegant greens that became the fashion by midcentury.[5] Remnants of calamanco from a petticoat or waistcoat could be repurposed for many items, including quilts or shoes.

If the calamanco shoe was so ubiquitous, why is it important historically, and what makes it worthy of study? Perhaps more than any other piece of material culture, calamanco elucidates important aspects of everyday life in Early America by revealing the multiple meanings of goods in a world of scarcity. It crossed socioeconomic boundaries. Martha Washington wore calamancos, and so did John Hancock's serving girl. Yet paradox underlies this particular fabric. A perusal of colonial advertisements or a tour of a modern museum collection would suggest the dominance of more-luxurious footwear—silk damasks, brocades, and the like. The number of calamanco shoes sold in British America—and in New England in particular—was significantly higher than silk or leather shoes, however.[6] There is a preponderance of eighteenth-century advertisements for calamancos, yet there are not many shoes of this type that still exist. Conversely, colonial newspapers featured fewer advertisements for silk shoes, but more survive in museums and similar institutions. Despite the large numbers of calamancos purchased both as imports and from colonial production, such shoes are now relatively scarce in North American collections.

Notwithstanding its past popularity, today's costume or material-culture historian may be unfamiliar with shoes fashioned from calamanco, although well aware of the textile through its use for quilts, petticoats, and small furnishings. It was the pedestrian nature of calamanco that rendered it a common and favorite type of shoe in Early American life. For museum visitors and researchers, the survival of a disproportionate number of silk shoes distorts the sense of what the elites, the "middling sorts," and working-class people wore in the eighteenth century.

Calamanco shoes were a nearly universal piece of material culture in Early America, yet they remain underrepresented, understudied, and underappreciated in the historiography of fashion. There are reasons for the paradox between what was then and what is now. Their absence from modern collections is understandable when one remembers that few examples have actually survived. Wool shoes face a particular threat that is common to historic fabrics: the decay and insect infestations that commonly deteriorate textiles. Apparently, the wool blend made it a particularly satisfying meal for moths, insects, and other vermin, all of which found calamanco nourishing and good for nesting.[7]

Second, the ordinariness of calamanco may also be responsible for its rarity in modern collections. As a workaday shoe, calamancos were simply tossed into a privy—the Early American form of trash dump—when worn out, serving a secondary use as compost. In contrast, more elaborate, costly footwear, such as shoes made from silk damask or silk brocade, were frequently special-occasion shoes. These were the shoes that were saved, passed down through generations, and treasured by families. Calamancos, on the other hand, were not highly prized. Perhaps their very ubiquity made them virtually invisible to the eighteenth-century eye. Further, for both "middling sorts" and those with wealth, calamanco shoes simply did not last long, due to the frequent hard wear accorded to them as an everyday shoe. Shoes made of silk brocades and damasks and metallic lace were retained by families for their sentimental value. Up through the first half of the twentieth century, the kinds of footwear collected by museums and other institutions were based on the methodology of connoisseurship: the assessment of visual qualities of beauty and perfection. When confronted with a well-worn or very simple shoe, one that was utilitarian in appearance, museum curators with a limited budget might err on the side of beauty. Changes in the study of history, however—the "new social history" that became manifest after World War II—began to privilege everyday and commonplace objects. This bottom-up approach gained momentum in the 1960s and 1970s and continues today as interest in the lives of everyday people grows.[8]

Calamanco shoes are thus an important element of material culture in the nascent country. First, calamanco challenges the conventional wisdom that early generations of Americans lived in an "age of homespun." This mythology of self-sufficient households became firmly rooted during the colonial revival movement of the 1890s–1920s and has continued uncontested until recent decades. Yet evidence from advertisements, inventories, and correspondence reveals a different story regarding these wool shoes, offering a rich example of how a textile was transferred from Europe and adapted to a multitude of American uses.[9] Even those shoes manufactured domestically, in places like Lynn, largely relied on wool produced in Norwich, England.[10]

Second, by the eve of the American Revolution, goods like calamanco shoes carried powerful messages that signaled one's political leanings. As historians such as T. H. Breen have observed, items imported from London or Bristol brought revenues into the royal treasury and the coffers of English merchants, rather than into the pockets of struggling neighbors. As early as the 1750s (see chapter 5), voices rose in protest against the corrupting aspects of luxury imports, calling on colonial consumers to purchase shoes made by local cordwainers in Lynn or Newport.[11]

When consumers were faced with a choice between a domestic shoe and an English- (and, later, French-) made shoe, those with sufficient means frequently opted for British shoes, even in the period leading up to and following the Revolutionary War. The purchase of calamanco shoes, because of the significant output from Lynn (and, no doubt, lesser-known regions of shoe production), in some small way came to represent colonial economic independence. Despite attempts by Patriot leaders to co-opt and politicize the wearing of imported goods, personal taste and the desire to look fashionable and genteel appear to have overridden those efforts. By 1770, Lynn shoes had such a good reputation in Boston that merchants proudly made note of and trumpeted their origin. Moreover, Lynn-made calamanco shoes appear in the same advertisements with calamancos from England. The *Essex Antiquarian*, in its 1901 discussion of shoemaking, revealed that in 1767, 80,000 pairs of shoes were made in Lynn. The same source reports that in 1770, Lynn-made shoes were even advertised for sale in London shops.[12] An intriguing moment occurred in February 1770, at the height of Boston's non-importation picketing. Isaac Vibird defended his wife Mary from the charge of buying tea from an importer by publicly offering to swear that she had gone into Jackson's shop only to pick up "a Number of Shoes from Lynn."[13] Surely Whigs would praise her for supporting local industry.

Complicating a curator's efforts to categorize a collection is the fact that not all wool shoes are calamancos, yet all calamancos are wool. In addition to calamanco, women could purchase russell or broadcloth, both made from wool. An excellent example of brocaded wool shoes is found in the collection at Historic Deerfield and can serve as a representative example of what might have been imported into the colonies during the 1730s–1740s.[14] These multicolored, rococo, buckle shoes feature substantial French heels.[15] On the surface, it might seem surprising to find such shoes in rural western Massachusetts at this date, but access to high-end consumer goods is readily apparent in the settlement of Deerfield. Evidence housed within the collection at Historic Deerfield reveals, for example, the use of a Spitalfields silk brocade that was made into a mantua, or dress, in the Springfield area of western Massachusetts in the 1740s, as well as a 1738 probate inventory for twenty-one-year-old Sarah Williams, replete with references to luxury clothing and shoes.[16]

The actual provenance of these stylish shoes at Historic Deerfield is unspecified, as they were purchased from a collector. Even if they have no known connection with Massachusetts or the colonies, it would not have been surprising to find a similar pair proudly secured to the feet of the owner by paste- or gemstone buckles. A pair of shoes like these could have easily caught the admiring eye of the wife of a successful country merchant or physician—and possibly the disapproving gaze of a minister such as Rev. Jonathan Edwards, who delivered his most famous sermon, "Sinners in the Hands of an Angry God," in neighboring Northampton in 1735. Further distinguishing the shoes and their wearer is the paper label, pasted to the footbed, which can just barely be deciphered. It reveals that these bold, brocaded wool shoes came from the shop of John Hose & Son in London.[17]

There is a bit of a clue, however, regarding the possible importance of these shoes to their owner or owners. An unusual gusset was placed on the vamp in order to accommodate a change in the owner's feet—perhaps due to illness or pregnancy, or to fit a new wearer. They may be examples of the secondhand clothing trade to British America, or perhaps they never fit properly in the first place, an issue the Washingtons and their London boot- and shoemaker, John Didsbury, discussed in their correspondence.

Advertisements that included calamanco footwear first appear in British American newspapers around 1739.[18] Commensurate with the consumer revolution that swept the provinces by midcentury, these announcements situate colonial America both within an expansive Atlantic-world economy and a cohesive cultural community. Ads that emphasized goods "lately imported from England," from "the latest ships," for "the season," suggest that many consumers preferred to buy their calamancos from Great Britain rather than from American cordwainers. Calamanco shoes were purchased and worn even among the "middling sorts," revealing a bit about a person's station. Among the earliest notices announcing the availability of calamanco shoes in the colonies is a wonderful example from Philadelphia, a shopper's haven, appearing in the *American Weekly Mercury* on 12 November 1741: "To be sold by George House in Chestnut-street near the Three Tons. Variety of choice neat Women Shoes with both Russell, Cloath, Callimanco and Morocco; Golloshoes black and red, very neat Clogs with Morocco and Sattin Tyes, all at 6 s[hillings] 6 per pair. Pattern Shoes at 7 s[hillings] and silk from 15 to 18 s[hillings] per pair. Also good live Geese Feathers, and sundry other Goods very Cheap."[19] Among the advertisement's prices for the various shoes, note the difference in cost between the calamanco shoes, at 6 shillings and 6 pence, and those made of silk, at 15 to 18 shillings a pair. The silk shoes were also two to three times more expensive than shoes of various other textiles or of Morocco leather.

Calamanco shoes were very popular in the American colonies from the 1740s to the 1780s, particularly in New England, as they offered more warmth than those made of silk. The shiny and colorful wool also had other advantages over silk, in that it was more durable and could be surface cleaned on a regular basis. Calamanco shoes, featuring a calendered, or glazed, surface, could withstand a little dirt and survive poor weather. Moreover, they were an affordable choice, available in differing qualities. During the mid-1700s, calamancos usually cost 4 to 8 shillings a pair, roughly equivalent to one to two days of a man's wages

To be Sold by GEORGE HOUSE,
In Chestnut-street, near the Three Tons.
VAriety of choice neat Women Shoes both Ruſſel, Cloath, Callimanco and Morocco; Golloſhoes black and red, very neat Clogs with Morocco and Sattin Tyes, all at 6 ſ 6 per pair. Pattern Shoes at 7 ſ. and Silk from 15 to 18 ſ. per pair. Alſo good live Geeſe Feathers, and ſundry other Goods very Cheap.

4.3 A newspaper advertisement. Note the selection, including "callimanco," and the cost of women's shoes. The silk shoes are more than double the cost of ones made of wool or Morocco leather. *American Weekly Mercury*, Philadelphia, November 1741

at the time, depending on his occupation.[20] Dozens of references to these shoes appear in the account books of merchants and country traders found in collections at sites such as Deerfield, Williamsburg, Boston, and Lynn. Numerous mentions, such as in George Washington's correspondence with John Didsbury, indicate that black calamanco shoes were perhaps the eighteenth-century equivalent to today's black pumps—they were a wardrobe staple for women. Other colors were available, of course, and there are frequent references to pink calamancos for young girls in account books and advertisements.

British American consumers had to import this type of woolen cloth from England, and references to "callimanco" textiles and shoes fill the correspondence, invoices, ledgers, and advertisements of the times. Most calamanco fabric was produced in Norwich, England, and distributed from there throughout Britain. It was then exported from London or Bristol to the colonies.[21] By the mid-eighteenth century, calamanco shoes were produced in large quantities in Lynn, Massachusetts (located fifteen miles north of Boston), and advertisements in Salem, Boston, Portsmouth, and Virginia newspapers offered consumers a locally fabricated version of the popular footwear made in Lynn.[22]

Examining a handful of surviving calamancos reveals the wide range of shoes available—for a price—to the British American consumer. For instance, although none of Martha Dandridge Custis Washington's calamanco shoes are known to survive, there is sufficient evidence found in her correspondence to say with certainty that she wore calamanco shoes, as did both her daughter Patsy and Martha's mother. The nuptials of wealthy widow Martha Custis and George Washington in 1759 marked one of the social season's premier events in Fairfax County, Virginia. Yet after the reels had been danced and the toasts drained, the couple returned to the everyday challenges of planting tobacco and managing several plantations, including the enslaved on them. Like other newlyweds, they also began the tricky process of consolidating their complicated financial affairs. George began to contract with Martha's London-based factor, Robert Cary & Company (who had also handled purchases for Martha's first husband) in an effort to streamline the buying power of both estates.[23]

While individual household members, such as Martha's children from her first marriage, had expenses billed directly to their own accounts, Washington assumed the costs for the majority of his wife's purchases. Among the orders for Martha that he sent to London in the 1750s and 1760s were ones for luxurious shoes "of the latest fashion." He also ordered everyday shoes, such as a pair of "black calamanca pumps." He sent many repeat orders to boot- and shoemaker John Didsbury in London over a twelve-year period, not only for footwear for himself and Martha, but also for his stepchildren Jacky and Patsy, as well as his mother-in-law and the household slaves.[24] There are orders for dozens of black calamanco pumps for Patsy over the years, such as one in 1763 that included "6 pr bla: Callimanca" pumps, which were to be made according to her measure (the size of her foot). Martha had also requested three pairs of "black Callimanca" pumps in an extensive order sent to Didsbury.

A pair of calamancos could be purchased and worn for a wedding and then subsequently serve as the owner's best shoes, worn for the Sabbath, visiting, or other special events. One lovely example is the pair of rosy red calamanco shoes worn by Mary Flint Spofford for her wedding in 1765 (see chapter 2), which are ensconced in the collection at Historic Deerfield. While there is no reason to dispute the paper label accompanying these shoes, attributing them to a British maker, by 1765 a similar pair could certainly have been produced in Danvers, Salem, Lynn, or Rowley in Massachusetts, or in Stratham, Haverhill, or Plaistow in New Hampshire. These geographically close towns and villages were associated with New England shoemaking. For instance, in the daybook of Colonel Welch, of Plaistow, in addition to crafting shoes, he noted making repairs to a calamanco shoe.[25]

A second pair of calamanco shoes are also housed within the collection at Historic Deerfield. This pair of pink infant's or toddler's shoes, circa 1763, were worn by a child with the delightful name of Wealthy Peck Bardwell. They are another particularly fine example of surviving calamancos.[26] An 1888 note accompanies the shoes, assigning them to the Root family of Connecticut. Further research indicates that Wealthy was born in Connecticut in 1762 to Gideon and Irene Peck. She married Elias Bardwell, who was born in 1763 in Whately, Massachusetts. They had at least two children: Robert Bardwell (1788–1849) and Gideon Peck Bardwell (1800–1876). According to family genealogy, she lived most of her adult life in Chenango County, New York. Elias died there in 1819.[27]

Due to the careful preservation efforts at Historic Deerfield, Wealthy's shoes have been recently conserved. The process often sheds more light on the construction of the shoes, however, than on the owner. This pair were probably American made, possibly in Connecticut. They appear to have been fashioned from an earlier garment or textile, as the wool upper is pieced across the toes. With so many household items and clothing made from calamanco, there would have been small remnants available, perfect for making shoe coverings, once again illustrating the economical use of textiles in colonial America. A delicate pink silk ribbon for fastening the shoe to the foot and a lighter

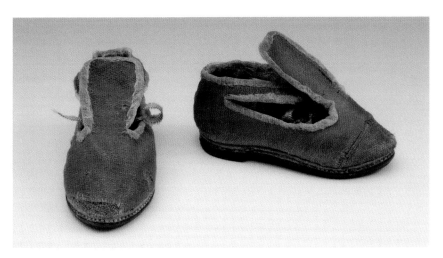

4.4 Rosy pink wool shoes, probably calamanco, made from an earlier textile, circa 1765. These baby shoes probably belonged to Wealthy Peck Bardwell (attribution through a family note). The upper of one shoe is pieced across the toe, and the shoes feature a thick leather sole and silk ribbon ties. Historic Deerfield, Mr. and Mrs. Hugh B. Vanderbilt Fund for Curatorial Acquisitions, object number 2001.56.1, photograph by Penny Leveritt

linen ribbon to bind each shoe complement the calamanco upper. The slightly molded heel is offset by a hand-stitched leather sole. It is possible to discern some significant use through the wear pattern in the wool fabric.[28]

These are possibly toddler's shoes, suggested by the sturdily crafted, layered sole; the leather insole; and the extensive wear on the toes. Wealthy's diminutive shoes, measuring only 3.5 inches in length, roughly comparable to a contemporary infant's size 1 shoe, are appropriate for a child up to nine months old who may not have been learning to walk yet but perhaps spent time twirling in a child-minder or crawling.[29] In addition, while the toes exhibit wear, there is very little on the soles, indicating the pair's use by an infant. Of particular interest in identifying or confirming a point of origin, a similar pair of infant's shoes survive in the collection of the Connecticut Historical Society. According to a note written across the sole of these shoes, they were worn in 1763, the same year young Wealthy Peck Bardwell most likely wore hers. Although the former are made of leather, both pairs feature an especially high, square tongue and a thick, hand-sewn leather sole. The two pairs of shoes may point to a particular regional Connecticut shoemaking style or, perhaps, even the same maker.[30]

Another surprise survival is found within the Irma Bowen Collection in the

University of New Hampshire Museum and Special Collections. This later pair of black-brown wool shoes, most likely calamancos, are in good condition. Unfortunately, neither the maker nor the wearer is known.[31] The wool upper retains a bit of a sheen, consistent with the glazed surface of calamanco, and it points to another reason calamancos are often not identified as such—the shiny surface wears away over time. They have pointed toes and lower heels—a "transition" shoe style—which give a nod to circa 1780s-1790s fashion. The straps, on the other hand, require buckles, carrying on an earlier tradition. They may well have been the best shoes of someone from a "middling," or merchant, sort, or perhaps they were made for a slightly older woman who wanted a more traditional shoe. They are both wide and long, dimensions accentuated by the low heel. The shoes are well constructed and finished with neat binding along the edges. Given their dark hue and dearth of ornamentation, they lack the instant visual appeal of silk shoes. Nonetheless, the style was no doubt common for women's shoes, although footwear of this type rarely survives. Because their quality is good, these were perhaps dress shoes for a middle-class woman, fit for church or visiting.[32]

Sometimes evidence does not manifest itself in the form of an actual shoe, but rather in a random bill of sale or letter or receipt, which leads to another, often unexpected story. Two tantalizing examples related to the Hancock family survive: one housed at the Massachusetts Historical Society, in the form of a receipt for "a pair [of] Calaminco Shoes," and the other in a letter from John Hancock to his fiancée, Dorothy Quincy.[33]

In June 1775, John Hancock was a busy man. Just a few months earlier, he and Samuel Adams had fled Boston, fearing that the British patrols sent out by General Gage would target them. Hancock was attending the Second Continental Congress in Philadelphia, where he was involved in the debates following the battles of Lexington and Concord, which would plunge the colonists into war with Great Britain. He was also planning his wedding. Moreover, he was cranky. His letter of 10 June to his future bride complains that he has written repeatedly "but not one word in answer," having "ask'd million questions & not an answer to one." Hancock was frustrated by her reticence and could not determine if it stemmed from the gendered constraints of the times or if he was not "agreeable" to her. He lamented, "I Really Take it extreme unkind, pray, my dear, use not so much Ceremony & Reservedness, why can't you use freedom in writing, be not afraid of me, I want long Letters."[34]

He was especially perturbed because he had sent presents to her and to Lydia Henchman Hancock—his favorite aunt as well as being the family matriarch—and was desperate to know how they had been received.[35] He tried

4.5 Late eighteenth-century brown-black wool shoes. Both the wearer and the maker are unknown. The wool upper retains a bit of a sheen, consistent with the glazed surface of calamanco. This points to another reason calamancos are often not identified as such, since the shiny surface wears away over time. They are a "transition" style of shoes, with pointed toes and lower heels, which gives a nod to fashion circa the 1780s–1790s. On the other hand, the straps, requiring buckles, carry on an earlier tradition. They may well have been the "best shoes" of the "middling," or merchant, sort, or perhaps they belonged to a slightly older woman who wanted a more traditional shoe. Courtesy of the Irma Bowen Textile Collection, the University of New Hampshire Museum and Special Collections, object number 438, photograph by Andrew Davis, February 2017

again, sending a "paper box" of presents to them via Dr. Benjamin Church. The package included a pair of black satin shoes and the promise of "1 pair Calem Co." that "shall be sent when done."[36] Latter-day historians may wonder if Church had purloined the goods referred to in this correspondence, as he was later found to be a British spy.

The shoes mentioned in Hancock's letter, however, are not the extant pairs of Dorothy's shoes that are housed in the collection of the Bostonian Society's Old State House Museum, which bear the label of London cordwainers Bragg & Luckin and John Gresham (who also provided shoes for Martha Washington). One pair, of ivory satin, may have been the shoes that she wore for her nuptials (see chapter 2), although stylistically they appear closer to ones from the 1780s.[37]

Two years later, John Hancock was back in Boston, the country had declared

4.6 A bill from Isaac Basset[t] (Lynn) to John Hancock for shoes, 8 April 1775.
Collection of the Massachusetts Historical Society, microfilm edition of the Hancock
family papers, 1728-1885, reel 2, call number P-277

its independence, and the theater of war had been removed to the middle
states of New Jersey and Pennsylvania. A surviving receipt, with two different
dates—8 April 1775 and 28 February 1777—reveals that he ordered a pair of
calamancos, made in neighboring Lynn, "for his Servant girl." The order was
placed with a well-known local shoemaker, Isaac Bassett. What is curious
about the note is that it appears as though Hancock had initially ordered the
shoes in 1775, but perhaps had not received them until two years later. It may
be that in his haste to leave Boston in 1775, the order was forgotten until he
returned to the city in 1777. The shoes cost 4 shillings and 8 pence—about the
rate of a working man's wage for one to two days—which was fairly standard
throughout the region at this time, as was the price of the calamanco shoes.

The particulars of the transaction aside, the receipt tells us a bit about the
Hancock household amid the ebb and flow of the Revolutionary War.[38] A man
of Hancock's station needed to equip his domestic servants with a respectable
but not overly expensive livery. Moreover, as a prominent figure who had,
early on, decisively declared his allegiance to the Patriot cause, he needed to
demonstrate the family's loyalty to local artisans, such as Boston shoemaker
Robert Twelves Hewes (1724-1840), or tanner and American songwriter William Billings (1746-1800), who made clothing for Hancock himself, such as a
pair of "black Cloth Leggins."[39] John could not afford the suspicion of buying
black-market British goods.

These pieces of evidence may suggest that the purchase of calamanco shoes
was politically correct on the eve of the American Revolution. Yet in 1775,
when it came to obtaining calamanco shoes in Philadelphia for his fiancée, we
assume—based on the London labels of Dorothy's extant shoes—that they
were the latest fashion, exported from that great metropolis. Hancock does
not mention the shoes in any detail, or even state where he purchased them,

making a final determination difficult. He does note, however, that the black calamancos will be sent to him when they are done, suggesting a special custom order, perhaps from London.

Alternatively, Quaker shoemakers, such as Steven Collins and Ebenezer Breed, had relocated from Lynn to Philadelphia by 1780, although they continued to maintain relationships with their Lynn colleagues.[40] There were dozens of skilled cordwainers working in Philadelphia, as evidenced by the many shoemakers who placed advertisements seeking the return of runaway apprentices. One of these Quaker shoemakers was Thomas Williams. In her diary, Elizabeth Sandwith noted on 19 December 1760 that she had stayed in all day and "T. Williams had measure'd me for a pair shoes." This order may well have been for her wedding to Henry Drinker on 13 January 1761, less than a month away. Elizabeth routinely patronized shops run by fellow Quakers.[41]

The shoemakers of Lynn, Massachusetts, offered customers such as John Hancock an opportunity to navigate the turbulent waters of revolutionary politics, allowing them to bedeck their households in attire appropriate to their station yet avoid the scandal of purchasing imported goods. Lynn was already a well-known shoemaking center by the mid-1700s, renowned for its ladies' silk and woolen shoes. With the onset of war, Lynn's cordwainers turned to supplying boots for Washington's Continental Army.[42] Newspaper advertisements reveal that Lynn-made calamancos were so well known throughout the region that the designation "Lynn" set them apart. In Portsmouth, New Hampshire, around sixty miles north of Boston, a local shoemaker, Samuel Foster, noted in a 1768 advertisement that he could make "womens Silk, Cloth, Calamamco and Leather Shoes, as neat and strong as ever was Made or brought from the famous Shoe Town of Lynn."[43]

In 1774, however, the *Boston Gazette and Country Journal* advertised items "imported from England by John Welsh, and sold in his shop No. 5, Union Street, Boston A general assortment of English GOODS, suitable for all seasons . . . women's English & Lynn shoes & pumps."[44] It is important to note that both British- and Lynn-manufactured shoes were sold side by side, providing Boston shoppers with an opportunity to make a selection that was best for their pocketbooks and their political leanings. The connection between shoe purchases and patriotism is evinced by Philadelphia shoemaker Alexander Rutherford. In 1765, he alerted women customers "as are resolved to distinguish themselves by their patriotism and encouragement of American manufactures, that he makes and sells all sorts of worsted or wool shoes, of all sizes, as neat and cheap as any imported from England."[45]

While the evidence does not support the notion that fines were imposed for wearing shoes from Britain, there certainly was the potential to be subjected to public shaming for doing so. This will be explored in more detail in chapter 6, but a few examples are instructive at this juncture. On 20 August 1764, an anonymous writer in the *Newport Mercury* criticized London cordwainer John Hose—and, by extension, those who wore his shoes—when he observed, "Great Virtue may even be exerted by the Ladies . . . preferring the well-turn'd Shoes of Hall and others in Newport, to those of John Hose of London, only made for Lump sale."[46] Another writer in that newspaper, identified as "Sophia Thrifty," opined that every virtuous woman must feel pride that "any part of her dress has employed the poor of her own country, provided food for the Orphan, or made the widow's heart leap for joy." She closed with a pointed, chastising query: why would any American prefer "pampering Mr. HOSE with his Army of Journeymen"?[47] In the minds of many, there clearly was no longer an excuse for not standing with your neighbors during this time of political tumult.

The various non-importation agreements were a direct challenge delivered to those supplying luxury goods from Britain. As noted recently by Meaghan Reddick, the numbers of shoes produced in Lynn began to rise dramatically after 1760: from several thousand before that date to 20,000 by 1767, and double that amount in the next few years. By the time George Washington

4.7 Wool shoes (although not calamancos) with metallic lace, English, circa 1700-1729. The shoes feature a robust geometric embroidery pattern known as bargello, or flame stitch. It was a popular style for upholstery and accessories in the late seventeenth and eighteenth centuries. Courtesy of the Brooklyn Museum Costume Collection at the Metropolitan Museum of Art, gift of Mrs. Clarence R. Hyde, 1928, and gift of the Brooklyn Museum, 2009, accession number 2009.300.1411a, b

visited Lynn in 1789, he noted that 175,000 shoes were produced there.[48] With the availability of so many Lynn calamancos and the clear popularity of this shoe type, why did more-affluent women, such as Martha Washington and Dorothy Hancock, or women of modest means searching for special-occasion footwear, such as Mary Flint Spofford, chose calamancos made in Great Britain rather than in America? The answer, no doubt, is more complex than what we can glean from surviving records. Nonetheless, those in a position to make a statement via their clothing—one of gentility, civility, and wealth—appear to have chosen a product from the country that many still considered their homeland, although they would soon engage in war with it. Perhaps Abigail Adams summed up the conflict many felt when she wrote to her husband John, "A little of what you call frippery is very necessary towards looking like the rest of the world."[49]

Alonzo Lewis's 1829 *History of Lynn* boasted: "The principal business of Lynn is the manufacture of Ladies' shoes. For the first hundred years from the settlement of the town, this business was very limited. Few persons followed it constantly, and the farmers only pursued it in the intervals of their common employment. The shoes were generally made of neats' leather or woolen cloth." He further noted: "In 1750, Mr. John Adam Deaggeor [or Dagyr] came from England, and gave this business its first impulse. After his arrival, shoes were manufactured of finer stuffs: calamanco, silk, and satin. They were made with long straps, for the ladies, like the gentlemen, wore buckles, and the rands were commonly white. The reputation of Lynn shoes soon found way to the cities of the south, and the manufacturers began to extend their business by taking apprentices and employing journeymen."[50]

Calamancos were also popular in the southern colonies. As Linda Baumgarten notes in *What Clothes Reveal*: "Plantation owner Rawleigh Downman sent single shoes from himself and his wife to use for sizing. For his daughters, Downman ordered shoes by foot length: 'Rose colour'd calamanco Shoes with low flat heels for my Girls; that is 2 pair for a foot 8-1/4 inches long, and 2 pair for a foot 7-3/4 long.'"[51] Whether in the northern or southern colonies, accurate shoe sizes could be a problem, and shoes were frequently ordered by the length, in inches, of a person's foot. At other times, customers used an existing, older shoe as a pattern.

In the depths of the deprivations of 1775, Abigail Adams wrote to her husband regarding the scarcity of calamanco.[52] She described in detail her (favorable) opinion of General Washington, the troubles those left in Boston had in procuring food, the health of the troops, and the ruthless actions of General

4.8 A pair of red broadcloth women's buckle shoes, with leather-clad heels and silk embroidery, English, circa 1720-1740. Courtesy of the Museum of Fine Arts, Boston, accession number 44.351a-b

Gage. She also bemoaned: "Every article here in the West India way is very scarce and dear. In six weeks we shall not be able to purchase any article of the kind. I wish you would let Bass get me one pound of pepper, and two yards of black calamanco for shoes.... You can hardly imagine how much we want many common small articles, which are not manufactured amongst ourselves. ... It is very provoking to have such a plenty so near us, but, Tantalus-like, not be able to touch."[53]

Abigail, however, only required the textile to have uppers made. This suggests that she had access to a local shoemaker. In one letter to John, she mentions needing help farming, confiding that a local man, a shoemaker by trade, would like to hire himself out for the growing season and then return to his shoemaking for the winter months. She assured her husband that she had good reports of the Richards family, who had long been associated with a local dairy.[54] It is also noteworthy to recall that, though her would-be father-in-law had died before Abigail and John married, he had been not only a deacon, but also a shoemaker and farmer. These small details indicate the presence of shoemaking activities in this small New England enclave, similar to those found north of Boston and continuing up the seacoast to New Hampshire and Maine.[55]

By the mid-1700s, the consumer revolution that connected ports throughout the Atlantic world was in full sway, and newspaper readers in bustling seacoast towns such as Portsmouth, New Hampshire, could scan the "Ship

News" for regular passages between America and Great Britain.[56] Successful merchant families—such as the Atkinsons, Hunkings, and Wentworths—had strong ties to Great Britain and the Crown, and they frequently traveled back and forth across the ocean. As John Wentworth wrote to Mrs. Fisher in a letter dated 17 January 1777: "I think it probable that Mr. Fisher and Rindge will be here early in the spring. . . . I have a box qt 16 pr. childrens shoes—3 pr. woms. silk and 3 pr. Calamanco shoes . . . which Mr. Fisher sent for you, by Mr. Brinley."[57]

This brief reference to calamancos is of interest. Given the date of 1777, it is clear that calamancos from England were still a valued gift and were items for sale in Portsmouth, although few had access to such goods. It is also evident that merchants, sea captains, and the wealthy could circumvent importation duties by bringing shoes back to the colonies with them after conducting business in Britain. English shoes and boots carried a substantial customs duty, or import tax, but it was a cost that customers willingly bore as in their efforts to be fashionable.[58]

Those in less elevated positions could also have access to shoes such as calamancos. If one could not afford them new from London or Lynn, there were auctions that sold every variety of secondhand clothing. There was also the somewhat curiously named translator, who would assemble a "new" shoe from old pieces. Shoes were commonly handed down or given as gifts to relatives and friends. Once the initial investment had been made, any number of alterations could be carried out by a local shoemaker or cobbler, from cutting down heels to refurbishing and refashioning uppers. It seems that all but those in the most modest positions could potentially purchase a small bit of luxury: an item of fashion.

4.9 A green and teal wool shoe, possibly American, given the heel and sole finishing, circa 1750-1760. Courtesy of the Colonial Williamsburg Foundation, museum purchase, accession number 1954-905-1

A Lift *of the* Prices *of*
Boots and Shoes, &c.

*As agreed to by the Mafter Cordwainers of the City
and Liberties of Philadelphia, at a Meeting
held the 8th November,* 1790.

Boots.

		£		
Beft plain boots	-	2	12	6
Laced do.	- -	1	5	0
Bootees	- - -	1	17	6
Footing boots	- - -	1	5	0
Soaling & foxing do. with ben foals		0	17	6
Do. do. country leather		0	15	0
Soaling & heeltaping do. ben leather		0	10	0
Do. do. country leather		0	7	6
Heeltaping & toe-piecing		0	4	0
Toping do. with ruffet leather		0	7	6
Extra work paid for				

Mens Shoes.

Cork fhoes	- - -	0	18	9
Foxed or double vamped		0	18	9
Channel pumps	- -	0	18	6
Plane fhoes		0	11	9
Do. with bound tops		0	12	6
Quarters bound, do.		0	13	0
Lined and bound do.		0	13	6
Stiched feats do.	- -	0	16	0
Soaling and healing do.		0	4	2
Soaling do.	- - -	0	3	0

Womens Shoes.

Lined and bound fhoes		0	10	0
Plane do	- -	0	9	0
Soaling and foxing do.		0	3	9
Do. and heeltaping do.		0	3	0

Boys welted Shoes.

Size.				Prices.	
4	- - -	£.	0	9	0
3	- -	-	0	8	6
2	- -	-	0	8	0
1	- -	-	0	7	6
13	- -		0	6	9
12	- -		0	6	6
11	- -		0	6	0
10	- -		0	5	6
9	- -		0	5	3

Back-ftitched Shoes.

2	-	-	0	7	0
1	-	-	0	6	6
13	-	-	0	6	0
12	-	-	0	5	9
11	-	-	0	5	3
10	-	-	0	5	0
9	-	-	0	4	9
8	-	-	0	4	3
7	-	-	0	4	0
6	-	-	0	3	9
5	-	-	0	3	6
4	-	-	0	3	3
3	-	-	0	3	0
2	-	-	0	2	9
1	- -	-	0	2	6

5.1 "A List of the Prices of Boots and Shoes . . . 8th November, 1790." Note that this broadside refers to "Master Cordwainers," suggestive of its roots in the British guild-and-apprenticeship system. "Philadelphia Master Cordwainers Price List" broadside, published in numerous historical imprint volumes

5

THE CORDWAINER'S LAMENT

• Benjamin Franklin and John Hose Testify
on the Effects of the Stamp Act •

On Thursday, 3 June 1773, Mary Simpkins (c. 1754) married Robert Rand (b. 1719) in Boston. It was her first marriage and his second. Mary's father, William, was a well-known jeweler and silversmith. Rand was a Boston merchant from an established New England family with strong Whig leanings. Although the groom had supported the Patriots' various boycotts of British goods—the famous non-intercourse acts—and opposed the hated Tea Act that precluded American merchants like him from selling tea, the bride wore wedding shoes imported from London. Mary was most likely quite pleased with her ensemble, made complete by the stylish silk brocade shoes. These cream-colored silk shoes, brocaded with delicate pink and green flowers, were especially prized because they boasted the label of cordwainers "John Hose & Son, At the Rose in Cheapside near Milk Street, London."[1] She was one of hundreds, perhaps thousands, of British American women to don shoes by the prolific Hose family.

5.2 A composite view of the types of textiles found in eighteenth-century clothing and accessories: brocaded silks, silk damasks, and hand-blocked chintz, among others. Author's collection, photograph by Andrew Davis, February 2017

With the Boston Tea Party a mere six months away, Mary's Hose & Son shoes were hardly a simple pleasure. They carried multiple meanings, each deciphered and understood by those observers who were well versed in the language of eighteenth-century fashion. For the genteel folk of colonial Boston, they signified taste and style. For raging Whigs who practiced a puritanical frugality, such as Samuel Adams, they represented a decadent luxury that had the potential to corrupt the morals of a free and enterprising people. For John Hose, whose London shop crafted the shoes' delicate and elegant form, their purchase on the far side of the Atlantic Ocean heralded burgeoning new markets, robust sales, and an exalted reputation.[2]

The various interwoven and complicated meanings that invested a pair

5.3 A composite view of the types of textiles found in eighteenth- and early nineteenth–century clothing and accessories: brocaded silks and silk damasks, featuring spangles, chenille, and silk and metallic threads. Author's collection, photograph by Andrew Davis, February 2017

of eighteenth-century wedding shoes intrigue costume historians. There are several interrelated questions regarding the maker of Mary Simpkins Rand's shoes specifically, as well as about the countless pairs, produced and shipped by other London cordwainers, that made their way to the shops and dressing rooms of colonial America. Although we may never know how Mary came into possession of her shoes, some answers to these questions can be found by tracing the journey of several pairs of Hose shoes to America. The passage encompassed their production in a London shop; their stint as cargo in the hold of a Yankee ship sailing across the Atlantic; their sale in the shops of Boston, New York, and Philadelphia merchants; and their display on the feet of elite customers in British America.

Mary Simpkins and her fiancé, Boston merchant Robert Rand, most likely had heard of John Hose and his shoes. By the mid-1700s, British America's elite were avid consumers of Hose shoes, as well as the pumps, slippers, and calamancos of his Cheapside competitors. As goods, ladies' shoes tended to be listed separately, even in shop advertisements and handbills. Gilliam Butler, Robert Trail, Samuel Penhallow, and John MacMaster were among those Portsmouth, New Hampshire, shopkeepers who singled out women's shoes from their lists of available products. Ships' logs and manifests, shopkeepers' advertisements in newspapers, and customshouse records all support the importance of the shoe trade for fashionable ladies—and the British economy. Shoe authority Giorgio Riello observes that Britain exported 300,000 pairs of shoes in 1760, of which America imported 42 percent.[3]

While calamancos and leathers from Lynn, the shoemaking center of Essex County, Massachusetts, were for sale in Portsmouth by the 1780s, the cost of London shoes was higher. One Portsmouth shopkeeper advertised Lynn-made calamanco shoes, indicating their wide availability, yet elite women who could afford the additional costs of fabrication and import duties would frequently choose the latest styles from London over a domestically made product.

English shoes and boots carried a significant amount of customs duty, but it was a cost that wealthy customers willingly bore.[4] Moreover, it brought in revenues that governments throughout the Atlantic world's economy were unwilling to pass up. Consequently, customers could expect to pay a premium for such items, even after the American Revolution. In 1789, the new nation's Congress called for tariffs in its first major piece of legislation, ordering, "for the support of government, for the discharge of the debts of the United States, and the encouragement and protection of manufactures, that duties be laid on goods, wares and merchandise." George Washington, the new president, signed the bill into law on Independence Day.[5] The next year, Secretary of the Treasury Alexander Hamilton recommended that Congress pass a customs duty on "boots, per pair, fifty cents; shoes, slippers and goloshoes, made of leather, per pair, seven cents; shoes and slippers, made of silk or stuff, per pair, ten cents," and so on.[6] The cash-strapped legislature happily complied.

While wages fluctuated from region to region and from job to job, the average payment for labor in northern New England in the 1780s was roughly between 3 and 6 shillings a day. Based on various sources, such as account books in Deerfield, Massachusetts, and Haverhill, New Hampshire, a pair of woman's shoes cost about 6 shillings, and a man's, 8 shillings or more, especially for men's well-made shoes or boots. This translates into roughly one to two days' labor to purchase a pair of shoes.

A published broadside pictured at the beginning of this chapter, with a price list from Philadelphia in 1790, is consistent with these costs: good men's shoes, such as channeled pumps (with the soles fastened to the uppers by stitches concealed in the channel), started at 18 shillings and 6 pence, while a good ladies' shoe, "lined and bound," started at 10 shillings.[7] Shoe buckles were needed to fasten both men's and women's shoes, which added an extra cost. While buckles could be transferred to different shoes, they, too, came in differing qualities, based on their initial expense. A pair of shoe buckles outlasted a pair of shoes, so only one or two pairs of buckles were actually needed. They could also be used to update an earlier pair of shoes, or to add extra shine if they were embellished with paste stones or even gems. A simple steel-plated buckle cost approximately one-half to one-third of a day's labor in New England at that time. In Virginia, the least expensive buckles could be had for two pence.[8]

Whether it was because of declining purchases after an initial investment in footwear, the intervening Revolutionary War, or a combination of both, one finds a great number of women's shoes available in the period leading up to 1770-1775, and then the supply tapers off. Various non-intercourse acts were put in place in the colonies, beginning as early as 1764 and culminating with the closing of Boston Harbor in 1775. A gap follows until about 1784, with the end of the conflict. In 1784, a new, easily identifiable style emerged, and the London merchants attempted to glut the American market with their excess stock. This is the time period mentioned by John Hose's son Thomas in his correspondence with Morden College.

Fortunately, shoes made by the Hose family have found their way into public institutions, due to their link with significant people and events, their high level of craftsmanship, and their sheer numbers. Mary Simpkins Rand's 1773 wedding shoes are housed in the Connecticut Historical Society's collection. Among several other noteworthy examples of the Hose family's popular shoes are those found in the collections of the Charleston Museum, Historic Deerfield, Colonial Williamsburg, the DAR Museum in Washington, DC, and Historic New England. They may have been shipped to the colonies as special, or bespoke, orders, requiring makers' labels to identify their country of origin, in order to assess importation duties. Or perhaps the labeling was simply to promote the products, or brand, of individual cordwainers in a profitable North American colonial marketplace. Surviving evidence reveals that the labeling of shoes did not begin much before the fourth decade of the eighteenth century. American shoemakers (or British or European shoemakers who set up shop in America, to capitalize on a market thirsty for such goods) would soon follow suit, with labels appearing in shoes made in Rhode Island, New York, and New Jersey shortly after the mid-eighteenth century.

AGENTS OF VICE AND CORRUPTION

Seven years before Mary Simpkins married Robert Rand in Boston, wearing a pair of elegant, silk brocade Hose & Son shoes, John Hose was in trouble. So, too, was George III's empire. A century of overseas wars, culminating in the Seven Years' War, which ended in 1763, had left the Crown's treasury bare. The nation needed revenues, and His Majesty's advisers in the Exchequer had cast their eyes on British America, where much of the fighting had taken place, insisting that the colonies must shoulder their share of the burden. The passage of the Stamp Act, on 22 March 1765, was Parliament's attempt to remedy the shortfall. The law, which would go into effect on 1 November, required colonists to attach a special stamp to every piece of paper they purchased. The cost, at one shilling per stamp, was especially burdensome for lawyers such as John Adams, plantation owners like George Washington, and merchants such as Robert Rand, all of whom used ample quantities of paper for letters, bills of lading, and so forth. In addition, as observed by historian J. L. Bell, the Stamp Act could be equated with a tax on marriage (due to the stamps required for the license and other documents), and there appears to be evidence to support a greater number of marriages taking place before the tax was enacted. This governmental innovation—the imposition of a direct tax on the colonies—was unlike anything that Parliament had ever previously attempted, and the colonists' responses were proportional. In Washington's Williamsburg, the House of Burgesses passed the Stamp Act Resolves, which rejected Parliament's authority to tax the provinces. In Samuel Lane's Portsmouth, angry protesters burned effigies of stamp distributor George Meserve and Lord Bute, whose administration had added to England's debt by placing a large number of British troops in the colonies to protect lands gained in the Seven Years' War. In Mary Simpkins's and Robert Rand's Boston, mobs tore down warehouses, and even ransacked the home of Lieutenant Governor Thomas Hutchinson. On a fundamental level, Parliament had failed to appreciate how British Americans understood their rights, as well as the role of imported British goods in the colonists' comprehension of their vaunted British liberty. As T. H. Breen observes: "During the 1760s and 1770s something unprecedented occurred in Britain's mainland colonies. Americans managed to politicize common consumer goods and, by so doing, suddenly invested manufactured items with radically new symbolic meaning."[9]

Benjamin Franklin's testimony before Parliament on 13 February 1766, concerning the sentiments of the American colonists regarding the Stamp Act, is one of the more famous moments leading up to the Revolutionary War. The transcript from the proceedings demonstrates that Franklin gave a polished, eloquent, direct performance, despite the lengthy questioning to which he was subjected. His testimony would later be referred to as "Franklin in the Cockpit." By all accounts, he was impressive, and unflappable.[10] But it is likely that the testimony from the man who followed Franklin—the sixty-six-year-old cordwainer John Hose—carried even greater weight in Parliament. Hose, with his extensive workforce, represented both employment for workers in the trades and revenue for England's coffers. Hose, as well as the other British merchants and tradespeople who testified, contributed substantially to the repeal of the tax in the following month. Hose told the committee that he had sold shoes to America for thirty-seven years, and in recent years he had sent £2,200 worth of shoes to New York alone. Through his trade with American merchants—such as colonial merchant Allen Trecothick, brother of London alderman Barlow Trecothick (who later became lord mayor of London)—he was able to employ more than three hundred workers. With the Stamp Act boycotts that followed, however, "he employed only forty-five." When asked "To what is this owing?" Hose's retort was clear: "To the Stamp Act for no Body never made better Shoes. Hopes and bets he sho[ul]d Employ his Men if the Stamp Act was Repealed."[11] His testimony reveals that he was fully cognizant of his importance as an employer, as a master craftsman who trained others up in the trade, and as a source of revenue for the Crown.[12] Exports, such as shoes, to British America would incur additional duties that were imposed by the Stamp Act (and the related non-intercourse proclamations), along with the general impact the act had on trade in terms of receipts, letters, bills of lading, and so forth. Hose's once-prized shoes were now reviled in some quarters by Patriots, who called for non-intercourse agreements.

It is something of a paradox, then, that the John Hose who shared a stage with Benjamin Franklin in opposing the Stamp Act had become a focal point for the Patriots' anger and the object of British American disdain. Mary Simpkins and Robert Rand might well have relished lovely shoes, but others

Glorious News.

BOSTON, Friday 11 o'Clock, 16th *May* 1766.

THIS Inftant arrived here the Brig Harrifon, belonging
to *John Hancock*, Efq; Captain *Shubael Coffin*, in 6
Weeks and 2 Days from LONDON, with important
News, as follows.

From the LONDON GAZETTE.

Weftminfter, March 18th, 1766.

THIS day his Majefty came to the Houfe of Peers, and being in his royal
robes feated on the throne with the ufual folemnity, Sir Francis Moli-
neux, Gentleman Ufher of the Black Rod, was fent with a Meffage
from his Majefty to the Houfe of Commons, commanding their atten-
dance in the Houfe of Peers. The Commons being come thither accordingly,
his Majefty was pleafed to give his royal affent to
An ACT to REPEAL an Act made in the laft Seffion of Parliament, in-
tituled, an Act for granting and applying certain Stamp-Duties and other Duties
in the Britifh Colonies and Plantations in America, towards further defraying
the expences of defending, protecting and fecuring the fame, and for amending
fuch parts of the feveral Acts of Parliament relating to the trade and revenues
of the faid Colonies and Plantations, as direct the manner of determining and
recovering the penalties and forfeitures therein mentioned.
Alfo ten public bills, and feventeen private ones.

Yefterday there was a meeting of the principal Merchants concerned in the
American trade, at the King's Arms tavern in Cornhill, to confider of an Ad-
drefs to his Majefty on the beneficial Repeal of the late Stamp-Act.
Yefterday morning about eleven o'clock a great number of North American
Merchants went in their coaches from the King's Arms tavern in Cornhill to the
Houfe of Peers, to pay their duty to his Majefty, and to exprefs their fatisfac-
tion at his figning the Bill for Repealing the American Stamp-Act, there was
upwards of fifty coaches in the proceffion.
Laft night the faid gentleman difpatched an exprefs for Falmouth, with fifteen copies of the Act for repealing the Stamp-Act, to be forwarded immediately for New York.
Orders are given for feveral merchantmen in the river to proceed to fea immediately on their refpective voyages to North America, fome of whom have
been cleared out fince the firft of November laft.
Yefterday meffengers were difpatched to Birmingham, Sheffield, Manchefter,
and all the great manufacturing towns in England, with an account of the final
decifion of an auguft affembly relating to the Stamp-Act.

When the KING went to the Houfe of Peers to give the Royal Affent, there
was fuch a vaft Concourfe of People, huzzaing, clapping Hands, &c. that it
was feveral Hours before His Majefty reached the Houfe.
Immediately on His Majefty's Signing the Royal Affent to the Repeal of the
Stamp-Act the Merchants trading to America, difpatched a Veffel which had been
in waiting, to put into the firft Port on the Continent with the Account.
There were the greateft Rejoicings poffible in the City of London, by all Ranks
of People, on the TOTAL Repeal of the Stamp-Act,—the Ships in the River
difplayed all their Colours, Illuminations and Bonfires in many Parts. — In
fhort, the Rejoicings were as great as was ever known on any Occafion.
It is faid the Acts of Trade relating to America would be taken under Con-
fideration, and all Grievances removed. The Friends to America are very powerful, and difpofed to affift us to the utmoft of their Ability.
Capt. Blake failed the fame Day with Capt. Coffin, and Capt. Shand a Fort-
night before him, both bound to this Port.
*It is impoffible to exprefs the Joy the Town is now in, on receiving the
above, great, glorious and important NEWS—The Bells in all the Churches
were immediately fet a Ringing, and we hear the Day for a general Rejoicing
will be the beginning of next Week.*

PRINTED for the Benefit of the PUBLIC, by
Drapers, Edes & Gill, Green & Ruffell, and *Fleets.*
The Cuftomers to the Bofton Papers may have the above gratis at their refpective
Offices.

July THE No. 467.
NEW - YORK MERCURY.
Containing the freſheſt ADVICES, *'Foreign and Domeſtic.*

MONDAY, JULY 13, 1761.

To be SOLD,
At JAMES M'EVERS's Store,
TRUNKS of Women's Shoes,
made by John Hoſe and Son, Bohea Tea by the Cheſt, choice Beaver in Packs, Boxes of Spices and Boxes of China, well ſorted ; Pepper in Bales, beſt French Indigo, New-England Rum by the Hogſhead, Tobacco in Tierces. Alſo, a general Aſſortment of European Goods.

5.5 A typical advertisement for John Hose shoes, indicating the large quantity he exported to America. *New-York Mercury,* 13 July 1761

lambasted Hose as a corrupter of American virtue. In colonial newspapers, his name became synonymous with the ongoing internal turmoil regarding local production of both necessities and luxury goods.

It is no wonder that colonial shoemakers felt threatened by the merchandizing powerhouse that was Great Britain, with its seemingly unlimited resources. John Hose's 300-person workforce gave him the ability to send not just dozens, but trunks of luxury shoes to fill the shelves of British American shops. Moreover, he was abetted by colonial merchants. Their advertisements in the *New-York Mercury, New-York Gazette, New Hampshire Gazette,* and other newspapers boasted "imported in the last ships from London," "just Imported from London," and "suitable for the Season," with the intent that their customers' purses would be emptied for one of Hose's silk damask slippers or calamanco shoes.[13] Readers of the *New-York Mercury* on 13 July 1761 learned that "TRUNKS of Women's Shoes, made by John Hose and Son" were available at James McEvers's store, along with chests of bohea tea and boxes of "well sorted" china. Likewise, on 17 December 1764, the *New-York Gazette* alerted colonial consumers that Samuel Deall had received, in the "last ships from London, and to be sold very reasonable" at his shop on Broad Street, "Hose's satin and calamanco shoes."

The onset of resistance to Parliament's tax innovations does not seem to have diminished the colonists' desire for British goods. Amid reports of resistance to the Stamp Act by the Sons of Liberty in various towns, on 10 April 1766,

5.4 (*opposite*) "The EXAMINATION of Doctor BENJAMIN FRANKLIN," from the *London Gazette,* Westminster, 18 March 1766, appearing in Boston on 16 May, under the rubric "Glorious news. Boston, Friday 11 o'clock, 16th May 1766: This instant arrived here . . . important news, as follows," printed by Drapers, Edes & Gill, Green & Russell, and Fleets, 1766. Collection of the Massachusetts Historical Society, Bdses-Sm 1766 May 16 the *Pennsylvania Gazette* posted Mease & Miller's notice of "a few Trunks of Hose's Shoes sorted, two Thirds black, and one Third blue, green, and Cloth Colours." Even in Boston, where the infamous massacre had taken place the year before, the Hancocks and the Adamses could find Caleb Blanchard's notice in their *Evening-Post* for a "large and general Assortment of GOODS" from London that included "HOSE'S shoes."[14] As colonials debated the effects of the Coercive Acts in New York's coffee houses in autumn 1774, they could scan their *General Advertiser* to find "HOSE'S SHOES in small trunks," available at the shop of Francis Lewis & Son.[15] In many advertisements, the shoes are noted as "Hose's shoes," giving them their own appellation and making it clear that anyone reading the ads was familiar with his footwear. What is also of interest is that in the dozens of New England advertisements examined, no other cordwainer appears to be mentioned by name at this time.

While there seems to be little doubt that British women also wore shoes by Hose, to date only one pair from England have been identified in British collections. Speculation suggests that John Hose had no reason to label or in any other way identify his shoes, unless they were destined for export markets.[16] Even after the Revolutionary War, Rhode Island's gentility, and those who aspired to dress like them, could find an advertisement for "Hose's Shoes and toed Clogs" in the *Newport Mercury* on 12 March 1785. Consequently, New England shoemakers, such as Samuel Lane, still faced competition,[17] as did cordwainer Robert Perrigo of Providence, who crafted "BOOTS and SHOES after the neatest and most genteel manner, which he sells very reasonable." Perrigo's advertisements in the *Providence Gazette and Country Journal* touted, "those Persons who are pleased to favor him with their Custom may depend upon being served with Fidelity and Dispatch," but this would not help him gain the attention of Mary Simpkins Rand and her circle. Nor could he compete with merchants such as William Rogers, whose advertisements in the *Newport Mercury* boasted "all Sorts of European Goods," including "a few Pair of Women's neat Brocaded SILK SHOES."[18] T. H. Breen notes that angry letters condemning luxury and debt often appeared next to alluring advertisements for the latest British goods.[19]

There were additional reasons to fear the influx of London-made shoes. Colonial social critics had long fretted that something more invidious—more dangerous to their culture—was at play. For instance, as early as 1692, Massachusetts' Puritan minister Cotton Mather argued against debilitating foreign luxuries, such as silks and calicoes. He dreamed of a time when "the vertuous woman" would spin wool and flax to occupy her hands and her soul.[20] The influx of luxury goods, increasing as the eighteenth century wore on, included dresses, wigs, and shoes, as well as coaches, mirrors, and furniture. These all posed a marked threat the morals of Americans. Luxury, critics argued, was the enemy of virtue, and the ships that carried Hose's goods also brought corruption and dissipation, which eroded the fiber of American morality.

Complaints from both sides of the Atlantic appeared in the *Boston Evening-Post*, which, in December 1751, carried a warning from London for Bostonians such as Mary Simpkins and Robert Rand. Luxury was the "epidemical distemper of the age." It was found in "a man's living above what his Estate or Income will bear." It could be seen in "the immoderate gin-drinker, beer-guzzler, wine-bibber, punch-tippler, tea-sipper, &c." It could be found among "the resorters to plays, balls, operas, masquerades, concerts, beer-gardens, horse-races, cock-matches, and those that deal most with the print-shops than with the book-sellers." Moreover, the dissipation that was brought about by luxury was not confined just to the wealthy. The "lower Ranks and Conditions" would emulate those who had more.[21] Twelve years later, the moral problem of luxury goods became a political threat, when George III and Parliament sought to squeeze more revenue out of provincial taxpayers to pay for the Seven Years' War.

In the 1760s, as British American colonists mounted resistance to Parliament's innovations—increased taxes and regulation—goods imported from England, including shoes, became a political issue. Once Parliament passed the Revenue Act (known as the Sugar Act in the colonies) on 5 April 1764, it galvanized the sentiments of many British Americans. London merchants and artisans became a target for propagandists, who vocally promoted the virtue of homespun and local manufacture as a means of liberating Americans from Britain's mercantilist hold. In colonial newspapers and pamphlets,

5.6 Supposed matron "Sophia Thrifty" admonished against the purchase of a number of European goods, including the "pampering of Mr. Hose, with his Army of Journeymen." *New-York Mercury,* 24 December 1764

some merchants were vilified as examples of purveyors of the frippery and finery that American consumers should boycott. Instead, they should opt in favor of products made in the colonies. In the *Newport Mercury* on 20 August 1764, one opponent (whose page-one letter was signed simply "O. Z.") criticized London cordwainer John Hose, observing that "great Virtue may even be exerted by the Ladies in taking the snuff of Rhode-Island, or preferring the well-turn'd Shoes of Hall and others in Newport, to those of John Hose of London, only made for Lump sale, or as the Tradesmen phrase it, for the Plantations." Colonial ladies were encouraged to set a good example and eschew such luxury items.

In the same newspaper and on the same day in 1764 that the unknown correspondent "O. Z." submitted his thoughts, an equally important report was heralded from Boston. The news was greeted with much approbation by the Rhode Island editor of the *Mercury*:

> It is with pleasure we hear some of the principal merchants in Boston have come into a resolution to curtail many superfluities in dress and that upwards of 50 have already signed a certain agreement for that purpose. Lace, ruffles, &c. are to be entirely laid aside. No English cloths to be purchased but at a fixed price. The usual manner of expressing their regard and sorrow for deceased friend or relative but cover themselves in black is also in the list of superfluities and no part thereof but the crape in the hat is retained instead of which a piece of Crape is to be tied upon the arm after the manner of the military gentlemen.
>
> The causes of these prudent measures everyone will to easily suggest to himself to e[n]quire any mention as we have always manifested a great attachment and complacence to <u>Boston fashions</u> however ridiculous and extravagant it is hoped we shall not shew an Aversion to such as are decent prudent and of the expense reputable but that we shall cheerfully join in the above laudable resolutions and such others as may best tend to restrain the present Prodigality and Licentiousness. And if our ladies should cast an Eye of Prudence around them when they next figure out for a Ball or public Entertainment they may doubtless be convinced that their charms would receive as full as many compliments if bedecked with but one half of the expense.[22]

Similar letters (some of them frequently reprinted) appeared in numerous contemporary papers.

The number of British merchants, or factors, in the colonies was abundant. Historian Benjamin Carp has noted that by the 1760s, the influx of British factors into Boston threatened to crowd out local merchants.[23] Now, in the new climate of "patriotism," the same *Newport Mercury* (as well as the *Boston Evening-Post* and the *New-York Mercury*) lamented about "how much fever some of our young ladies may be smitten with [by] the charms of dress and gaiety." This was purportedly written "from a Lady" and was notable in that her declared station was a "matron," who represented "mothers and mistresses of families, and know that our husbands and sons must prosper or decline, with our flourishing or sinking country." In this missive, signed with the pseudonym "Sophia Thrifty," she chastened the "darling appurtenances," "gaudy plumes," and "modish expenses" that took trade away from the colonies' shopkeepers and craftsmen, who daily faced "the difficulty of procuring an estate or even providing for a large family." Against such luxury, the author extolled those who practiced household economy. Every female Patriot and virtuous woman should feel pride that "any part of her dress has employed the poor of her own country, provided food for the Orphan, or made the widow's heart leap for joy."[24]

"WHETHER A WOMAN OF FASHION NOT BE DECLARED A PUBLIC ENEMY?"

For British Americans, the consumer revolution that transformed the culture of the colonies after 1740 was a mixed blessing. Donning fashionable London-made shoes could be read either as a signifier of gentility and civility, or as a marker of economic and political betrayal. For those "Britons abroad," maintaining cultural connections with what they saw as their home country was a natural inclination. To others, however, the wearing of imported goods represented the dangers of indulging in luxury. Even a shopkeeper like Elizabeth Murray of Boston had to mediate between her niece Dolly and her brother James, Dolly's father, who feared that the teenager's frequent shopping trips would lead to a life of idle dissolution.[25] The political agitation of the 1760s, in response to Parliament's novel form of taxation, skewed the meaning of imported goods, especially those from England, toward the latter interpretation, making them antithetical to the goals of economic independence, as well as to the Patriot cause.

We see an example of this in the *Newport Mercury* on Monday, 27 August 1764: "Whether we are not undone by fashions made for other people and whether it be not madness in a poor people to imitate a rich one? Whether a woman of fashion not be declared a public enemy? Whether a lady set out with foreign silks and laces may not be said to consume more beef and butter than [a] hundred farmers?"[26] Less than two weeks later, the front page of the *New Hampshire Gazette*, on Friday, 7 September 1764, asked "whether the women may not sew, spin, weave, Embroider, sufficiently for the embellishment of their persons, and even enough to raise Envy in each other, without being beholden to foreign countries?"[27] A 1754 excerpt from "A Satire on Women's Dress" in the *Boston Evening-Post* captured the mood prevailing among many, while also conveying the thoughts of a traditionalist on the excesses of women's fashion:

Let your gown be a Sack, blue, yellow or green,
and frizzle your elbows with ruffles
furl off your lawn aprons with flounces in rows
puff and pucker up knots on your arms and your toes
make your petticoat short that a hoop eight yards wide
may decently show how your garters are tyed
with fringes of knoting, your Dicky cabob
on slippers of velvet, set gold À-la-baube
but mount on French heels when you go to a Ball
'Tis the fashion to totter and shew you can fall
throw modesty out from your Manners and Face
À-la-mode de François, you're a bit for his Grace.[28]

As a result of the Sugar Act—the effects of which can be traced in newspaper notices such as those quoted above—an alternative (which was supported by the anonymous Sophia Thrifty and many likeminded souls) was a new organization, the Society for the Promotion of Arts, Agriculture, and Economy.

In 1764, some of New York's most prominent figures—and thus likely customers for John Hose's footwear—came together to support colonial products. Concerned over "the present state of declining trade," "the vast luxury introduced during the late war," and the "numerous restrictions" on trade encumbered by the recent Sugar Act, they hoped to encourage American-made products. Publishing their plans in newspapers throughout the colonies, they invited "every real Friend and Lover of his Country," by which they probably meant the colony of New York, "of whatever Rank or Condition" to join them in the effort to support local industry and reject the craving for luxury goods that seemed to have captured British Americans. The new society took off quickly. By 24 December 1764, the *Newport Mercury* noted that "the subject of economy as a matter of unspeakable moment will be amply considered; and it is to be hoped, some happy expedients will be discovered to check the progress of our luxury and extravagance."[29] To this end, the publishers offered subsidies for domestic goods, including £10 for "the best made 100 Pair of Womens Shoes, the Soles to be of Leather tanned in this Province, and covered with Stuff."[30]

MARY SIMPKINS RAND'S SHOES

The comfortable world that Mary Simpkins Rand and John Hose had inhabited changed with remarkable suddenness. Ironically, by February 1766, Hose had become an incidental ally—as well as an inducement to British American interests to increase the domestic production of shoes—in challenges to the increasing regulation that Parliament sought to impose on colonial trade. When Hose lamented before Parliament that ever since the promulgation of the Stamp Act, his transatlantic business had withered, he therefore was able to employ only forty-five workers, and his future was bleak. American shoemakers were all too happy to fill the void. Hose died in 1769, just three years

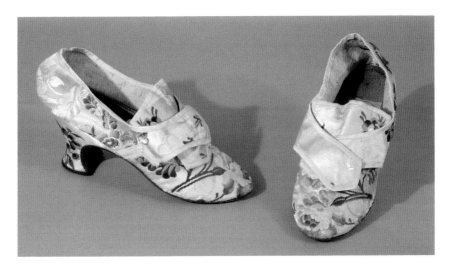

5.7   Women's brocaded, pattern-matched silk shoes, lined with linen, with a silk-covered wooden heel and leather sole. These stylish shoes most likely were worn by Mary Simpkins Rand for her 1773 wedding in Boston. Courtesy of the Connecticut Historical Society, museum purchase, accession number 1953.16.0a,b

5.8 A pincushion, made by Mary Simpkins Rand of Boston. This small object, made for her firstborn child, reads "WELCOME LITTLE STRANGER TO BOSTON THO THE PORT IS BLOCK'T UP 1774." Sadly, her infant daughter died and was buried in Boston. Family tradition notes that Mary carried this memento with her, past British soldiers, when she evacuated from the city. Courtesy of Massachusetts Roots

after his testimony regarding the Stamp Act followed that of Benjamin Franklin. Although Hose may not be remembered by most for his appearance before Parliament, many a curator, costume historian, and scholar will come into contact with the "fashionable fripperies" that began their long journey from his shop "at the Rose, Cheapside." Writing to his wife Abigail in 1778, John Adams made it clear that abundant concerns remained regarding the "plague of Europe" and the "bewitching Charms" of luxury in America, stating, "If I had Power I would forever banish and exclude from America, all Gold, silver, precious stones, Alabaster, Marble, Silk, Velvet and Lace."[31]

Mary Simpkins Rand's wedding shoes, clearly a treasured heirloom, were passed down through the family and eventually found their way into the collection of the Connecticut Historical Society. There is an additional artifact that survives from Rand, which sheds further light on her connection with the opening events of the American Revolution. In June 1773, about a year after their marriage, Mary and Robert welcomed their firstborn: a daughter. The child did not survive and, according to family sources, was interred at the Granary Burying Ground.[32] A poignant memento survives from this troubled period in Mary's life. Amid the imposition of Parliament's Intolerable Acts, the soon-to-be or new mother made a pincushion for her firstborn, which bore the inscription "WELCOME LITTLE STRANGER TO BOSTON THO THE PORT IS BLOCK'T UP 1774."

It was a token to her new role as mother, and also to the tumult of revolutionary politics. Enraged over the Boston Tea Party, Parliament had passed the Boston Port Act in March, and the Royal Navy had formed a blockade around

Boston Harbor. Patriot families fled the city, and Boston's population fell from approximately 15,000 to fewer than 3,000. Mary was one of those who departed the besieged city. While Robert fought against the British, serving as a sergeant with the Bedford minutemen at Concord in April 1775, Mary went to nearby Chelmsford. She did not return to Boston until sometime in 1777, after Washington's artillery forced the British forces to move on to New York. In her flight to Chelmsford, Mary had to cross British checkpoints, where suspicious Redcoats examined the few personal goods that frightened Bostonians could pack. For the grieving mother, few items were more precious than the modest keepsake that held the memory of her lost child.[33]

6.1 "Washington's Family," by Edward Savage, oil on canvas, painted between 1789 and 1796. *Left to right*: George Washington Parke Custis, George Washington, Eleanor Parke Custis, Martha Washington, and an enslaved servant (probably William Lee or Christopher Sheels). Courtesy of the National Portrait Gallery, Andrew W. Mellon Collection, accession number 1940.1.2

"FOR MY USE, FOUR PAIR OF NEAT SHOES"

• George Washington, Virginia Planter, and Mr. Didsbury,
Boot- and Shoemaker of London •

Play not the peacock, looking every where about you,
to see if you be well decked, if your shoes fit well, if your stockings
sit neatly and clothes handsomely.

George Washington, rule number 54 from his 110 "Rules of Civility
and Decent Behavior: In Company and Conversation"

The papers of George Washington, at the University of Virginia, hold a remarkable series of correspondence: a set of letters from the Virginia plantation owner to John Didsbury (d. 1803), a well-known London boot- and shoemaker to the colonial elite. The future commander-in-chief penned numerous missives—a dozen or so of them have survived—in which Washington placed orders for footwear from the London cordwainer. He requested calamancos for Martha, slippers for nieces, boots for nephews, all manner of footwear for his step-children, and work shoes for the family's servants and slaves. Yet, despite references to Didsbury's business on both sides of the Atlantic, as of this writing, there are no known surviving shoes or boots attributed to this cordwainer. Perhaps Didsbury, unlike many of his competitors, did not label or otherwise identify his shoes.

June ..... 1768.

6.2 A shoe order from George Washington to John Didsbury, 20 June 1768. George Washington purchased shoes from London boot- and shoemaker John Didsbury for more than a dozen years. Some of his orders were extensive, such as the order he placed on 27 September 1763 for more than forty pairs of shoes (for the family and the enslaved servants within the household), while others, such as this order from June 1768, were smaller. Just above his signature is a complaint regarding Mrs. Washington's shoes—which did not fit well, being made of poor materials—noting that she has sent her measure (the size of her foot) again. George Washington Papers, series 5, financial papers: copybook of letters and invoices, 1767–1775, manuscript / mixed material, retrieved from the Library of Congress, https://www.loc.gov/item /mgw500004/

But how does a shoe scholar proceed without a shoe? With a clientele "of the quality"—especially well-heeled planters in colonial Virginia as well as landed gentry in Britain—the absence of artifacts necessitates a different approach: the more conventional strategy of examining and decoding the paper documents that reveal clues to an object's provenance. Receipts, bills of lading, and advertising show the context for fashion choices. Assisted by well-trained archivists, work of this sort shifts from tidy back-of-house collection rooms or the dusty attics of historic homes to the well-appointed, wainscoted reading rooms of the Massachusetts Historical Society, beneath the watchful portraits of John and Abigail Adams and Governor Francis Sargent, or to tattered family papers, deeds, and probates in the basement of a local historical society.

The Washington/Didsbury letters and orders for merchandise shed light on one of the most important themes in the transatlantic shoe trade: consumption. First, the documents elucidate the ways in which elite Americans purchased and distributed shoes. Second, Washington's selection of footwear would have reflected his concepts of civility and gentility vis-à-vis dress and fashion. As he noted in rule number 54 of his "Rules of Civility," one should ensure that "your shoes fit well, if your stockings sit neatly and clothes handsomely." Lastly, the footwear orders Washington placed highlight his evolving role as a family man and show how one went about clothing a "well bred" family in Early America.

During the period of the Didsbury correspondence, Washington established himself as a leader in Fairfax County, an important figure among the cohort of planters who dominated Virginia. His interest in politics made him a visible presence, and he was acutely aware that the eyes of Virginia were scrutinizing him. The first step in his advancement was holding a place on the county court, where twenty-six-year-old Washington joined the eminent George Mason and George William Fairfax as justices of Fairfax County. He also became a vestrymen of Truro Parish.[1] Washington then sought election to the House of Burgesses. He decided that his chances were better in Frederick County, where he owned land, than in Fairfax, the site of Mount Vernon, which was roughly fifty miles to the east. Even so, he was defeated in his first attempt in 1755, and three years later he organized a full-scale campaign to reach the heights of political power in the colony. Other responsibilities, however, distracted his efforts.

As a colonel in Virginia's militia during the French and Indian War (1754–1763), Washington's presence was required at Fort Cumberland when the 24 July 1758 election took place. He turned to Lieutenant Charles Smith to manage much of the election business for him in Frederick County that year. At this time, it was common to treat the voters to refreshments. Washington may not have gone all out in "swilling the planters with Bumbo" (a drink made from rum, water, sugar, and nutmeg), but he certainly paid handsomely. Smith sent him receipts for itemized accounts of the sums he had paid out to five persons who supplied refreshments for the voters. The costs could be quite steep, as Smith billed the candidate for twenty-eight gallons of rum, fifty gallons of rum punch, thirty-four gallons of wine, forty-six gallons of beer, and two gallons of cider royal. The strategy had its desired effect, as Washington handily entered the House of Burgesses.[2]

Much of Washington's campaign to establish himself among the leaders of Virginia politics and society depended on appearance. A young man on the make in the colonial Chesapeake region had to demonstrate more than an aptitude for plantation management. This was a rigidly hierarchical domain, in which one's station brought deference from the "middling sorts" below and connections with the "great men" above. Consequently, an aura of graceful gentility was requisite. Washington trained himself to be alert to the nuances of appearance and manners. The world to which Washington sought entry was marked by coordinates of race, family, and inherited wealth (in land and slaves)—traits that he could not control—as well as material possessions and manners, which were displays that he could acquire through learning and consumption. Fashion played an essential role. In his famous and frequently copied 110 "Rules of Civility and Decent Behavior: In Company and Conversation," we see how the then sixteen-year-old Washington attuned himself to the subtleties of fashion in carving out the identity of a respectable plantation owner:

51. Wear not your clothes foul, or ripped, or dusty, but see they be brushed once every day at least and take heed that you approach not to any uncleaness.

52. In your apparel be modest and endeavor to accommodate nature, rather than to procure admiration; keep to the fashion of your equals, such as are civil and orderly with respect to time and places.

53. Run not in the streets, neither go too slowly, nor with mouth open; go not shaking of arms, nor upon the toes, kick not the earth with your feet, go not upon the toes, nor in a dancing fashion.

54. Play not the peacock, looking every where about you, to see if you be well decked, if your shoes fit well, if your stockings sit neatly and clothes handsomely.[3]

Washington understood how clothing was "read" in Early America, how polished boots and a well-turned heel displayed an air of gentility and civility. His sense that one lived under a microscope, carefully observed for any faux pas, shows through in his orders for shoes, whether they were "double channel pumps," "strong shoe boots" for walking, riding boots and saddlery, shoes with "middling to high heels," or Moroccan leather slippers. He was very specific about the necessity of a good fit and the use of quality materials. In other words, it did not matter if it was a coat, waistcoat, or shoes—he was making a statement regarding gentility and civility through his sartorial selections. His purchases reflected his writing, as a young man, a set of "Rules of Civility."

Once George and Martha wed in January 1759, his reflections on matters of clothing and decorum from that period also provide a rare glimpse into his role as husband and stepfather. Washington ordered the clothing required for his stepson, John Parke Custis (1754–1781), known as "Jacky," who was Martha's son from her first marriage. Jacky was four years old when Martha and George married. In one letter, Washington appears in a rare domestic role, noting that the boy was still growing, so his clothing must be made to accommodate that circumstance. In 1764, Washington noted that Jacky's foot was eight inches long.[4]

The significance of Washington's role as a stepfather and father figure was underscored by selecting the right sort of clothes for a young gentleman who not only was still developing physically, but would also inherit a substantial fortune. Years later, he expressed a similar concern with fashion and decorum in a letter of "advisory hints" to his nephew, seventeen-year-old George Steptoe Washington. Writing as "Uncle and friend" from Mount Vernon on 23 March 1789, a month before he would assume the presidency of the new nation, Washington observed that for a young gentleman on the cusp of adulthood, "it is therefore, absolutely necessary, if you mean to make any figure upon the stage, that you should take the first steps right." These first steps included the correct decisions about a gentleman's wardrobe:

The article of clothing is now one of the chief expenses, you will incur; and in this, I fear, you are not so economical as you should be. Decency and cleanliness will always be the first object in the dress of a judicious and sensible man. A conformity to the prevailing fashion in a certain degree is necessary—but it does not follow from thence that a man should always get a new coat, or other clothes, upon every trifling change in the mode, when, perhaps he has two or three very good ones by him. A person who is anxious to be a leader of the fashion, or one of the first to follow it, will certainly appear in the eyes of judicious men, to have nothing better than a frequent c[h]ange of dress to recommend him to notice. I would always wish you to appear sufficiently decent to entitle you to admission into any company, where you may be,—but I cannot too strongly enjoin it upon you—and your own knowledge must convince you of the truth of it—that you should be as little expensive in this respect as you properly can—You should always keep some clothes to wear to church, or on particular occasions, which should not be worn every day. This can be done without any additional expense; for whenever it is necessary to get new clothes, those which have been kept for particular occasions, will then come in as every day ones, unless they should be of a superior quality to the new. What I have said with respect to clothes will apply perhaps more pointedly to Lawrence than to you,—and as you are much older than he is, and more capable of judging of the propriety of what I have here observed, you must pay attention to him, in this respect, and see that he does not wear his clothes improperly or extravagantly.[5]

Once Jacky was breeched—a term that was employed when a small boy was first dressed in trousers, which generally occurred between the ages of four and eight, according to the prevailing tradition—he was expected to spend more time in his stepfather's sphere, leaving the circle of his mother and that of female domesticity.[6] For Jacky, Washington ordered clothes of a similar style and decoration to his own.[7] Further, he also ordered clothing for the boy's household slave and servant (most likely this was Julius, who was assigned to wait on Master Custis). Washington referred to Julius as a young man of sixteen in 1763, while Jacky was about ten.[8] Despite the increase in Washington's household after the marriage, he only covered the costs of his and Martha's attire. His stepson's clothes were paid for through Martha's income from her late husband's estate, as was the custom. As for his orders for Jacky (whom he then called "Mr. Custis"), they continued much the same throughout the youth's teenage years and as he reached adulthood. In 1772, when Jacky was in his late teens, there is a minor notation in Washington's correspondence to Didsbury regarding his stepson's footwear. In a postscript on 15 July 1772, he noted: "Mr. Custis desires his shoes may be made long and low in the hind quarters—in short that they may be made fashionable." In the main body of that letter, regarding his own shoes, Washington observed, "The shoes what you sent me last fitted very well but were in my opinion very ill shap'd; at least they do not please my taste as I am not fond of either long or low hindquar-

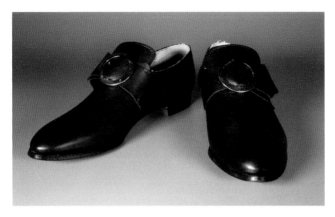

6.3 Reproduction black leather men's shoes, with buckles. Courtesy of the Mount Vernon Ladies' Association

ters or sharp toes."[9] The notation reveals Washington's conservative taste and signals that Jacky was now an adult. Although Jacky's footwear choices may no longer have aligned with those of his stepfather, Washington nonetheless honored the request.

This division between purchase and financing seems to have been in line with the English traditions described in Amanda Vickery's *Behind Closed Doors*. In general, the mother or the female head of the household was responsible for domestic items, such as linens, as well as for clothing for the females in the household and boys before they had been breeched, including all of their small clothes, or undergarments. She oversaw the mantuamakers and milliners, the physicians, and nursery and educational expenses. A husband was responsible for a boy's clothing after he was breeched, oversight of the tailor for his own clothing, and, in particular, all leather equipage associated with riding, such as saddlery.[10]

THE MYSTERIOUS JOHN DIDSBURY, SHOEMAKER OF LONDON

John Didsbury, whose work so impressed yet also frustrated the Washingtons, is something of a mystery to historians. In addition to them, his clients included Edward Shippen (1703–1781), a wealthy Philadelphian who laid out the town of Shippensburg and was a founder of the College of New Jersey (now Princeton University); Newmarket planter Colonel John Baylor, whose lasts were used to adapt several of Washington's shoes; and Virginian John Walker. D. A. Saguto, master boot- and shoemaker (emeritus), Colonial Williams-

6.4 An order for shoes, placed by Edward Shippen, Philadelphia, to J. Didsbury, London, 7 September 1767. Shippen was another of John Didsbury's customers. His order includes "measure of leg and foot taken according to Mr. Didsbury's Directions." For example, item 5 notes the length of the foot, at eleven inches. Courtesy of the Colonial Williamsburg Foundation, John D. Rockefeller Jr. Library, Special Collections, accession number MS 1989.10

burg Foundation, and consulting curator for archaeological footwear, Historic Jamestowne, and Colonial Williamsburg's apprentice shoemaker, Rob Welch, note that Baylor's lasts were UK size 8–8.5, comparable to a US size 9–9.5.[11] As historian Harold Gill notes, "Beginning around the middle of the 18th century, shoes made by John Didsbury of London became especially popular with Virginians."[12] Didsbury's apprentices emphasized their tutelage in Virginian newspaper ads.

Didsbury's receipts, as well as instructions for measuring for boots, advertisements, and even orders, survive in several manuscript collections in both North America and Great Britain. In England, receipts from 1760 to 1763 remain for landholder John Dunston, Esq., of Nottingham. They record payments for "shoes, pumps, goloshoes and new binding." Didsbury's will can be found at the National Archives in Kew, England.[13] As of this writing, however, no known examples of shoes by Didsbury are currently documented. He probably did not label his work, and even in his native country, it has been difficult to find any extant examples of his shoes or boots.[14] Despite a privileged clientele of planters, who were "men of quality" in colonial Virginia, as well as landed gentry in Britain, we have yet to locate any footwear associated with his workshop for either men or women.

Further, though Didsbury's name shows up in account books and advertisements from southern and mid-Atlantic newspapers, such as the *Virginia Gazette*, neither his work nor his name currently surfaces in New England collections or newspapers, underscoring the different manner of sending and shipping goods throughout the colonies. On large plantations, the owners needed a wide variety of different types of footwear, often paying for them with advances on their crops. Planters frequently worked through a factor. If that agent had several clients, why not route them through a purveyor whose goods were a known entity and satisfied the taste of the American clientele? This may help explain why the shoes of certain London cordwainers appear with more frequency in museum collections than others, or become favored by a particular region or group.

THE WASHINGTON–DIDSBURY CORRESPONDENCE

George Washington's relationship with cordwainer John Didsbury lasted more than a dozen years, from 1758 through 1773. Washington was a significant client, given his station as a gentleman of property, standing, and influence, as well as his position as an overseas customer who placed sizable requisitions for a large household of family, staff, slaves, and servants. In one query to Didsbury, dated 27 September 1763, Washington ordered no fewer than forty-six pairs of shoes, slippers, and boots for family members and household slaves (including Julius and Moll, the enslaved who waited on Martha's children, Jack and Patsy).[15] Nearly a year later, in a letter dated 10 August 1764, Washington again placed a substantial request with Didsbury, this time for thirty-one pairs of assorted footwear.[16]

The surviving correspondence brings us into Washington's family circle. It is a one-sided conversation, however, with letters and requests for goods coming from Washington only. It is not known if Didsbury responded to the correspondence directly, through the factors Cary & Company, or not at all. Finding the best clothes, the most exotic materials, the finest handwork, and the latest fashions presented a challenge to the up-and-coming young man,

6.5 George Washington's blue wool coat, American made, possibly in Hartford, Connecticut, circa 1790–1800. A note written by his granddaughter, Elizabeth "Eliza" Parke Custis, indicates that it is "made of the first American cloth sent to General Washington and much worn by him." The garment no longer retains its buttons, as Eliza gave them away as relics.
Courtesy of the Mount Vernon Ladies' Association, purchase, 1949, object number W-1514

even after his marriage to Martha Dandridge Custis in 1759 secured his place among Virginia's elite. Consequently, the correspondence reveals moments of both tension and satisfaction.[17]

Even the well-to-do and well-connected Washingtons had difficulty obtaining the clothes and shoes they desired from London during this time. The quality of the goods imported from Britain was uneven. Cargoes contained out-of-date wares or imperfect goods that had been repaired or refurbished. Consequently, Washington's letters are filled with complaints to his London factors, as well as to various tradesmen. In a letter from Mount Vernon to Didsbury on 27 September 1763, Washington observed, "Sir: The last Cargoe of Shoes you sent me, fit very well, and I hope you will continue to preserve my Last. You will please to send me (with the Goods Mr. Cary will forward) the following Shoes and according to the Inclosed measures."[18] Regarding Martha Washington's shoes, he noted in a June 1768 letter, also to Didsbury, "As

6.6 Martha Washington's brown satin-weave silk dress, probably made in England, circa 1790-1800. A description provided by the Mount Vernon curatorial staff notes: "Most of Martha Washington's apparel is known today to us through fragments, as her descendants disassembled and distributed these garments as treasured heirlooms. This gown, constructed of brown satin-weave silk, is the only intact example at Mount Vernon. Eliza Parke Custis Law (1776-1832) lovingly preserved it with a handwritten note identifying it as 'a favorite gown of my dear Grandmother Mrs. Washington.' The gown's styling, including its scoop neckline, three button flaps to secure the front closure, tight-fitting sleeves, and bustled skirt open at the front, suggest a 1790s date. Mrs. Washington possibly wore it while her husband was President, thereby setting an example of understated elegance for the nation and future presidents' wives." Courtesy of the Mount Vernon Ladies' Association, purchase, 1949, object number W-1523

Mrs. Washington's Shoes (last sent) did not fit her well She now sends her Measure again, and desires I will add that they were made out of bad materials having no last in them."[19] Despite disappointments, it appears that Washington continued to purchase Didsbury's wares in great numbers. The reason is apparent in the records of other Virginians, as this cordwainer's shoes were a particular favorite in the Chesapeake region before the American Revolution.

The earliest surviving requests from Washington for shoes made by Didsbury appear to be from 5 April 1758. He made the request, through Richard Washington, for "a Compleat hunting Saddle & Bridle with two neat Sadle Cloths to cost 40/ the whole. As much of the best superfine Blue Cotton Velvet as will make a Coat Waistcoat & Breeches for a Tall Man with a fine Silk button to suit it & all other necessary Trimmings & Linings together with Garters for the Breeches." He further requested "six pr of the very neatest Shoes (viz.) 2 pr double Channel pumps — 2 pair turnd Ditto & 2 pr Stitchd

6.7 A fragment of Martha Washington's yellow-gold silk lampas dress, circa 1730-1750. This vibrant fragment features a central bouquet motif with tulips, berries, pineapples, and pomegranates in a vase. Courtesy of the Mount Vernon Ladies' Association, gift of Colonel and Mrs. Edward Parke Custis Lewis Cumming, 1961, object number W-2370/B

Shoes to be made by one Didsbury on Colo. Beilers [Baylor's] Last but to be a little wider over the Instep."[20] It may well have been Colonel Baylor who first introduced Washington to the boot and shoemaker, since he was mentioned by George in an enclosed invoice to Robert Cary & Company:

Willmsbg 1 May 1759.
Invoice of Sundry Goods to be Shipd by Robt Cary Esq. and Company for the use of George Washington—viz.

Half a dozn pair of Men's neatest Shoes and Pumps, to be made by one Didsbury on Colo. Baylors Last—but a little larger than his—& to have high Heels—6 pr Mens riding Gloves rather larger than the middle size One neat Pocket Book, capable of receiving Memorandoms & small Cash Accts to be made of Ivory, or any thing else that will admit of cleaning Fine soft Calf Skin for a pair of Boots—Ben. leathr for Soles.[21]

On 30 November 1759, Washington again wrote to Didsbury, notifying him of further specifications:

The first Shoes which I desir'd might be made by you for me, on Colo. Baylors Last are come in, and fit me tolerably well except that some of them are (if any thing) rather too short; as I imagine you will now be able to suit my foot exactly I beg you will for the future observe the following Directions in making the Shoes.
    Let the hind Quarters always be high and very short so that they may Buckle high up on the Instep; the Heels midling high also.

Never more make any of Dog leather except one pair of Pumps in a Cargoe (which let be very neat) unless you send better Leather than they were made of before, for the two pair of Shoes scarcely lasted me twice as many days and had very fair wearing. If I shou'd find occasion to alter at any time these Directions you shall be timely advis'd of it—at present please to send me

2 pair strong Shoes 1 pr dble Channel Pumps
2 pr neat and fine Do 1 pr very neat turnd Ditto.[22]

These surviving orders, from a very particular customer, who knew his mind, to one of London's finest shoe- and bootmakers, underscore that, for Washington, clothing and accessories of the highest quality were a sine qua non, intended to convey his position among the society of genteel southern planters. In 1759, Washington requested middling- to high-heeled shoes from Didsbury. Although elevated heels for men were fading from popularity by the mid-eighteenth century, heeled shoes could have added half an inch, or even an inch, to his six-foot frame.[23] By donning shoes with even slightly higher heels, he understood that his height could be connected with power and authority. In this respect, Washington recognized, and indeed embraced, the importance of space and stature in eighteenth-century society—an appreciation of the idea that how much space one took up had much to do with wealth and power. It was also, in a manner of speaking, a performance accentuating the way one moved in luxury clothing and accessories, the play of light and shadow, and one's ability to create delight or drama. It was part of the complexity of the rococo style. The conquest of physical space (and filling it with lavish, shiny garments) explains much of the eighteenth century's penchant for panniers, or side hoops in undergarments, for women, along with high, lavishly decorated wigs and hats. Much of the same intent applied to men, with their full-skirted coats, wigs, and tall hats.[24]

Of course, relationships will alter and sour in the face of financial disputes and inequities of trade. By the late 1760s, the political situation in the colonies placed additional stress on the already uneasy relationship between Washington and Robert Cary's British firm. He placed his last order with Didsbury, via Cary & Company, on 10 July 1773. The connection between Washington and his shoemaker appears to have closed unceremoniously with the former's request for "3 pr of strong Shoes, 3 pr dress'd Do Calf, 1 pr Mens Clogs, or Goloshoes to fit the above Shoes—[all] Short Quartd & high."[25]

7.1 George Washington's brown broadcloth suit, possibly of American-made cloth, circa 1795-1799. Courtesy of the Mount Vernon Ladies' Association, gift of John Murray Forbes, with appreciation to William D. McGregor, 1877, object number W-574/A-B

BOSTON'S CORDWAINERS
GREET PRESIDENT WASHINGTON, 1789

On Saturday, 24 October 1789, President George Washington returned to Boston, the site of a standoff between his Continental Army and General Gage's redcoats thirteen years earlier. Revolutionary leaders, including Washington, had no intent for the country they envisioned to dissolve the social bounds that distinguished "the quality" from the "middling sorts," but that is exactly what happened when thousands of ordinary citizens—no longer subjects of a monarch—joined the Continental Army. Washington fought for liberty—taxation *with* representation—but many, including women, African Americans, and working-class people, also wanted equality. Their participation in the Revolutionary War transformed the loose set of colonies into that rarest of political entities in the eighteenth century: a republic.

One unanticipated effect of this change was in fashion. Once Washington learned of his unanimous election as president of the new nation, he no doubt reflected on the impression that he, as the first leader of a people's republic, should make. In January, he wrote to Henry Knox, his confidant and former artillery commander, requesting that, "having learnt from an Advertisement in the New York Daily Advertiser, that there were superfine American Broad Cloths to be sold at No. 44 in Water Street; I have ventured to trouble you with the Commission of purchasing enough to make me a suit of Cloaths." In this missive, Washington revealed a remarkably current knowledge of such sartorial details as fabrics, textures, and dyes: "If the dye should not appear to be well fixed, & clear, or if the cloth should not really be very fine, then (in my Judgment) some colour mixed in grain might be preferable to an indifferent (stained) dye. I shall have occasion to trouble you for nothing but the cloth & twist to make the button holes. If these articles can be procured & forwarded, in a package by the Stage, in any short time your attention will be gratefully acknowledged." As to the color, Washington elected to "leave it altogether to [Knox's] taste." Having selected what was needed for his own dress, the president-elect then took pains to place an order for Martha, requesting cloth in a fashionable new color, "what is called (in the Advertisement) London Smoke," for a riding habit. Washington was particular about the style. If Knox could not acquire the desired items, then, his commander queried, "could they be had from Hartford in Connecticut where I perceive a Manufactury of them is established."[1]

When the day came for the inauguration of both the president and the new nation, on 30 April 1789, Washington famously wore a suit of chestnut brown broadcloth from the Connecticut manufactory, a symbol not of the military man on horseback, but of republican simplicity. Later, for formal occasions, he could be seen in the black velvet long coat captured in Gilbert Stuart's magisterial portrait.[2]

By the end of the summer, Washington had determined that the legitimacy of the new republic, and the authority of his presidency, required a wider stage. His visit to Boston in October was part of an extended tour of the northern states, an exhibition that would announce to all the national reach of the new federal government. The commander-in-chief would stay in Boston for several days. An elated populace planned a grand procession for his arrival, one that included prominent dignitaries and, of particular interest to us, representatives of the various trades.[3]

As part of the preparations for this event, the city's artisans and tradesmen fabricated banners to be carried in the procession. The banners were of uniform size, each representing the insignia or coat of arms of the individual trades. Two examples survive in the collection of the Bostonian Society's Old

7.2   "View of the triumphal ARCH and COLONNADE erected in Boston in honor of the president of the UNITED STATES, Oc[tober] 24, 1789," engraving by Samuel Hill, detached from the *Massachusetts Magazine*, vol. 2, no. 1 (January 1790): 3, published in Boston by Isaiah Thomas and Ebenezer Andrews. The triumphal arch was designed by well-known Federal architect and Boston native Charles Bulfinch. It was eighteen feet high, with a central opening fourteen feet wide, displaying the requisite grandeur and classical attributes, as well as the appropriate inscribed accolades for the president's much-anticipated visit. Collection of the Massachusetts Historical Society, Graphics-Sm Boston, Views 01

State House Museum: those of the mastmakers and the cordwainers. The Bostonian Society also has a broadside, dated 19 October 1789, that lists instructions for those taking part in the procession, as well as specifying the order in which they were to march.[4] The creation of the banners by artisans is not surprising, as a significant number of tradespeople had participated in the Boston Tea Party nearly twenty years earlier, many of them as young apprentices or journeymen.[5]

The participation of the cordwainers is particularly noteworthy. Boston's shoemakers had chosen to model their emblem on a centuries-old counterpart: the Worshipful Company of Cordwainers, one of London's esteemed livery companies, which was formed in 1272 and received a royal charter in 1439 from King Henry VI. The ancient guild system never took hold in the colonies, however, for a variety of political and economic reasons. The cordwainers probably came closest, as they were the only artisans to be granted a

7.3 The cordwainers' processional banner of painted silk, maker unknown, carried to welcome President George Washington to Boston, October 1789. The banner depicts the cordwainers' crest and was carried in the procession by cordwainer (and Boston Tea Party participant) Matthew Loring of Boston. Courtesy of the Bostonian Society, object number 1910.0033

complete charter. Still, the ability to set prices, and to support needy members and their survivors through traditional charities, was denied them by the local authority. Nonetheless, the cordwainers in the British colonies were permitted to have some jurisdiction over quality control and craftsmanship, and the system of apprenticeships and indentures remained strong.[6]

The banner paraded by the city's proud shoe- and bootmakers represented these ancient traditions. The background is silk, with the ornament painted freehand. While the armored figures (centuries earlier, these were to represent the third century AD's martyred saints, Crispin and Crispinian) are somewhat awkward, they nonetheless exude a certain charm. Significantly, St. Crispin is the patron saint of cordwainers.[7] The banners were held aloft on poles, visible from a distance above the throngs who lined the parade grounds, rather than being displayed at eye level. The primary attributes of the Worshipful Company of Cordwainers' coat of arms are present, including three goat heads

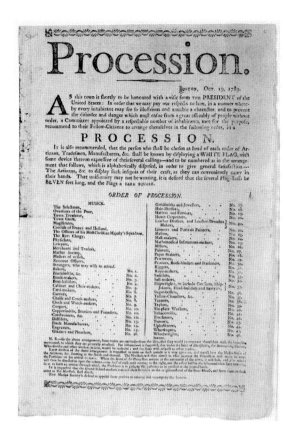

7.4 "Procession. Boston, Oct. 19, 1789. As this town is shortly to be honoured with a visit from the President of the United States." The broadside lists instructions for those taking part in the procession, as well as specifying the order in which they were to march.

Collection of the Massachusetts Historical Society, Bdses 1789 Oct. 19

(signifying cordovan, the white goat leather that London's shoemakers had originally imported from Moorish Cordoba in Spain) against a blue and gold field, flanked by knights in armor.

Cordwainer and leatherworker Matthew Loring had the honor of carrying the banner. Born in 1751, he had participated in the Boston Tea Party at the age of twenty-one. Loring went on to become a respected member of the leatherworker's trade, conducting business on Devonshire and Brattle Streets. He spent time in the lucrative role of leather sealer, a peer-appointed position. By the time of the president's visit, Loring was a family man in his late thirties, with a young daughter, Sarah. Loring was married three times and had nine children, most of whom lived to adulthood. He had means enough to send his daughter Hannah (1800–1842) to Miss Perkin's Academy in Boston when she was twelve, in order to learn silk embroidery.

The survival of the genealogical register for Hannah's family, held in the

Metropolitan Museum of Art's collection, adds another rich material-culture artifact to what little we currently know of the Lorings.[8] Her sampler painstakingly records not only the names of Loring's wives, but also notes their marriage dates, who officiated at the weddings, and the children from each marriage. Matthew died on 7 November 1829, at the age of seventy, and is interred in Boston's Granary Burying Ground, tomb 75. As of this writing, there are no surviving shoes identified as having been made by his hands.

Although Matthew Loring did not leave a record of his experiences in the Boston Tea Party—as did his older compatriot, shoemaker Robert Twelves Hewes—the cordwainers' banner and his daughter's instruction in needlework throw a sliver of light onto the status of shoemaking in Early American society. Some historians have incorrectly situated shoemaking at the bottom rungs of economic endeavor. Yet the banner used in the 24 October procession, and the academy where Hannah learned embroidery, convey a different social position.[9]

One outcome of President George Washington's travels in 1789 were the many artifacts collected and preserved by those who met him or interacted with him in some way. In addition to the distinction that "George Washington slept here," museums and families can boast of glassware, tankards, quilts, and coverlets used by the president. And then there are the shoes.

Women saved the shoes that they wore when they met Washington, or when they danced or dined with him. One example is a surviving silk brocade shoe worn by Sally Brewster Gerrish of Portsmouth, New Hampshire, now in the collection of the Portsmouth Historical Society. Her father, an innkeeper, ran Brewster's Tavern, where Washington slept while in Portsmouth. He arrived in the seacoast town on 31 October, to great fanfare. Family tradition indicates that Sally wore the shoes when she accompanied the president in his carriage, traveling to a gala ball at the downtown Assembly House. Washington noted in his journal that there were "about 75 well dressed, and many of them very handsome Ladies."[10] It is likely that Sally danced with the president, as well. The surviving shoe—it appears that one shoe from the pair was given to one of her children, and the second shoe to the other—shows its wear, but something of its earlier sparkle and sheen may be seen in the silk. The current heel may have been altered from its original, approximately 2 to 2.5-inch height to reflect the lower heels associated with burgeoning neoclassical fashion.

After the Revolutionary War, fashion inspired the same inducements as before to shopping, as well as the same criticisms of the opulence and extrava-

7.5 A single silk brocade shoe with metallic threads, circa the 1770s, with later alterations to the heel, probably British, maker unknown. Family tradition records that this shoe belonged to Sally Brewster Gerrish
and was worn when she accompanied President George Washington in the carriage that conveyed him
to a ball in Portsmouth, New Hampshire. Sally's father was William Brewster, who ran the tavern where
Washington stayed during his visit in October 1789. Courtesy of the Portsmouth Historical Society, gift of Samuel
Gerrish, object number 847, photograph by Andrew Davis, February 2017

gance that had teased society before the war. With the return of peace, British merchants emptied their warehouses, brimming with goods unsold during the war, and dumped their overstock onto American markets. The seeming tidal wave of luxury wares was received with delight by consumers, and with foreboding by critics. Playwright and Continental Army veteran Royall Tyler of Walpole, New Hampshire, was a prominent voice in this dichotomy. Tyler penned the first American play, *The Contrast*, and took this opportunity to rail against the new nation's obsession with fashion. One of the central vices identified by ardent republican thinkers—and the bane of social life, they contended—was luxuriance. In act 3, scene 2, Tyler delivered his influential monologue through the words of Colonel Manly: "And it is not all the types of mandibles that she'll convince me that a nation, to become great, must first become dissipated. Luxury is surely the vein of a nation. Luxury! which enervates both soul and body by opening a thousand new sources of enjoyment, opens also a thousand new sources of contention and want. Luxury! which renders a people weak at home and accessible [vulnerable] to bribery, corruption, and force from abroad."[11]

J. Hector St. Jean de Crèvecoeur, a French American writer, was another influential voice against what he called the "dark spots" that oppressed this "flourishing" country. In particular, he lamented "the number of debts" that plagued Americans, which would "greatly astonish" foreigners. Among the sources of indebtedness that Crèvecoeur identified, Americans' appetite for imported luxury wares loomed large: "Another reason which keeps us in debt is the multiplicity of shops with English goods. These present irresistible temptations. It is so much easier to buy than it is to spin. The allurement of fineries is so powerful with our young girls that they must be philosophers indeed to abstain from them. Thus one fifth part of all our labours every year is laid out in English commodities. These are the taxes that we pay."[12]

Abigail Adams's response to the thrills and dangers posed by London-made shoes was complicated. Her letters reveal a personality that was feisty, even opinionated, but her portraits suggest the appearance of a rather plain, perhaps even dowdy matron. The reality was both, and more. Fifteen years earlier, in 1775, she was the wife of an up-and-coming lawyer who had left in her care a sprawling Massachusetts farm, and five children, while he met with Thomas Jefferson, George Washington, and John Hancock in Philadelphia to debate the colonies' course into revolution. Her letters to John, while he was in Philadelphia, describe the British assault on Bunker Hill, a smallpox epidemic and her decision to inoculate the children, the deaths of neighbors, and the suffering of Boston's populace. Yet, amid her loneliness and anxiety, Abigail adds a curious plea. During this time of scarcity and sacrifice regarding material goods, she nonetheless requested John send a bit of woolen textile, known as calamanco, to her, to make fashionable shoes.[13]

Over the next fifteen years, Abigail Adams penned two other revealing letters, in which shoes help tell her story and allow us to gain a deeper understanding of her life and times. In a later missive, written in 1785, we find Abigail writing to her frequent correspondent (and close friend at that time), Thomas Jefferson, who was then in Paris, to ask for French-made shoes. The United Colonies were now independent—thirteen separate republics—and she was the wife of the American ambassador to the Court of St. James in England. Her entreaty is revealing, as it shows a side of her that we rarely see: "You were so kind sir as to tell me you would execute any little commission for me, and I now take the Liberty of requesting you to let petit go to my paris shoemaker and direct him to make me four pair of silk shoes 2 pr. sattin and two pr. fall silk; I send by Mr. Short the money for them. I am not curious about the colour, only that they be fashonable. I cannot get any made here to suit me, at least I have faild in several attempts. Col. Smith proposes visiting Paris before he returns, and will be so good as to take Charge of them for me."[14]

Abigail Adams's letters to both her husband and to the man who would soon become his enemy fascinates us, in part because the correspondence portray a woman who seems to present two quite different personas. They intrigue us, also, because her request to Jefferson, that the shoes be "fashionable," suggests priorities that might seem to contradict her identity as a simple Yankee matron. She was clearly ordering bespoke, or custom-made, shoes. But it is the qualifying constraints that tell us what she was about.

She does not care what color her four pairs of silk shoes should be, whether they should have any additional adornments or embellishments, or even if they should have heels—high or low—or be flats. The key is her observation to Jefferson, a man who understood matters of genteel diplomacy in Europe's capitals, that she could not receive satisfaction from her own London cordwainer. As the wife of the American ambassador, presenting herself before the royalty and aristocracy of Great Britain, it was essential that Abigail Adams appear as a genteel and fashionable woman. "A little of what you call frippery is very necessary towards looking like the rest of the world," she quipped to John.[15] As Massachusetts politician Fisher Ames would later lament: "Until that contest [the Revolutionary War] a great part of the civilized world had been surprisingly ignorant of the force and character, and almost the existence, of the British colonies. . . . They did not view the colonists so much a people, as a race of fugitives, whom want, solitude, and intermixture with the savages, had made barbarians."[16]

In a later letter, written in 1790 and sent from the family farm in Braintree to John in New York, the capital of the young country, Abigail presents herself as a frugal Yankee goodwife, counting pennies and telling her husband that the only expenditure she had made that winter was for a pair of her own shoes: "For myself I have Spent only 2 dollors and half through the winter and that was for shoes. The whole of the Family expences are upon my Books."[17] Much had changed, both in the affairs of her country and in her station. The United Colonies were now a new nation, and she was the wife of the vice president, second in importance only to George Washington, reputedly the most famous man in the world. Yet the question haunting the recently formed country remained one of identity. "What then is the American, this new man?" asked Crèvecoeur. Would Americans seek to imitate the opulent courts of Europe? Or would they remain true to the republican principles that had fueled the Revolutionary War? For Abigail and John Adams, how they presented themselves, and their choice of clothing and footwear, said as much as about the values of the new nation's people as what they wrote and how they behaved.

In 1790, Abigail Adams wrote to her sister, Mary Smith Cranch, and conveyed her reflection on shoes as a metaphor for life: "I hate to complain. . . . No one is without difficulties, whether in high or low life, and every person knows best where their own shoe pinches."[18] During a fifteen-year time period, the vicissitudes of Abigail's middle years are reflected in something seemingly as mundane as her shoes. Her footwear choices tell us where her own shoe pinched and where it stretched. A pair of buttercream yellow leather shoes, roughly contemporary with her quote, survive at the Smithsonian Institution.[19] The leather is printed with a stylized, neoclassical symbol in a contrasting blue color. They are flats, lined with linen. Inside, a label is affixed to the sock, revealing that these shoes were made in England—not in America or in France. They were crafted by popular London cordwainers Hoppe & Heath and appear to have very little wear. Several similar pairs from the late eighteenth century, made by the same shoemaking concern, survive in North American collections. One pair, connected with the Hancock family, are in the Bostonian Society's collection. They are made of blue leather, with an impressive tassel, and were most likely dancing shoes. The label—reading "Hoppe & Heath, Ladies Shoemakers, No. 156 Minories, London"—is fixed in the footbed, and they are stylistically from the same time period. A version in pink is extant at the Royal Ontario Museum in Toronto, Canada.

These 1790s shoes are especially revealing, as they date to about the time that Abigail made her remark to her sister about where one's shoes pinch. As her husband's political career rose, and her own status along with it, she would begin to feel those "pinches" associated with political jealousy and backbiting. John's enemies—allies of the Adams's erstwhile friend, Thomas Jefferson— would frequently hint that Abigail stepped outside the boundaries of genteel womanhood by expressing her own opinions.

In her own stint as the country's first lady (1797–1801), Abigail Adams sought to influence the fashion styles of the "republican court." The diaphanous, or semisheer, neoclassical clothing that adorned the fashionable women in Europe's aristocratic circles had no place among the respectable women of the new nation, she maintained. Perhaps she had forgotten that she, too, had once sought to be à la mode: while in London, writing to her friend Thomas Jefferson in Paris. Nonetheless, Abigail Adams knew shoes. She was well aware that they could tell stories, not just about the shoes themselves, but also about the people who wore them.

C.1 A pair of silk shoes, with gold and black painted decoration, maker unknown, circa the 1780s. These shoes were probably fabricated from a piece of a banner, flag, or standard. The Connecticut Historical Society notes in their records that "these shoes were made about 1780, from a military flag carried in the Revolutionary War." Courtesy of the Connecticut Historical Society, gift of Mrs. Horatio Fitch, accession number 1950.28.0a,b

CONCLUSION

The years following President George Washington's visit to Boston reveal a marked change in the technology of shoe production, as well as in the availability of footwear. With mechanization employed in established Massachusetts shoe-making areas—such as Lynn, Haverhill, and Brockton—the New England shoe trade grew so large that it would have surprised the cordwainers of previous generations. The existence of the home-shop system, which was already in place, allowed this rapid development. One of the most expansive areas of growth in the shoe business was making "coarse" shoes for the enslaved who labored in fields and on farms. The supply of shoes for enslaved people is a little-mentioned aspect of New England's complicity in the slave trade. For example, Zerubbabel Porter sent thousands of boxes of shoes from Salem to various distribution points, including Baltimore, Norfolk, Wilmington, and Charleston. While his accounts do not specifically mention making shoes for the enslaved, the sheer numbers, the shipping locations, and the low cost of the items reveal their purpose. Further, the terminology used—coarse or sturdy—employs a language quite different from that used for customers who were free, particularly affluent ones.[1]

Standing alongside the innovations in mechanization, production, and manufacture, however, are examples of highly personal, custom-made shoes. One notable pair of woman's shoes, which appear to be tied to the American Revolution, were fabricated from a piece of a banner, flag, or standard. Their maker is unknown. The Connecticut Historical Society notes in their records that "these shoes were made about 1780, from a military flag carried in the Revolutionary War."[2] They were presented to the historical society by Mrs. Horatio Fitch, and both her family and her husband's were probably involved in the revolution.

The uppers are crafted from red silk damask and painted with gold and black highlights. The letters OIT are discernible on one shoe and N on the other, and they include decorative swirls. The straps would have buckled across the vamp. The interior is lined with linen. They are hand stitched, and the historical society's description notes that the edge was hastily whipstitched. This may indicate that the shoes were fabricated quickly, for a special commemorative event. The materials are typical of those used for banners at that time. Indeed, during President George Washington's Boston visit, the processional banners for the various trades were made of painted silk.[3]

The diminutive white heel adds a visual contrast to the red silk upper. Given the dimensions and angle of the heel, it seems appropriate to date the shoes to circa the 1780s, most likely closer to 1784. The shoe's length of 8.25 inches corresponds roughly to a woman's US size 5 today.

Another example of a one-off shoe, fashioned from an earlier textile by a local or regional shoemaker, is at the Currier Museum of Art in Manchester, New Hampshire. Family tradition notes that the uppers of this pair of blue-green silk shoes were made from an embroidered silk waistcoat, circa 1738. The floral motif, as well as the color and style of the pattern, certainly indicate an earlier date of manufacture than that of the shoe itself. Judging by the style, height, and placement of the heel, and the contrast of the white, leather-clad heel with the blue green of the upper, suggests a date range from the 1780s to the 1790s. The shoes' construction appears to be hasty; the finishing a bit haphazard, with significant piecing; and the lining nothing more than a rough linen. A few small hooks remain along the upper edge of the shoe. These were most likely for a silk ribbon to lace up the front and the ankle, demonstrating the neoclassical penchant for shoes resembling classical footwear—in this

C.2 Embroidered blue-green silk shoes, maker unknown, circa the 1780s. Family tradition notes that the uppers were remade from an embroidered silk waistcoat, a textile from circa 1738. The style, height, and placement of the white, leather-clad heel suggest a date range from the 1780s to the1790s. Courtesy of the Currier Museum of Art, gift of Helen J. Stearns, accession number PC S19a,b (238)

case, a sandal. The shoes are straight lasted. It is highly likely that they were made by a local shoemaker, who attached the earlier English silk to his own leather sole for his customer.[4]

During the course of his life, John Hancock developed a reputation as something of a dandy. Many American men of his era loved fashion, as quite a few do now. In 1819, a New England groom who was married in Haverhill, Massachusetts, designed and made his own wedding shoes, which are housed in Haverhill's Buttonwoods Museum. This pair of leather wedding pumps from the early republic demonstrate an independent design aesthetic. They belonged not to the "quality"—people such as George Washington or John Hancock—but to one of the "middling sorts," a cordwainer named Leonard Phillips (1792–1832), who married Sarah Head (1796–1881) of Bradford, Massachusetts, on 20 January 1819. The groom was twenty-seven, and the bride was twenty-three. They later had two children.[5] These men's shoes were probably made in Haverhill in the early years of the nineteenth century. There is no question that they are a rare survival and offer a personal response to the shoemaker's impending nuptials.

These charming shoes, fashioned from leather and embellished with leather appliqués of animals, fish, peacocks and other birds, and trees, convey

C.3 A groom's wedding shoes, of leather with leather appliqués, most likely made and worn by Leonard Phillips of Haverhill, Massachusetts. There is no question that these shoes are a rare survival, as well as a very personal response to the shoemaker's impending nuptials. These charming shoes are embellished with leather appliqués of animals, fish, peacocks and other birds, and trees. They convey a "folk art" feel. Traces of original paint in red, yellow, and green originally accentuated these applied pieces.

Courtesy of the Buttonwoods Museum, accession number 2008.017

a folk art feel. Although now faded, the once-colorful shoes featured touches of green, yellow, and red dyes, still discernible in the house appliqué on the vamp. The shoes have low heels and squared-off toes and were fastened with buckles.

The shape of the shoe and the use of buckles at this late date indicate a conservative style.[6] Yet turning the shoes upside down reveals an unusual feature. The narrative cycle displayed on the uppers continues on the soles, which are incised with a man and a woman standing next to two houses, probably symbolizing the joining of their families. A peacock is incised on the heel. The clarity of the image on the sole and the condition of the heel suggests that the shoes were worn very little, perhaps just for this one occasion.[7] There are no doubt countless examples of highly personal responses to self-fashioning through footwear such as these, tucked away in museums, historical societies, private collections, and family attics, which will come to light in time.

C.4   Detail from a groom's wedding shoes, of leather with leather appliqués, most likely made and worn by Leonard Phillips of Haverhill, Massachusetts. The soles continue the narrative of marriage, with a man and a woman standing adjacent to two houses. Courtesy of the Buttonwoods Museum, accession number 2008.017

EPILOGUE

My intense interest in shoes began by chance in 2010, when I came across a single brocaded silk shoe by the London cordwainers Ridout & Davis at the Strawbery Banke Museum in Portsmouth, New Hampshire. The shoe held an aura of mystery. Although it had seen hard times, there was such quality, beauty, and craftsmanship invested in this relatively small object that it immediately captured my imagination. The silk is shattered, abraded, and missing altogether in some spots, yet even after two centuries, a sheen remains. Examining the elegantly carved heel and pointy toe for wear marks and alterations, I searched for some small key to the woman who once wore it. Inside, affixed to the insole, was a paper label—a link to its past. I was smitten.

In any number of recent blockbuster fashion exhibitions, often the stars are diminutive silk brocade or damask shoes, embellished with spangles or metallic lace—or both. They catch many a contemporary glance, with the viewer perhaps imagining what it may have been like to wear such shoes and pondering what eighteenth-century floors the wearer had walked. As beautiful as they may be as objects, putting Georgian shoes into a historic context amplifies their significance beyond simply a connoisseur's visual interest. How do we know that shoes were important to Georgian-era Americans? Lacking any letters, diary and journal entries, or odes written specifically about them by their owners, how can historians draw any conclusions about the importance of a sturdy pair of boots, an elegant silk brocade pump, or a favorite pair of dancing slippers?

Without the historians' conventional print documents, the most compelling evidence remains the objects themselves. North American collections alone contain thousands of pairs of shoes, humble or luxurious, filling the drawers and shelves of museums, house sites, historical societies, and archives. The "keptness" of shoes, generation after generation, reminds us that these were loved objects that carried significant meanings, deep associations, and both personal and historical connective memories. Shoes could hold the goals and aspirations of a family, long after the original wearer had died. Because of the portability of shoes, children and grandchildren and great-grandchildren could pass them along as family heirlooms or place them into museum collections. Sometimes children, like those of Sally Brewster Gerrish, would each be given a shoe, dividing the pair. This is why, in many museum collections, only a single shoe has survived. Later generations understood that even a well-worn pair of shoes—frayed, damaged, dirty—could easily have historical importance. A number of these objects carry family memories in the form of handwritten notes attached to a shoe or inscribed upon it. In a sense, shoes have been treated like significant pieces of architecture, protected and treasured by preservationists. Their value is seen not only in primary characteristics—such as style, age, materials, and exemplars of a particular type—but also in who used them.

In this book, shoes have told us stories. They have revealed the hopes, dreams, and disappointments of the people who made them and those who wore them. Shoes allowed their owners to reimagine themselves as elegant and refined, to adorn themselves in the regalia of the gentry, and to identify with the cosmopolitan values of a prosperous and powerful empire.

In Georgian America, these acts of self-fashioning began even before the consumer revolution of the 1740s. British American shoppers craved the elegant footwear, crafted by London cordwainers, that filled the shelves of shops in Boston, Philadelphia, New York, Williamsburg, and beyond. These were sophisticated, selective consumers. They sought out particular makers, ordering and purchasing shoes from cordwainers they associated with high quality and upscale fashion, and buying from shops that presented goods they equated with gentility. They also adapted the shoes they bought, according to their own needs and tastes. They engaged in reuse, modifying the shoes to their own specifications, thereby making them their own. In effect, their British shoes became British American ones, connoting their own identity. This was a process of self-fashioning, a projection of an Anglo American identity. The stories that the lives of Samuel Lane and John Hose tell are Atlantic-world stories, revealing how these master craftsmen sought to keep up with the changing fads and fashions their customers sought. Their stories tell us how elite American colonists attempted to revitalize their ties to Old England in the second half of the eighteenth century, and how this effort spread to middle-class consumers and beyond.

During the 1760s, resistance to the so-called innovations imposed by a novice king and a pliant Parliament challenged comfortable identities and loyalties and called into question customary purchasing arrangements. Throughout these years, Americans navigated the boisterous seas of consumption. Leaders and consumers debated the role of "enemy" goods, attempting to impose non-intercourse agreements and encourage the wearing of American-made clothing, yet many continued to don their favored British shoes.

In post-revolutionary America, consumers could again enjoy their purchases without enduring the political taint of disloyalty. British cordwainers (and now French shoemakers as well) accommodated this hunger for elegant shoes, emptying their bulging warehouses of stock that then sold for a fraction of its original cost. Yet eighteenth-century Americans were not just consumers of goods foisted on the former colonies. They were also active agents in the selection of which goods to purchase. By the early republic, the "middling sorts"—consumers of modest means—could take advantage of inexpensive surpluses that now trickled down to them.

As the eighteenth century came to a close and the nineteenth century dawned, mechanization made it possible for individuals in most economic strata to have one or perhaps several pairs of shoes, often made for specialized purposes. In these stories, even working-class consumers became active participants in their purchases and their imitation of luxury tastes. As shoes became readily available, however, the stories so often captured by footwear in the eighteenth century begin to fade into the background. This volume is an attempt to bring these shoe stories back into contemporary notice.

Appendixes

1

AN EIGHTEENTH-CENTURY SHOE TIMELINE

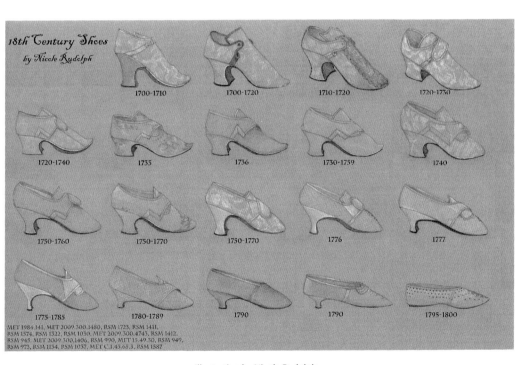

18th Century Shoes
by Nicole Rudolph

1700-1710 1700-1720 1710-1720 1720-1730
1720-1740 1735 1736 1730-1759 1740
1750-1760 1750-1770 1750-1770 1776 1777
1775-1785 1780-1789 1790 1790 1795-1800

MET 1984.141, MET 2009.300.1480, RSM 1723, RSM 1411,
RSM 1574, RSM 1322, RSM 1050, MET 2009.300.4743, RSM 1412,
RSM 945, MET 2009.300.1406, RSM 990, MET 15.49.30, RSM 949,
RSM 973, RSM 1134, RSM 1037, MET C.I.43.65.3, RSM 1587

Illustration by Nicole Rudolph

2

PRIMARY COMPONENTS OF AN EIGHTEENTH-CENTURY SHOE

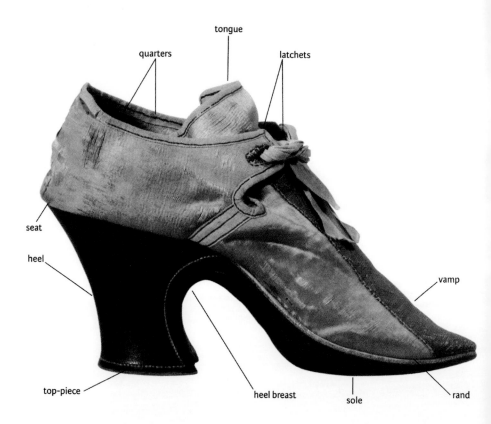

Image from Althea Mackenzie, *Shoes and Slippers* (London: National Trust, 2004),
unnumbered page [95], photograph by John Hammond

3

THE PARTS OF A SHOE BUCKLE

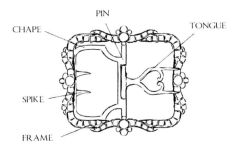

Image courtesy of American Duchess Historical Footwear,
www.americanduchess.com

4

COLLECTIONS VISITED

American Textile History Museum, *Lowell, Massachusetts*
   (no longer in operation)
Bata Shoe Museum, *Toronto, Ontario, Canada*
Bostonian Society's Old State House Museum, *Boston, Massachusetts*
Brick Store Museum, *Kennebunk, Maine*
Buttonwoods Museum, *Haverhill, Massachusetts*
Charleston Museum, *Charleston, South Carolina*
Chester County Historical Society, *West Chester, Pennsylvania*
Colonial Dames, *Boston, Massachusetts*
Colonial Dames, *Portsmouth, New Hampshire*
Colonial Williamsburg Foundation, *Williamsburg, Virginia*
Currier Museum of Art, *Manchester, New Hampshire*
Dedham Historical Society, *Dedham, Massachusetts*

Haverhill Historical Society, *Haverhill, New Hampshire*

Historic Deerfield, *Deerfield, Massachusetts*

Historic New England Collections, *Haverhill, Massachusetts*

Ipswich Museum, *Ipswich, Massachusetts*

Massachusetts Historical Society, *Boston, Massachusetts*

Mount Vernon Ladies' Association, *Mount Vernon, Virginia*

Newmarket Historical Society, *Newmarket, New Hampshire*

Old Berwick Historical Society, *South Berwick, Maine*

Peabody Essex Museum / Phillips Library, *Salem, Massachusetts*

Portsmouth Athenæum, *Portsmouth, New Hampshire*

Portsmouth Historical Society/John Paul Jones House,
   Portsmouth, New Hampshire

Saco Museum, *Saco, Maine*

Salem Maritime National Historic Site, *Salem, Massachusetts*

Strawbery Banke Museum, *Portsmouth, New Hampshire*

University of New Hampshire Museum
   and Special Collections, *Durham, New Hampshire*

Warner House, *Portsmouth, New Hampshire*

Glossary

back strap   A strip of material covering the back seam of a shoe.

bespoke   Clothing items and accessories made for an individual order.

brocade   A fabric, often silk, with a plain ground and a pattern of extra wefts in a contrasting color, producing a slightly raised surface. Today, the term is used to describe any woven, patterned textile.

calamanco   A textile of worsted wool, which could come in various weaves. It was distinguished by its glazed, calendered surface, created by being pressed through hot rollers.

cordwainer   The historical name for a shoemaker, most likely derived from cordwain or cordovan, a Spanish leather originally used for shoes from Cordoba, Spain.

custom-made   An item that is not ready-made or mass produced.

damask   A figured, woven fabric with a pattern visible on both sides, often of silk, but also of linen or cotton.

dogskin   Generally a type of leather made from the skins of sheep or goats.

footbed   *See* insole.

galosh	A shoe construction in which the vamp and quarters are cut in one piece and seamed at the back. The term also refers to waterproofed overshoes.
heel	A solid base under the back of the foot, usually a carved wooden shape covered in leather or fabric, or built up with strips of leather. The heels of ladies' eighteenth-century shoes were generally made of carved wood and are often called a French heel. A French heel was of medium height, flared out or widened at the base. The term Louis heel (named for the Sun King, Louis XIV) to describe the shape of the French heel was not in use until after the mid-nineteenth century. Stacked leather heels for women began to appear with more regularity in the late eighteenth century.
insole	The sole to which the upper is attached and on which the foot rests. An outside sole was added beneath the insole.
lachets	The tops of the uppers that extend from the quarters, crossing over at the front of the shoe and over the tongue. Lachets could be tied or buckled, though when long enough to require buckles, lachets tended to be known as straps.
last	A wooden form, resembling the shape of the desired shoe, over which the upper was made.
metallic lace	A type of lace made from metal or metallic threads, such as gold, silver, or copper. The designs were worked directly on a textile ground, or the lace was completely made from metallic threads. Metallic lace was used as an embellishment in all manner of clothing, from shoes to waistcoats, gowns, and caps.
Morocco leather	Usually goatskin that was tanned with sumac, meant to imitate leather from Morocco. It was frequently dyed red.
mule	A shoe without heel quarters.
patten	A patten includes various types of footwear with a thick sole, usually made of leather, that is used to elevate the foot from mud and muck in streets and roads, protecting the shoes. During the Georgian period, a patten often

made use of silk brocade or damask uppers, attached via lachets with a leather lace. Although the term clog is frequently interchanged with the term patten in current use, originally the former word meant a type of shoe with an inflexible sole, frequently made of wood, with an open heel.

polychrome   A term referring to a multicolored item

quarters   The sides of the uppers that joined the vamp at the front and were seamed together at the back. They were so named since they were, in effect, one quarter of a shoe.

rand   A narrow strip of leather inserted between the upper and the sole. A rand was often used as an integral part of the decoration for the shoe. For example, if it was white, it contrasted with the color in the rest of the shoe.

sock   A piece of fabric or leather inside the shoe, covering all or part of the insole.

sole   The undersurface of any footwear. The sole rests on the ground.

sole stamp   Small, sealed holes made by nails, used to attach the soles to the last before attaching the upper. Occasionally, a design is evident, such as a star or fleur-de-lis.

spangles   A small, thin piece of glittering material, typically used in quantity to embellish a shoe. Today, these are more commonly known as sequins. In French, they are called *paillettes*.

stiffener   Reinforcement for the quarters, usually giving extra support to the back of the shoe. Stiffener was also found in many of the pointed toes, to maintain their shape.

straight last, or straights   A pair of shoes made with no differentiation between the left and right shoes. This required only one last to make a pair of shoes, and the shoes could be worn on either foot.

straps   *See* lachets.

taffeta   A plain-weave silk fabric.

throat   The center front of the vamp.

tongue	An extension of the vamp over the instep and under the lachets or straps.
translator	One who assembled, remade, or refashioned shoes (and other items) from various older bits and pieces of textile, leather, metallic lace, and so on.
turnshoe	A method of fabrication, where a shoe is initially made inside out and then is turned, so the sole seam is on the inside. Many of the shoes discussed in this book are of turnshoe construction.
upper	The part of the shoe that covers the top of the foot, normally consisting of the vamp, quarters, and lining.
vamp	The front section of the upper, covering the toes and part of the instep.
waist	The narrowest part of the sole, under the arch of the foot.
welt	A narrow strip of leather, sewn around the edge of the upper and insole prior to the attachment of both.

Notes

INTRODUCTION

Epigraph. Letter from Abigail Adams to Mary Smith Cranch, 21 March 1790, Adams family correspondence, vol. 9, *The Adams Papers: Digital Edition*, Massachusetts Historical Society, https://www.masshist.org/publications/apde2/browse-volumes/.

1. In a 1992 interview, international authority on shoes June Swann noted: "'The shoe is the only garment you wear that retains your shape and your personality . . .' Ms. Swann explained. 'You take off your clothes, they're just a heap of rags on the floor. But the shoe is moulded to your foot. It's got the essence of the wearer in it.'" Paula Weideger, Lifestyle, *Independent*, 23 August 1992, www.independent.co.uk.

2. For information on eighteenth-century textiles and shoes generally, see Anishanslin, *Portrait of a Woman*; Anonymous, *Shoepedia*; Baumgarten, *What Clothes Reveal*; Bossan, *Art of the Shoe*; Graddy and Pastan, *Smithsonian First Ladies' Collection*; Farrell, "Silk and Globalisation"; Haulman, *Politics of Fashion*; Hopkins and Hopkins, *Footwear*; Johnston and Woolley, *Shoes*; Mackenzie, *Shoes and Slippers*; L. Miller, *Selling Silks*; Rexford, *Women's Shoes in America*; Riello, *Foot in the Past*; Rudolph, *Turn Shoe Construction*; Saguto, *Art of the Shoemaker*; Shephard, *In Step With Fashion*; Swann, *Shoes*; Walford, *Seductive Shoe*; Thompson, "'Invectives . . . Against the Americans'"; Melinda Watt, "Textile Production in Europe: Silk, 1600–1800," *Heilbrunn Timeline of Art History*, 2003, Metropolitan Museum of Art, www.metmuseum.org/toah/hd/txt_s/hd_txt_s.htm; Young, *Shoemaker*.

3. The archaic term "cordwainer" refers to a person who worked with cordovan leather, from Cordoba, Spain. In "What Is a Cordwainer?: An Ancient Calling," the Honorable Cordwainers' Company, www.thehcc.org/backgrnd.htm: "'Cordwainer' is an Anglicization of the French word *cordonnier*, which means shoemaker, introduced into the English language after the Norman invasion in 1066. The word was derived from the city of Cor-

doba in the south of Spain, a stronghold of the mighty Omeyyad Kalifs until its fall in the 12th century. Moorish Cordoba was celebrated in the early Middle Ages for silversmithing and the production of cordouan leather, called 'cordwain' in England. Originally made from the skin of the Musoli goat, then found in Corsica, Sardinia, and elsewhere, this leather was tawed with alum after a method supposedly known only to the Moors. Crusaders brought home much plunder and loot, including the finest leather the English shoemakers had seen. Gradually cordouan, or cordovan leather, became the material most in demand for the finest footwear in all of Europe."

4. For a recent and important study on American shoe labels, see Reddick, "American Identity."

5. British Americans were little different from their counterparts in England in coveting Georgian shoes, as underscored by a 2016 exhibit held at Fairfax House in Castlegate, United Kingdom, called "A Century of Shoes: The Rise and Fall of the Georgian Heel," www .fairfaxhouse.co.uk/whats-on/a-century-of-shoes/.

6. Examples of the reuse of and repairs to shoes are found in the daybooks of the Pingry family (Salem, Massachusetts), the Pope family (Salem, Massachusetts), Colonel John Welch (Plaistow, New Hampshire), Colonel John Montgomery (Haverhill, New Hampshire), and Samuel Lane (Stratham, New Hampshire), to name just a few.

7. The idea of anglicization was introduced and given its fullest expression in Murrin, "Anglicizing an American Colony." The quote is taken from the introduction to Murrin, "The Legal Transformation," 540. Also see Breen, "Empire of Goods"; Myers, "Reinventing the American Wing"; Thompson, "'Invectives . . . Against the Americans'"; Gould, "Virtual Nation"; E. W. Carp, "Early American Military History"; Gallup-Diaz et al., *Anglicizing America*.

1 • THE CORDWAINERS

Epigraph. Quoted in Brown, *Life of Samuel Lane*, 9.

1. Bow Lane and Queen Street run along a north–south axis through the ward, Watling Street runs east–west, and Queen Street runs diagonally through part of the ward.

2. For the size of shoemaking concerns and the long working hours, see Saguto, *Art of the Shoemaker*, 2. For an excellent example of a shoe created by a translator, see one in the Museum of London, dating from circa 1720–1750, using some bits of an embroidered textile that possibly dates back to the 1620s. For more, see "A Rubbish Display: 2000 Years of Junk," Discover London through History, Museum of London, https://www.museumoflondon .org.uk/discover/.

3. Willcocks, *Cordwainers*, 174–175.

4. For information on working conditions and apprenticeships, see Campbell, *London Tradesman*; Saguto, *Art of the Shoemaker*; Willcocks, *Cordwainers*; Riello, *Foot in the Past*, and Swann, *Shoes*. Materials about historic trades, available on Colonial Williamsburg's website (http://history.org/Almanack/life/trades/tradehdr.cfm), are especially useful.

5. Hose family documents suggest a date of about 1699 for John Hose's birth, based on church records. He married Elizabeth Collver in Nottingham on 18 August 1731. In that same year, he acquired his freedman's papers from the City of London and established

himself in Cheapside. His only son, Thomas, followed him in the business. John Hose died on 31 March 1769 and was buried in a vault at St. Mary Islington. In addition to passing on his skill as a cordwainer to his son, he also served as master to apprentice William Chamberlain, another cordwainer whose shoes are found in North American collections and whose product quality was very high. The author is indebted to Colin Michael Hose and Linda Pardoe, descendants of the Hose family, for sharing their illuminating family documents.

6. Here, success is defined as having attained a substantial amount of material goods, a business or trade to pass on, and at least modest sums of money to distribute.

7. Bossan, *Art of the Shoe*.

8. One method for ascertaining the number of thefts of shoes is to search under "shoes" on the Old Bailey Online website, https://www.oldbaileyonline.org. This database is searchable by date, offense, and, frequently, by footwear type (shoe, pump, boot, etc.). Further, in many cases where there is little accessible information about a shoemaker, researchers can glean biographical details if that individual was the victim of a theft or shoplifting.

9. For images of St. Mary-le-Bow, see the Museum of London website, www.museum oflondonprints.com.

10. Old Bailey Online website, https://www.oldbaileyonline.org.

11. Among the dozens of taverns and hostelries in this part of the ward, there were also two churches there in the mid-seventeenth century: St. Mary Aldermay and St. Mary-le-Bow. Given Mr. Hose's reference in his testimony to catching the culprit in the Bow churchyard, St. Mary-le-Bow seems likely.

12. Thomas Hose, City of London, "Petition to Morden College," Hose family papers, courtesy of the Hose family. The author is indebted to Michael Colin Hose and Linda Pardoe for making these family papers available.

13. Urban residential areas with access to trade imports included Boston; New York; Salem; Philadelphia; Newburyport, Massachusetts; Charleston, South Carolina; Norfolk; Williamsburg; Portsmouth, New Hampshire; Kittery, Maine; and Providence. By the mid-eighteenth century, customers could make purchases of both locally manufactured and imported (especially British and, less frequently, French) wares directly from shoe shops, as well as from stores selling various drygoods and West India goods.

14. Smith, *Generall Historie of Virginia*. In the copy of Smith's first edition (rare books, call number 69259) in the Huntington Library, San Marino, California, he included a dedication to the Worshipful Company of Cordwainers, indicating that the members had supported him and his book. The imprint date was altered in the manuscript to 1626, and the binding is stamped with royal arms.

15. W. Wood, *New England's Prospect*, 189.

16. To this day, Ladd Lane and Tannery Road stand on opposite sides of the Dartmouth College Highway, along Oliverian Brook

17. Colonel Joseph Welch, account book, Plaistow, New Hampshire, 1762–1768, MSS 1492, Phillips Library, Peabody Essex Museum, Salem, Massachusetts.

18. Colonial Williamsburg journeyman shoemaker Brett Walker, commenting on Lane family shoes.

19. Lieutenant Colonel Joseph Welch was the highest-ranking officer from Plaistow, New Hampshire, to serve in the Revolutionary War. He participated in the New Hampshire Provincial Congress during 1775 and commanded a regiment of New Hampshire militia in autumn 1777 to bolster the Continental Army forces at Saratoga. See "Participants in the Battle of Saratoga," Saratoga NYGenWeb Project, http://saratoganygenweb.com/batlwe .htm. Welch is mentioned in correspondence from George Washington to Colonel Thomas Tash, 13 October 1776, *Founders Online*, National Archives, https://founders.archives.gov.

20. Colonel Joseph Welch, account book, MSS 1492, Phillips Library, Peabody Essex Museum. It includes accounts of shoes made and repaired, customer accounts, and goods sold. The Putnams, Popes, Pingrys, and Porters were among the Salem, Danvers, and Rowley shoemakers who have left account books to that effect, also located in the Phillips Library. Other opportunities were prevalent in smaller urban communities, such as Lynn or Ipswich in Massachusetts, and especially along Boston's North Shore and throughout Essex County. The existence of ten-footers, a vernacular building type that could be used for a number of small trades, was frequently associated with preindustrial shoe production.

21. Letter from George Washington to John Didsbury, 30 November 1759, *Founders Online*, National Archives, https://founders.archives.gov. For information on uses for dog leather, see Yvette Mahe, "History of Gloves and Their Significance," 12 November 2013, *Fashion in Time*, www.fashionintime.org/history-gloves-significance/.

22. Master boot- and shoemaker D. A. Saguto of the Colonial Williamsburg Foundation and Historic Jamestowne, as quoted in "Revisited Myth #17: The Most Stylish Shoes Were Made of Dogskin, Hence the Expression 'Puttin' on the Dog,'" History Myths Debunked, https://historymyths.wordpress.com.

23. Samuel Lane, "Almanack," December 1775, ser. I, box 1, folder 5, New Hampshire Historical Society, Concord, New Hampshire.

24. The author thanks D. A. Saguto, master boot- and shoemaker (emeritus), Colonial Williamsburg Foundation, and consulting curator for archaeological footwear, Historic Jamestowne, for clarification of this point.

25. The document appears in Gannon, *Short History*. The statement about fifty dollars after he had completed his apprenticeship was interlined before the document was signed. As of this writing, the author has not been able to locate any shoes made by Putnam or his apprentice, Joseph Verry, although there are numerous references to a shoe shop being part of the large Putnam family holdings (now administered by the Danvers Historical Society, Danvers, Massachusetts). It was occupied by Daniel Putnam and family members until the mid-nineteenth century.

26. Samuel Lane, "Almanack," December 1741, ser. I, box 1, folder 5, New Hampshire Historical Society. In colonial New England shoemaking, there were frequently small shops set up within larger farmhouses, such as by Deacon Adams (John Adams's father) in Braintree, Massachusetts; the Putnams and Verrys in Durham, New Hampshire; Samuel Lane in Stratham, New Hampshire; and the home later owned by the Rasielis family in Maine. Apprenticeship records reveal that in addition to learning the trade of shoemaker, half of their tenure would be spent "at farming." Shoemaking became a growing occupation in the early nineteenth century.

27. "Agreement between Timothy Jones and Samuel Lane, October 8, 1741," accession number 1991.095, New Hampshire Historical Society.

28. "Receipt from Daniel Mason to Samuel Lane, September 26, 1751," accession number 1991.095, New Hampshire Historical Society.

29. "The Little Ice Age was a period of regionally cold conditions between roughly AD 1300 and 1850. The term 'Little Ice Age' is somewhat questionable, because there was no single, well-defined period of prolonged cold. There were two phases of the Little Ice Age, the first beginning around 1290 and continuing until the late 1400s. There was a slightly warmer period in the 1500s, after which the climate deteriorated substantially, with the coldest period between 1645 and 1715. During this coldest phase of the Little Ice Age there are indications that average winter temperatures in Europe and North America were as much as 2°C lower than at present." See "Little Ice Age," Environmental History Resources, https://www.eh-resources.org/little-ice-age/. Also see Golinski, *British Weather*.

30. Samuel Lane, "Almanack," February 1748, ser. I, box 1, folder 5, New Hampshire Historical Society.

31. Ulrich, *A Midwife's Tale*.

32. Letter from Abigail Adams to John Adams, 8 February 1794, "Letters between John and Abigail," *Adams Family Papers: An Electronic Archive*, Massachusetts Historical Society, www.masshist.org/digitaladams/archive/browse/.

> Quincy Febry. 8th 1794
> My dearest Friend
> I was very sorry to learn by your last Letters that you had little hopes of getting home til May. There are so many new Arrangements to make upon our places that I really feel unequal to the Task, but if it must be so, I will do the best I can according to my Ability, and if I fail in the execution, You must at least allow for the intention. I would wish you to think what you would have done upon the several Farm's: Humphries is gone into the Country, and I doubt very much, whether Porter will not be so quidling that I shall not be able to agree with him. His woman is so weakly, and Maids are so nice now, that they cannot drive a Cow to pasture, &c I mentiond to you in a Former Letter that I had offers of several persons, and I have seen the Son, and daughters of the Richards Family, and told them my Terms. They have them under consideration; I have inquired their characters of Dr. Tufts and he approves of them. He thinks I could not do better. They are an able Family and have been used to a dairy upon a large scale. The Young Man is a shoe maker but would like to let himself for 6 or 8 months. The rest of his Time he would work at his trade. What his terms would be he could not tell, yet.

33. Ferling, *John Adams*, 10. Deacon John Adams purchased the Braintree homestead, built in 1681, in 1720. The president was born there on 30 October 1735. When Deacon Adams died in 1761, John inherited the house, along with lands his father had purchased in 1744. John and Abigail married in 1764 and made the Braintree site their home, which is now the Adams National Historic Site in Quincy, Massachusetts.

34. The recently renovated ten-footer, brilliant in yellow-gold clapboards with white trim, now graces the courtyard of the Lynn Museum in Lynn, Massachusetts, where it stands in the shadow of the old, eight-story Vamp Building. The latter is appropriately

named, as it was, at one time, reputed to be the largest shoe factory in the world. The Vamp Building housed the next generation of shoe manufacturing, after the introduction of shoe machines such as Jan Matzeliger's shoe-lasting machine. The juxtaposition of these two structures provides a unique contrast of historical eras gone by.

35. Ten-footers, such as the Lye-Tapley Shoe Shop (in the Federal Garden area of the Peabody Essex Museum), circa 1830, were common at one time on the North Shore—a center for shoemaking in the nineteenth century. Comparatively few ten-footers survive today. The building currently houses a collection of significant preindustrial shoemaking tools. Other examples are located at the Ipswich Museum (Ipswich, Massachusetts), the Maine State Museum (Augusta, Maine), and the Lynn Museum, among other sites.

36. A list of the holdings in Samuel Lane's library late in his life does not include any work by Benjamin Franklin. Lane made gifts of his books and his psalm books and Bibles to family members and neighbors. He also specifically made a gift of a Bible to Dinah, his second wife's slave, who moved with her into Samuel's home once he remarried. The New Hampshire Historical Society holds this list, along with the Lane family papers.

37. Goldthwaite, *Boardman Genealogy*, 18. Also see Fea, *Way of Improvement*.

38. Samuel Lane, "Almanack," December 1775, ser. I, box 1, folder 5, New Hampshire Historical Society.

39. Understanding the methods of production for shoemaking in New England is a challenge, because so few documented or identified shoes by local shoemakers exist until those made after the American Revolution.

40. Brett Walker, journeyman shoe- and bootmaker, Colonial Williamsburg Foundation, has been studying and researching Samuel Lane for sixteen years.

41. The collection was carefully preserved by family members before being deposited at the New Hampshire Historical Society.

42. Will of John Hose, cordwainer of London, 20 February 1769, National Archives, Kew, United Kingdom.

43. Will of Samuel Lane, Stratham, New Hampshire, 20 May 1789, New Hampshire Historical Society. All known copies of Samuel Lane's will are housed in the Lane Family Papers in the New Hampshire Historical Society.

44. Ibid.

2 · WEDDING SHOES

Epigraph. Letter from George Washington to Martha Washington, 23 June 1775, George Washington's Mount Vernon, www.mountvernon.org.

1. Samuel Richardson's *Pamela; or, Virtue Rewarded*, published in London in 1742, was exceedingly popular, and it was well known in British America. For example, Eliza Lucas Pinckney reported reading it.

2. General sources on weddings in the eighteenth and early nineteenth centuries include Jabour, *Marriage in the Early Republic*; M. Miller, *Eye of the Needle*; Metzger, *Wedded Bliss*; Kenslea, *Sedgwicks in Love*. Also see Knight, *Journal of Madam Knight* (her journal of a horseback ride from Boston to New York in 1704), which tells of curious marriage customs in Connecticut and other rural New England towns. For an online version, see "Journal

of Madame Knight," *Early Americas Digital Archive*, http://eada.lib.umd.edu/text-entries
/journal-of-madam-knight/.

3. Historic New England's collection includes a pair of shoe buckles worn by a New England bride. Extravagant examples, such as sapphire- and diamond-laden shoe buckles dating from the mid-eighteenth century, were exhibited at the Victoria and Albert Museum in 2015. For additional information on buckles as a fashion and economic statement, see Riello, *Foot in the Past*, 75–82.

4. See, for example, an extant gown and matching shoes, circa 1760, Bunka Gakuen Costume Museum, Tokyo; a green Spitalfields silk damask ensemble (textile c. 1743–45; dress and shoes c. 1775), Metropolitan Museum, www.metmuseum.org/art/collection/search /80403?img=1/.

5. Recent research by historian John Bell notes the uptick in the number of colonial weddings in several Massachusetts communities prior to the enactment of the Stamp Act. Bell's work shows that to avoid what was essentially a marriage tax (because of the stamps required), many couples married before 1 November 1765, when the act went into effect. The cost of a marriage license was 10 shillings, approximately two *days'* labor for a working man. For more, see Bell's blog piece, "The Stamp Act as a Marriage Tax," 20 December 2015, *Boston 1775*, http://boston1775.blogspot.com.

6. Rexford, *Women's Shoes in America*, includes a table listing wedding shoes from 1790 on that are housed in various collections. Although outside the scope of this book, a rare early example of a wedding shoe from circa 1651 survives in the collection at the Pilgrim Hall Museum, Plymouth, Massachusetts. According to family tradition, this slipper is one of a pair worn by Penelope Pelham when she married Josiah Winslow in 1651. The surviving shoe is a square-toed, heeled, silk mule, encrusted with metallic lace, that was made in London.

7. Nylander, *Our Own Snug Fireside*; Richter, *Painted with Thread*; Ulrich, *Age of Homespun*; Vickery, *Behind Closed Doors*.

8. See the conservation report, prepared for the Bostonian Society, for Elizabeth Bull's wedding dress.

9. For an English context, see Vickery, *Gentleman's Daughter*.

10. Goodwin, *Archaeology of Manners*.

11. According to the Bostonian Society (the caretakers of this rare pre-revolutionary garment): "Miss Bull began designing, sewing, and embroidering her own China silk wedding gown while in school, a project undertaken by young women to practice and perfect the advanced needle arts. She had already been working on the gown for several years when, in 1734, she met Reverend Roger Price at Trinity Church. The gown was still not completed when Miss Bull wore it for their wedding the following year."

12. Foote, *Annals of King's Chapel*, 424.

13. Judge Wetmore served as deputy to the General Assembly for forty-eight terms, as well as being a judge of the county court in Hartford, Connecticut.

14. Sources for the consumer revolution in specific regions are Murrin, "Anglicizing an American Colony"; Breen, *Marketplace of Revolution*; Hoffman, "Consuming Women." For the consumer revolution generally, see "The Consumer Revolution," *Colonial Williams-*

burg e-Newsletter, vol. 5 (December 2006), www.history.org/history/teaching/enewsletter/volume5/december06/consumer_rev.cfm.

15. Schoelwer, *Connecticut Needlework*. For the Stoddard-Williams-Edwards family tradition of needlework and its relationship to women from clerical families in Connecticut, see 8–10 and appendix, "The Stoddard-Williams-Edwards Tradition," 17–21. For the Mary Edwards dress fragment, see 36–37.

16. Ibid, 14.

17. Ibid., 9–10, 38. Information on the Edwards' shoes may be found at the Connecticut Historical Society, Hartford. For comments applying to the sisters' education, see note 26. On the topic of needlework in general, see Nylander, *Our Own Snug Fireside*; Richter, *Painted with Thread*; Ulrich, *Age of Homespun*; Vickery, *Behind Closed Doors*.

18. According to Schoelwer, *Connecticut Needlework*, 38: "They were originally owned and made by Hannah Edwards (1713–1773). The shoes feature hand-stitched, embroidered silk and metallic threads on silk and linen. Labels attribute the embroidery alternatively to Hannah and her older sister, Mary. Both may be accurate: separate pairs of hands were almost certainly engaged in the embroidery."

19. For information on the Seth Wetmore House, see Historic Buildings of Connecticut, http://historicbuildingsct.com. On the paneling and so forth at the Wadsworth Atheneum, see "American Decorative Arts," Wadsworth Atheneum Museum of Art, https://thewadsworth.org/collection/americandecorative/.

20. The theft from the Wetmore home was noted in the *Connecticut Journal and New Haven Post-Boy*, 13 July 1770.

21. Ibid.

22. For information on the Byles family, see the Massachusetts Historical Society collection guides, www.masshist.org/collection-guides/.

23. Lieutenant Governor William Tailer's splendid embroidered waistcoat, circa the 1720s–1730, is in the collection of the Massachusetts Historical Society.

24. For information on silk weaving at Spitalfields, see Anishanslin, *Portrait of a Woman*; Farrell, "Silk and Globalisation"; "Industries: Silk Weaving," British History Online, www.british-history.ac.uk.

25. It is not entirely clear why deep emerald green was such a popular color choice for silk in the 1730s–1750s. The author has been unable to ascertain whether there was a new technology or dye that enabled dyers to create this lush color. Its desirability, however, may be linked to the costliness of producing such a rich tone, available only to the wealthy. Early in 1749, Jean Leonard Roederer (also referred to as Koederer), a dyer in Strasbourg, made several developments in what was known as Saxon blue and Saxon green. Though he was working with wool, his efforts reveal the potential for color development, which could be perfected for different textiles, such as silk. See Sarah Lowengard, "Techniques and Innovations: Saxon Blue and Saxon Green," *The Creation of Color in Eighteenth-Century Europe*, www.gutenberg-e.org/lowengard/C_Chap34.html. The popular Scheele's green was invented in 1775 and named after its inventor, Carl Wilhelm Scheele. It was based on copper arsenite. During the Regency period, a highly toxic chemical was used to create an emerald green. See "Emerald Green or Paris Green, the Deadly Regency Pigment,"

https://janeaustensworld.wordpress.com/2010/03/05/. The use of copper arsenite, however, falls outside the period under examination. The discovery of a new deposit of emeralds is not mentioned in the literature of that time, yet sapphires, rubies, and emeralds were quite popular for jewelry in the 1750s. Perhaps emerald green was just a very fashionable color, as certain palettes are today. Also see Ed Crews, "Weaving, Spinning and Dyeing: Dexterity and Detective Work," *Colonial Williamsburg Journal* (Winter 2007), www.history.org /foundation/journal/winter07/weaving.cfm/.

26. There are several items of baby clothing associated with the Byles family, but no connection is made with Rebecca in the family papers. It is a long held—and frequently mistaken—belief that all elite colonial women created examples of their sewing or needlework. For example, a large quilt or bed covering at the Bostonian Society has been assumed to have been made by Dorothy Quincy Hancock, when it was most likely professional made in England and may have originally belonged to John Hancock's aunt, Lydia Henchman Hancock. Further, John repeatedly beseeched his betrothed to send him something by her own hand, even as simple an item as a watch string.

27. The shoe is stamped along the interior with the name of the shoemaker and point of origin, although it is difficult to decipher his name. It could be Robert Dasson or Basson, or something else entirely. Little is currently known about Dasson/Basson, although there was a Robert Dasson, born in 1690 in London, which would make him a prime candidate.

28. Consultation with scholars Rebecca Shawcross (shoe operations manager at the Northampton Shoe Museum, United Kingdom) and D. A. Saguto (master boot- and shoemaker [emeritus], Colonial Williamsburg Foundation, and consulting curator for archaeological footwear, Historic Jamestowne), and assistance from the Massachusetts Historical Society's curatorial staff, yielded no additional information on the marking.

29. Eaton, *Famous Mather Byles*, 73.

30. Ibid., 72. Rebecca's remains are interred in Granary Burial Ground No. 2.

31. Wedding shoes, Massachusetts Historical Society, purchased from Margaret Callet-Carcano of Brussels, Belgium, in 1967, accession number 1111.01-.02.

32. Letter from George Washington to Martha Washington, written from Fort Cumberland, 20 July 1758, George Washington's Mount Vernon, www.mountvernon.org.

33. On Martha Washington's clothing purchases in 1759, see George Washington, "Invoice of Sundry Goods to be Shipped by Robt. Cary, Esq., and Company for the use of George Washington," May 1759, in "George Washington Invoices and Orders Project," Mount Vernon's Midden Project, http://mountvernonmidden.org. Also see "Shoe Shopping with Martha Washington," George Washington's Mount Vernon, www.mountvernon.org.

34. While this letter is penned to Lady Frances Shelbourne in London and attributed to Charlotte Chamberlain of New Kent County, it is used with some caution, as its provenance has not been verified. There are a number of questions surrounding the source, date, and accuracy of this letter. A full account, written by Donald N. Moran, is included in the attached link from the Revolutionary War Archives, www.revolutionarywararchives.org /washcourtmartha.html. The original article was published in the December 2001 Edition of *The Liberty Tree Newsletter*.

35. Visiting the Mount Vernon collection on 24 June 2016, the author had the opportu-

nity to discuss Martha's wedding clothing at length with assistant curator Amanda Issac. There are numerous yellow-gold dress fragments at Mount Vernon that were preserved by Martha Custis Washington's descendants. Ascertaining those that were bits of her wedding attire either for her 1750 or her 1759 nuptials has not yet been definitely determined, leaving the question of her ensemble still to be investigated thoroughly. Although the date of 1759 for Martha's extant purple wedding shoes has never been in question, the close proximity between her two marriages raises the same possibility as the one regarding her dress.

36. Martha Washington's shoe size was provided to the author by D. A. Saguto, Colonial Williamsburg Foundation and Historic Jamestowne. Also see "Shoe Shopping with Martha Washington," George Washington's Mount Vernon, www.mountvernon.org.

37. Eliza Pinckney receipt book, 1756, shelving number 43/2178, South Carolina Historical Society, Charleston.

38. John Gresham's will was proved on 31 July 1787. His probate is available at the Public Record Office, National Archives, Kew, United Kingdom.

39. Author's electronic correspondence with Rebecca Shawcross, shoe operations manager, Northampton Shoe Museum, United Kingdom.

40. The draft 1738 trade card for John Gresham is in the Heal Collection at the British Museum, London.

41. "Nearly every merchant sold Didsbury's boots and shoes. Catherine Rathell, a Williamsburg milliner, advertised in 1768, 'Didsbury's best shoes and pumps for Gentlemen, red, blue, and yellow slippers for do. Didsbury's best and neatest black and white sattin and callimanco pumps Ladies.'" See Harold B. Gill Jr., "Leather Workers in Colonial Virginia," August 1966, 52, Colonial Williamsburg Foundation Library Research Report Series 0107, Colonial Williamsburg Foundation Library, http://research.history.org/DigitalLibrary/.

42. John Didsbury's will was proved on 7 November 1803. His probate is available at the Public Record Office, National Archives, Kew, United Kingdom.

43. The color purple, similar to the color red, was costly both to obtain and to manufacture. Martha's purple shoes would have signaled wealth to an onlooker. For information on obtaining purple dye, see Sarah E. Bond, "The Hidden Labor behind the Luxurious Colors of Purple and Indigo," 24 October 2017, Hyperallergic, https://hyperallergic.com/406979/.

44. These shoes date to circa the 1750s and feature metallic thread placed in much the same pattern as on Martha's shoes. Shown with actual gem buckles, they offer a good comparison.

45. For specifics on the wedding of George and Martha Washington, see Ashby, *George & Martha Washington*, 17; "George and Martha's Courtship," George Washington's Mount Vernon, www.mountvernon.org.

46. George Washington's height has been a point of discussion for some time. Renowned footwear authority D. A. Saguto, Colonial Williamsburg Foundation and Historic Jamestowne, in electronic correspondence with the author on 9 January 2016, generously shared his unpublished research on this point, concluding that "George Washington only wore [a] US size 9 -9.5 shoe," and stood "but 6 feet tall" in life.

47. Letter from George Washington to Martha Washington, 23 June 1775, George Washington's Mount Vernon, www.mountvernon.org.

48. For the genealogy of the Wise and Farley families, see Waters, *Ipswich.*

49. From catalog information at the Ipswich Museum: "Pair of brocade slippers, worn at wedding of Mrs. John (Mary) Wise (John was grandson of Rev. John Wise) of Chebacco (Essex) to Nathaniel Farley in 1764. The shoes are made of a beige material with a gold pattern and some pink fabric crosses over the front of the shoe. Miss Wise was born in Chebacco in 1741 and died in Ipswich in 1792." Mary Wise Farley's shoes were on view in "Cosmopolitan Consumption: New England Shoe Stories, 1750–1850," a 2015 exhibition at the Portsmouth Athenæum, www.PortsmouthAthenaeum.org.

50. Her mother, Deborah [Lincoln] Thaxter, had married Deborah's father on 29 November 1739.

51. Textile fragment, accession number HD F.393A, Historic Deerfield. See "Collections Database," Five Colleges and Historic Deerfield Museum Consortium, http://museums .fivecolleges.edu/index.php.

52. Mary Caroline Crawford, "Hancock's Dorothy Q.," in *The Romance of Old New England Rooftrees,* Kellercraft Studio, www.kellscraft.com/RomanceOldNERooftrees/Romance OldNERooftrees07.html.

53. "John Hancock letter to Dorothy Hancock, March 10, 1777," Revolutionary War and Beyond, www.revolutionary-war-and-beyond.com/american-historical-documents.html.

54. Mackie, *Commerce of Everyday Life.*

55. Padilla and Anderson, *Red Like No Other*; Greenfield, *A Perfect Red.*

56. Mackie, *Commerce of Everyday Life,* 559. So popular was the *Tatler* among the cosmopolitan readers in Britain and British America that it spawned a number of imitators, including the *Lady Tatler* and the *Spectator.*

57. Advertisement by James Vincent, Boston silk dyer, in the *New England Weekly Journal,* 7 April 1729, 4.

58. On "Saturday the 17th of this instant August," Isaac Lawrence also had twenty-six yards of Irish poplin stolen and noted that "whoever will apprehend the thief or thieves so they may be brought to justice and the owner may have his goods again should have paid by Isaac Lawrence." See *Pennsylvania Gazette* (Philadelphia), 22 August 1771.

59. Letter from John Adams to Abigail Adams, 12 October 1782, "Letters between John and Abigail," *Adams Family Papers: An Electronic Archive,* Massachusetts Historical Society, www.masshist.org/digitaladams/archive/browse/.

60. Wheeler, "Albany of Magdalena Douw."

61. A pair of red wool shoes with lace detail from roughly the same time period (c. the 1750s), accession number P87-0032AB, survive in the Bata Shoe Museum, Toronto. The author thanks the museum's collections manager, Suzanne Petersen, for her assistance. The Bata Shoe Museum has at least one other pair of red wool shoes, and there are examples at Colonial Williamsburg and the Museum of Fine Arts in Boston, among others.

62. See D. Hill, *Record of Births,* vol. 1; "Death Notice for Mrs. Catherine Haven, Widow of the Late Reverend Jason Haven of This Town, Age 77," *Dedham Gazette,* 2 September 1814; death notice for Reverend Samuel Dexter, *Boston Evening Post,* 3 February 1755. The author thanks librarian and archivist Sandra Waxman at the Dedham Historical Society, Massachusetts, for her assistance with the Dexter/Haven family genealogy. As a relevant

aside, a reference in the Dedham Historical Society from Abigail Adams mentions a carriage ride from her home to Dedham to hear Reverend Haven preach—an excursion that, she noted, was worth the effort. This opens the possibility that Abigail Adams and Catherine Haven may have been acquainted, as Catherine would most likely have been present during her husband's sermon.

63. Catherine Dexter Haven's wedding shoes came into the collection of the Bata Shoe Museum, accession number P99.0085.A-C, through a purchase from a family descendant.

64. "Just imported from London and to be sold by Edward Green," *Boston Gazette and Country Journal*, 28 June 1756.

65. Spofford family papers, Phillips Library, Peabody Essex Museum.

66. Historic Deerfield, accession number 2004.46. The author thanks Ned Lazaro, curator of textiles, Historic Deerfield, for his generous assistance over the years.

3 • THE VALUE OF A LONDON LABEL

1. Von La Roche, *Sophie in London*.

2. Walsh, "Shop Design," 110.

3. A number of excellent British scholars—such as June Swann, Rebecca Shawcross, Giorgio Riello, and others—have traced the rich history of English shoes and shoemaking. Outside the scope of their studies, however, is the fate of these accessories once they were exported to the colonies. An invaluable resource for the study of shoes in the colonies is Saguto's *Art of the Shoemaker*, which includes extant and archaeological examples of British shoes worn in America. Nancy Rexford, a renowned American scholar, turned her attention to the problem in her classic work, *Women's Shoes in America*, although her study begins in 1795, just as this volume ends. The recent work of Reddick, "An American Identity," delves into the use of shoemakers' labels in British American imports, seeing this as an early effort at branding in the Georgian era. Also see Breen, *Marketplace of Revolution*; Murrin, "Anglicizing an American Colony"; Gallup-Diaz et al., *Anglicizing America*.

4. According to the author's electronic correspondence with Professor Giorgio Riello, it is not known how many pairs of shoes were contained in a trunk, or if it was a standardized shipping size.

5. The author extends thanks to Emily Murphy, the curator at the Salem Maritime National Historic Site, for sharing this information regarding making and transporting shoes from Salem to Philadelphia.

6. Advertisements for goods such as shoes appear with regularity.

7. John Gerrish of Boston handled the Caine auction; Samuel Larkin's auction house was located in Portsmouth, New Hampshire, by the early years of the nineteenth century; and William Lang's auction house was in Salem, Massachusetts. For additional information, see "Samuel Larkin House," 23 November 2011, *Walk Portsmouth*, http://walkportsmouth .blogspot.com; Raiselis, *Elegant to the Everyday*, 3; Alexander, "Second Hand Clothing."

8. For information on tariffs prior to 1789, see W. Hill, "Colonial Tariffs." Also see "Estimated English Shoe Export, 1700–1800," fig. 25, in Riello, *Foot in the Past*, 50.

9. Lemire, "Consumerism"; Styles, *Dress of the People*; Alexander, "Second Hand Clothing."

10. For more on Henrietta Maria East Caine, see Cleary, *Elizabeth Murray*, 45–46, 57, 60, 62–63, 241n. For an example of the advertisements she placed and a partial list of her

inventory sold at auction in 1754, see "The Unfortunate Tale of Boston Shopkeeper Henrietta Maria East Caine, 1750s," SilkDamask, www.silkdamask.org/2014/04/the-unfortunate-tale-of-boston.html.

11. Cadwalader family papers, 1630–1900, collection 1454, Historical Society of Pennsylvania, Philadelphia. The author is indebted to textile authority Deborah Kraak for bringing this citation to her attention.

12. Johnston and Woolley, *Shoes*, 66. Also, the core of the author's research is work with Hose, Ridout & Davis, and Chamberlain, grouping shoes by their maker.

13. "Brocade silk lady's shoe—cream background with polychrome floral pattern. Trimmed with a narrow green braid. Lined with linen and has leather sole. Upturned pointed toe. The heel heavy and thick bottom flaring. Two straps from side to side over the instep. Tongue extends above the instep and is shaped with curved edges and pointed end," James Davis, accession number 1987-1034, Strawbery Banke Museum, Portsmouth, New Hampshire, under the search criteria "James Davis" in "Online Collection," http://strawberybanke.pastperfectonline.com.

14. The difference between pattens and clogs is roughly that a clog is a type of shoe with an inflexible sole, frequently made of wood, with an open heel, while pattens include various types of footwear with thick soles, generally used to elevate the foot. During the Georgian period, pattens often had silk brocade or damask uppers, attached by means of lachets (narrow leather straps that fasten a shoe on the foot) and a leather lace. In today's lexicon, the two terms are frequently used interchangeably when referring to footwear. Well-known shoe designer Lauren Stowell, of American Duchess, notes: "Pattens were ladies' shoe accessories worn to protect one's fancy shoes, to raise the wearer up out of the mud and muck of the street, and to keep the heels of the shoes from sinking into the various street substances. They served to protect hems, and prolong the life of the shoes they covered." See "18th Century Pattens for Shoes," 13 February 2013, American Duchess Historical Costuming, http://blog.americanduchess.com/.

15. For information on export arrangements for shoes, see Swann, *Shoes*; Saguto, *Art of the Shoemaker*; Riello, *Foot in the Past*.

16. The Ridout family history and genealogy has been well documented by descendants. For a full and detailed account of this family of cordwainers, see "Jeremiah & Porter Ridout: Yellow Silk Shoes and Blue Murder!," 16 April 2013, The Rideouts of Sherborne and Bath, https://the-ridouts.com.

17. Mehitable Rindge Rogers (1725-1803) lived in Portsmouth, and her shoes are now held in the Warner House collection in Portsmouth, New Hampshire.

18. Additional research on this aspect of the export trade is needed, but such materials are scattered widely.

19. For additional information, see "Woman's Brocaded Silk Shoes," result 371, in Online Collections: Costume Accessories, Colonial Williamsburg, http://emuseum.history.org.

20. For many years these shoes were in the collection of the United Shoe Machinery Corporation, before that collection was transferred to the Peabody Essex Museum.

21. "Invoice from Robert Cary & Company, 3 December 1771," Washington Papers, *Founders Online*, National Archives, https://founders.archives.gov.

22. An abundance of material regarding Eliza Lucas Pinckney is available online and in print, including Pinckney, *Letterbook*.

23. On 21 April 2015, the author ended a nearly five-year pilgrimage to view these shoes in person. She extends appreciation to Jan Hiester, the Charleston Museum curator of textiles, for her generous assistance. The author's continued thanks go to Colin Hose and Linda Pardoe for so generously sharing information on the Hose family.

24. Pinckney, *Letterbook*.

25. For more on Eliza's shoes, see the Charleston Museum, http://charlestonmuseum .tumblr.com/post/3701726426/.

26. A second wallet, which entered the Portsmouth Historical Society at the same time as the shoes and the salmon-colored wallet, is made of blue silk brocade from the late eighteenth century.

27. The author thanks Curator Emerita Sandra Rux, Portsmouth Historical Society, for sharing this discovery.

28. According to authority D. A. Saguto, master boot- and shoemaker (emeritus), Colonial Williamsburg Foundation, and consulting curator for archaeological footwear, Historic Jamestowne, a rand is "a strip of leather, rolled over, sewn in with the inseam to attach a sole to. Although the technological innovation appears after 1500, the term does not appear in English until at least 1598. It is suggested that this is derived from the German technique of the Rahme, [a] platform sole-cover on overshoes."

29. Shoemaker Winthrop Gray, of Lynn and Boston, used brocaded silk, as well as metallic thread, leather, and linen, for the pumps housed in the collection of Historic New England, Haverhill, Massachusetts. These shoes may well have been in the ownership of the family of the wearer before being gifted to Historic New England.

30. There is abundant information on Freemasonry in various publications and online. For a succinct overview, see "History of Freemasonry," Masonic Service Association of North America, www.msana.com/historyfm.asp.

31. The textile is most likely from a bit earlier, circa 1750-1760s.

32. Gray, *William Gray*.

33. Winthrop Gray was established in Boston by the 1770s and set up shop as a cordwainer.

34. According to Secretary of the Commonwealth, *Massachusetts Soldiers and Sailors*, volume 6, 783, Winthrop Gray and others signed a petition "asking that their resignations be accepted, as the Legislature had failed to redress their grievances. Resignations accepted in Council, Feb. 26, 1779."

35. See Gray, *William Gray*, 115-118. This may be the same Mary Gray who applied for a shop or tavern license during the war. There was also intermarriage between the Gray, Breed, and Bassett shoemaking families—all have some connection with the business in Lynn and Salem.

36. It is not known where John Gonsolve received his training or whether he was born in the colonies.

37. Details about Phebe's husband's life are hard to come by, with one significant exception: the recent discovery of his connection with the burning of the British cutter *Gaspee* in Providence, Rhode Island, in 1772. The couple was married for about five years at the time of the destruction of the *Gaspee*. For information, see Gaspee Virtual Archives, www .gaspee.org.

38. Published 10 August 1785 in Providence, Rhode Island.

39. Reddick, "American Identity."

40. General John Montgomery, daybook, 1793, held at the Haverhill Historical Society, Haverhill, New Hampshire.

41. Dr. Camper's original Dutch publication was translated by Scottish cordwainer James Dowie and included in Dowie's own treatise on shoes, *The Foot and its Covering* (London: Robert Hardwicke, 1861). The full treatise is available on Internet Archive, www.archive.org.

4 · COVETING CALAMANCOS

Epigraph. Roosevelt, "What the Westerners Had Done during the Revolution," chapter 13, 296, in *Winning of the West*, vol. 2.

1. There are many variations on the spelling of this word, such as callimanco, calamanco, or calamink. Calamanco is used here for consistency.

2. Nicole Rudolph, "Shoe Advertisements in the North East Colonies," 23 May 2014, *Diary of a Mantua Maker*, http://mantuadiary.blogspot.com. Also see Rudolph, *Turn Shoe Construction*.

3. See, for example, "Invoice from Robert Cary & Company, 3 December 1771," Washington Papers, *Founders Online*, National Archives, https://founders.archives.gov; letter from John Hancock to Dorothy Quincy, 10 June 1775, from Philadelphia to Fairfield, Connecticut, cited in Ellen C. D. Q. Woodbury, *Dorothy Quincy, Wife of John Hancock* (Washington, DC: Neale, 1905), 250n1; letter from Abigail Adams to John Adams, 16 July 1775, "Letters between John and Abigail," Massachusetts Historical Society, *Adams Family Papers: An Electronic Archive*, www.masshist.org/digitaladams/archive/browse/.

4. Meg Andrews, "Norwich Worsted Textiles 18th c," Meg Andrews: Antique Costumes & Textiles, www.meg-andrews.com/articles/.

5. Ibid.

6. Costume historian and shoemaker Nicole Rudolph has shared with the author some preliminary data on the occurrence of several ladies' shoe types, including calamanco shoes worn in New England from 1775 to 1783. She includes information appearing in newspapers from New York, New Jersey, Pennsylvania, Massachusetts, Connecticut, Rhode Island, and New Hampshire. Rudolph reveals that out of 408 unique descriptions of women's shoes for sale, the breakdown was: 105 calimanco/callimanco/calamanco/callimancoe; 84 leather; 62 stuff, and 55 silk.

7. David E. Lazaro, "Putting Our Best Feet Forward: Shoes Get Conserved at Historic Deerfield," in the "Textiles, Clothing, and Embroidery" section in Collections, Historic Deerfield, www.historic-deerfield.org/discover-deerfield/collections/. Abridged conservation reports, available from Historic Deerfield for their wool shoes, may also be accessed on their website.

8. Groundbreaking work in the new social history has been extensive. Some representative titles include Davis, *Return of Martin Guerre*; Ginzburg and Tedeschi, *Cheese and the Worms*; Lockridge, *New England Town*.

9. On this debate over economic self-sufficiency in early households in America, see Henretta, "Families and Farms"; Lemon, "Comment"; Henretta, "'Families and Farms' . . .

Reply"; Breen, "Back to Sweat"; Merrill, "Putting 'Capitalism' in Its Place"; Timm, "Hunting for the Market Economy."

10. References to textile production are found in several cordwainers' daybooks from Salem prior to 1750. The Eleazar Pope account book, held at the Phillips Library of the Peabody Essex Museum, references spinning and visiting the "weave shed" in Salem as early as the 1730s, but there is no indication of the purpose of the completed textile, or even if it remained with Pope. The Pope home still stands on Boston Street in Salem. Although the North River has since been redirected, at the time of Pope's business, this river (where Leslie's Retreat would take place many years later) would have provided a convenient waterway.

11. Breen, *Marketplace of Revolution*, 23.

12. *Essex Antiquarian* 5, no. 3 (March 1901), 67–68.

13. Lewis, *History of Lynn*.

14. Calamanco shoes, gift of Mr. and Mrs. Kendall Bancroft, accession number 76.095.1, Historic Deerfield.

15. It should be noted that Early Americans more frequently called these simply "wood heels," "carved heels," or "French heels." The term "Louis heel" (named for France's Sun King, Louis XIV, who died in 1715) came into use during the Victorian period, and it is the predominant term employed by the time of Georgian-revival shoes in the 1920s. Shoe scholar Rexford, in *Women's Shoes in America*, 84, notes that "the curved [French] heel went out of fashion about 1923, and from 1924 nearly all heels had relatively straight sides."

16. Polychrome brocaded silk dress, with a plain-weave linen lining, gift of Mrs. Arthur F. Draper, accession number F.495, Historic Deerfield. According to the records at Historic Deerfield, the fabric was possibly designed by John Vansommer (1705-1774) and woven in Spitalfields, England. It was made into a garment in the Springfield, Massachusetts, area in the late 1740s, with later alterations. For information on Sarah Williams's 1738/39 probate inventory, see www.historic-deerfield.org/files/4813/7450/7840/WILLIAMS _SARAH_1716-1737.pdf. Sarah came from a very wealthy family, as may be seen by the number and type of garments listed in her probate inventory. Among the extensive list: one taffeta robe at £6; one damask robe at £3 and 15 shillings; one chintz robe; one calico robe; one silk quilt; one shalloon (a lightweight twill fabric) quilt; and cloth and trimming cut for a riding habit. The reference to one riding hood, at £4 and 5 shillings, indicated it had been a quite costly purchase. Her inventory also listed three pairs of stays: black, yellow, and red. There are several references to unfinished garments or accessories, perhaps indicating, in the case of "cloth for a pocket," that Sarah was sewing the item just prior to her death. The range of items available to her in the 1730s certainly calls into question long-held mythologies regarding colonial dress and access to current fashions far distant from the colonies' seaport and coastal towns.

17. For Hose, see chapters 1 and 6 in this volume. For conservation information, see Lazaro, "Putting Our Best Feet Forward."

18. Pers. comms. in 2016 with Colonial Williamsburg milliners and mantuamakers Nicole Rudolph, Sarah Woodyard, and Abbie Cox, as well as Colonial Williamsburg apprentice shoemaker Rob Welch.

19. This is the first mention of calamanco shoes that the author has yet discovered.

20. See the costs to Pingry, Welch, and Pope from their account books and daybooks, Phillips Library, Peabody Essex Museum.

21. For background on Norwich wool and calamanco exports, see Meg Andrews, "Norwich Worsted Textiles 18thc," Meg Andrews: Antique Costumes & Textiles, www.meg-andrews.com/articles/.

22. For sources on Lynn shoemaking, see Rexford, *Women's Shoes in America*, 9–10; Richter et al., *Step Forward, Step Back*; Lewis, *History of Lynn*, and Gannon, *Short History of American Shoemaking*. Also see the Lynn Museum and Historical Society archives, Lynn, Massachusetts.

23. This information is from Martha Washington's account books at Mount Vernon. It is also found in Fields, *Worthy Partner*.

24. Letter from George Washington to John Didsbury, London, Boot & Shoemaker, 20 June 1768, George Washington Papers, series 5, financial papers: copybook of letters and invoices, 1767–1775, manuscript / mixed material, retrieved from the Library of Congress, https://www.loc.gov/item/mgw500004/. Just above his signature is a complaint regarding Mrs. Washington's shoes—which did not fit well, being made of poor materials—noting that she has sent her measure (the size of her foot) again.

25. The repair and mending of shoes was common. For example, the Francis Pingry account book, 1797–1804, MSS 1326, Phillips Library, Peabody Essex Museum, has the note "by mending Calamances shoes" on 23 April 1798.

26. Object number 2001.56.1, Historic Deerfield.

27. Bardwell family genealogy, https://www.ancestry.com/genealogy/records/wealthy-peck_86648595/.

28. Conservation report for object number 2001.56.1, Historic Deerfield.

29. For example, an early child-minder survives in the kitchen at the Crownshield-Bentley House, located on the grounds of the Peabody Essex Museum.

30. Although made of leather, the child's shoe from Connecticut is constructed much like the one for Wealthy Peck Bardwell and was made at the same time.

31. The author gratefully acknowledges Astrida Schaeffer, consulting curator, and Dale Valena, museum director of the University of New Hampshire Museum and Special Collections, for their unstinting generosity regarding access to the Irma Bowen Collection at the University of New Hampshire.

32. The shoes may well be of local New England manufacture.

33. Letter from John Hancock to Dorothy Quincy, 10 June 1775, from Philadelphia to Fairfield, Connecticut, cited in Woodbury, *Dorothy Quincy*, 250n1. For Hancock's purchase of calamanco shoes for his serving girl, whose name was either Vilate or Vitale [it is difficult to decipher the script], see Lynn shoemaker Issac Bassett's receipt for making her calamanco shoes, 8 April 1775, Hancock family papers, 1728–1885, 2 microfilm reels, call number P-277, Massachusetts Historical Society.

34. Letter from John Hancock to Dorothy Quincy, 10 June 1775, cited in Woodbury, *Dorothy Quincy*, 250n1.

35. Ibid. Other items that Hancock mentions in the letter include stockings, caps, a fan, "one pretty light hat, [and] one neat airy Summer Cloak."

36. See Mary Caroline Crawford, "Hancock's Dorothy Q.," in *The Romance of Old New England Rooftrees*, Kellercraft Studio, www.kellscraft.com/RomanceOldNERooftrees/Romance OldNERooftrees07.html.

37. For information on the shoemakers Bragg & Luckin at 21 St. Bartholomew Close, see London poll taxes and business directories. The members of Bragg family lived, worked, and were buried in the vicinity of Bartholomew Close. One of the most intriguing descriptions of the business is captured in the records of the Old Bailey for 28 October 1824. John Smith was indicted for stealing a pair of shoes, valued at 9 shillings, from Bragg & Luckin's shop. Smith asked to try on several pair of shoes and was served by Luckin. The culprit slipped a pair of shoes under his coat and headed toward the door. He was apprehended by the senior Luckin's son George. Found guilty, Smith was imprisoned for six months. Shoes and other small items were favorites with thieves and shoplifters—they were easy to hide and convenient to fence.

38. For biographies of John Hancock, see Fowler, *Baron of Beacon Hill*; Unger, *John Hancock*.

39. One of the oft-related stories regarding John Hancock's civility relates to a recollection by Boston cordwainer and Tea Party attendee Robert Twelves Hewes, in which he notes his interactions with Hancock. After the journeyman shoemaker returned a repaired shoe to Hancock, John invited him to visit the Hancock House on New Year's Day and drink a toast, a common ritual among the gentry. For more, see Young, *Shoemaker and the Tea Party*, 3–4. Hancock's tanner and tailor, William Billings (best known today for his patriotic songs) is mentioned in a letter from Hancock, in Rhode Island, to his wife Dorothy on 14 August 1778 (MS 0190, file unit 47, 1–2, Bostonian Society, transcribed 5 October 2014 by Gillian Cusak).

40. For additional information, see Reddick, "American Identity." Several shoes with Ebenezer Breed's label, made in Philadelphia, survive in various collections, including the Delaware Historical Society in Wilmington and the Lady's Repository Museum. The latter is a privately owned museum west of Trinidad, Colorado. It is dedicated to the collection, preservation, and study of unique Early American fashions for both women and children, the latter being a specialty. It is owned and managed by Rachael Kinnison.

41. Drinker, *Diary of Elizabeth Drinker*, 19. Drinker frequented other Quaker shops and artisans. In addition to Thomas Williams, she noted shopping at R. Steele.

42. For information on men's footwear and Lynn boot production during the American Revolution, see Alexander, "Footwear, Men's"; Reddick, "Footwear Industry."

43. Advertisement from the *New Hampshire Gazette* (Portsmouth), 24 June 1768, collection of the New Hampshire Historical Society, reproduced in Brown, *Life of Samuel Lane*, 185.

44. John Welsh advertisement, *Boston Gazette and Country Journal*, 3 January 1774.

45. Alexander Rutherford advertisement, *Pennsylvania Journal* (Philadelphia), 20 January 1765.

46. *Newport Mercury*, 20 August 1764.

47. Letter by "Sophia Thrifty," *Newport Mercury*, 20 August 1764.

48. Reddick, "Footwear Industry," 118. For her statistics, Reddick also draws on Dawley, *Class and Community*, 15, and Rexford, *Women's Shoes in America*, 9.

49. Letter from Abigail Adams to John Adams, 1 May 1780, "Letters between John

and Abigail," Massachusetts Historical Society, *Adams Family Papers: An Electronic Archive*, www.masshist.org/digitaladams/archive/browse/.

50. Lewis, *History of Lynn*, 162.

51. Baumgarten, *What Clothes Reveal*, 93–94.

52. Letter from Abigail Adams to John Adams, 16 July 1775, "Letters between John and Abigail," Massachusetts Historical Society, *Adams Family Papers: An Electronic Archive*, www.masshist.org/digitaladams/archive/browse/.

53. Ibid. Her letter suggests that the calamanco wool she wanted was not of local manufacture.

54. Letter from Abigail Adams to John Adams, 8 February 1794, "Letters between John and Abigail," Massachusetts Historical Society, *Adams Family Papers: An Electronic Archive*, www.masshist.org/digitaladams/archive/browse/.

55. Much evidence of shoemaking and shoe repair is scattered in New England homesteads from Massachusetts to Maine.

56. The population of Portsmouth, New Hampshire, at the time of the first census in 1790 was 4,720. Massachusetts' neighboring cities of Marblehead (5,661), Salem (7,921), and even Boston (18,320) did not approach the size of Philadelphia (28,522) or New York (33,131). While not among the ten largest towns or cities, Portsmouth was always a merchants' and traders' haven, dating from the first permanent English settlement in 1623. Fish and lumber were among the early commodities. Portsmouth's location at the mouth of the Piscataqua River made it possible for numerous surrounding towns to send timber and various cargo items along waterways by small local craft, such as gundalows and wherries.

57. See the letter from John Wentworth to Mrs. Fisher, 17 January 1777, in the Portsmouth Athenæum. This quote raises questions about the flow of goods across the Atlantic Ocean during the blockades. The author thanks Thomas Hardiman, keeper of the Portsmouth Athenæum, for bringing this correspondence to my attention.

58. For example, Alexander Hamilton's 1790 tariff proposal included ongoing duties on imported items.

5 • THE CORDWAINER'S LAMENT

1. Object number 1953.16.0a,b, Connecticut Historical Society.

2. Maier, *Old Revolutionaries*, 6–7.

3. Riello, *Foot in the Past*.

4. The use of labels may also be related to duties and tariffs on foreign goods brought into colonial ports. The appearance of shoes made by the Hose family and others, such as Ridout & Davis and W. Chamberlain & Sons, in North American collections underscores their importance as luxury trade goods in colonial American shops, which therefore were subject to duties or tariffs. As costume and fashion historians, we generally observe the final product rather than the fabricator of these sought-after accessories. Yet when one is able to establish even a rudimentary timeline, often related to the information found on shoe labels, it aids in dating these significant Georgian-era survivals.

5. Committee of Finance, *Comparison of Customs Tariff Laws*, 266–267.

6. The Act Laying Duties on Imports was communicated by Secretary of the Treasury

Alexander Hamilton to the US House of Representatives on 23 April 1790. In order to promote manufacturing in the United States, Hamilton proposed that imported goods be more costly, thereby forcing Americans to buy more local products. While the proposition failed, as it was essentially a tariff, it is nonetheless instructive regarding public sentiment at that time.

7. "A List of the Prices of Boots and Shoes . . . Philadelphia . . . 8th November 1790," published in numerous historical imprint volumes. The events that resulted in the creation of this document are outside the scope of the current volume. In 1760, while there was a certain degree of fluctuation in wages, a rural laborer earned about 3 to 4 shillings per day, roughly the same amount as an urban day worker.

8. The author thanks D. A. Saguto, master boot- and shoemaker (emeritus), Colonial Williamsburg Foundation, and consulting curator for archaeological footwear, Historic Jamestowne, for providing the information on shoe-buckle pricing in Virginia.

9. Breen, *Marketplace of Revolution*, 23. The proposed Stamp Tax may have incited another, unexpected effect in the colonies: an increase in marriages before November 1765. The tax included a ten-shilling liability on "certificates of intent" to marry, and historian J. L. Bell has found evidence that suggests that couples in Marblehead, Newton, and Springfield, Massachusetts, wed early in order to avoid the tax. See J. L. Bell, "The Stamp Act as a Marriage Tax," 20 December 2015, *Boston 1775*, http://boston1775.blogspot.com; J. L. Bell, "Massachusetts Marriages in 1765," 22 December 2015, *Boston 1775*, http://boston1775 .blogspot.com.

10. See an enlightening article on pre–Revolutionary War politics by Bob Ruppert, "Barlow Trecothick's Role in the Repeal of the Stamp Act," 18 January 2016, *Journal of the American Revolution*, All Things Liberty, https://allthingsliberty.com.

11. Green, "Repeal of the Stamp Act," 197.

12. See Bob Ruppert, "Barlow Trecothick's Role in the Repeal of the Stamp Act," 18 January 2016, *Journal of the American Revolution*, All Things Liberty, https://allthingsliberty.com.

13. See, for instance, *New-York Mercury*, 13 July 1761; *New-York Gazette*, 17 December 1764; *New Hampshire Gazette* (Portsmouth), 11 November 1763.

14. *Boston Evening-Post*, 23 September 1771.

15. *New-York Journal; or, General Advertiser*, 15 September 1774.

16. The author has queried the Northampton Shoe Museum, United Kingdom, and the Charles Paget Wade Collection in the National Trust's Snowshill Manor, as well as reviewed the collection database for the Victoria and Albert Museum, regarding Hose shoes in their respective collections. Further, consultation with leading British shoe scholars—including Rebecca Shawcross, June Swann, and Giorgio Riello—failed to turn up any Hose-made shoes in British collections. A pair of Hose-labeled shoes, however, is featured (with several photographs) in Hopkins and Hopkins, *Footwear*, 14-15. It is quite likely that additional examples will surface at some point.

17. Following the American and then the French Revolutions, French-made shoes and slippers also began to vie seriously for the contents of the American consumer's pocketbook. The latest-fashion shoes from France had a neoclassical flavor—silks and satins, with limited or no ornament, thus creating smooth surfaces, and, frequently, in pale tones, with diminu-

tive heels or as flats—which complemented the prevailing fashion of columnar, diaphanous gowns, patterned on Greek and Roman styles.

18. *Providence Gazette and Country Journal*, 7 January 1764; *Newport Mercury*, 20 August 1764.

19. Breen, *Marketplace of Revolution*, 28.

20. Eacott, "Making an Imperial Compromise," 739. For example, it was reported in Portsmouth, New Hampshire, on 22 April 1720 that an act of Parliament forbade the wearing of calicoes. The author thanks Jeffrey Hopper, manager of Warner House, Portsmouth, New Hampshire, for sharing this citation.

21. *Boston Evening-Post*, 16 December 1751.

22. *Newport Mercury*, 20 August 1764.

23. B. Carp, *Defiance of the Patriots*, 54–55.

24. Letter by "Sophia Thrifty," *Newport Mercury*, 20 August 1764. Also see *Boston Evening-Post*, 4 February 1765; *New-York Mercury*, 24 December 1764.

25. Cleary, *Elizabeth Murray*.

26. *Newport Mercury*, 27 August 1764.

27. *New Hampshire Gazette* (Portsmouth), 7 September 1764, 1.

28. Excerpt from "A Satire on Women's Dress, 1754," *Boston Evening-Post*, 4 February 1754. The original title of the piece is "A Receipt for Modern Dress," which was printed in London on 16 October 1753.

29. *Newport Mercury*, 24 December 1764. Similar sentiments appeared in the *New-York Mercury* on 3 and 24 December 1764.

30. The term "stuff," as it appears in eighteenth-century advertisements, account books, and so on, referred to shoes with a worsted wool upper. The author thanks D. A. Saguto, Colonial Williamsburg Foundation and Historic Jamestowne for clarifying this point.

31. Letter from John Adams to Abigail Adams, 3 June 1778, "Letters between John and Abigail," Massachusetts Historical Society, *Adams Family Papers: An Electronic Archive*, www.masshist.org/digitaladams/archive/browse/.

32. "A Boston Family Takes Refuge in Chelmsford," chapter 23, *Beside Old Hearth-Stones*, Massachusetts American Local History Network, Massachusetts History and Genealogy Project, www.ma-roots.org/books/hearth/.

33. Ibid.

6 • "FOR MY USE, FOUR PAIR OF NEAT SHOES"

Epigraph. George Washington, "Rules of Civility & Decent Behaviour in Company and Conversation," Papers of George Washington, http://gwpapers.virginia.edu.

1. Sydnor, *American Revolutionaries*, 84.

2. Ibid., 53–55, 66–67. Sydnor estimated that Washington spent amounts of £25, £39, and £50 for various elections.

3. Wood, *Radicalism*; George Washington, "Rules of Civility & Decent Behaviour in Company and Conversation," Papers of George Washington, http://gwpapers.virginia.edu.

4. Letter from George Washington to John Didsbury, 10 August 1764, *Founders Online*, National Archives, https://founders.archives.gov.

5. George Washington to George Steptoe Washington, 23 March 1789, in Washington, *Writings of George Washington*, vol. 11, ed. Ford, 371–372.

6. For information on the role and significance of breeching, see "Lifecycle," under "Clothing," in Historic Threads: Three Centuries of Clothing, Colonial Williamsburg, www.history.org/history/museums/clothingexhibit; Linda Baumgarten, "Children's Clothing," Colonial Williamsburg, www.history.org/history/clothing/children/childor.cfm.

7. For an excellent short biography on Jacky Custis and his relationship with his stepfather, see Mary V. Thompson, "John Parke Custis," *George Washington Digital Encyclopedia*, George Washington's Mount Vernon, www.mountvernon.org/digital-encyclopedia/.

8. Letter from George Washington to John Didsbury, 27 September 1763, *Founders Online*, National Archives, https://founders.archives.gov.

9. Letter from George Washington to John Didsbury, 15 July 1772, *Founders Online*, National Archives, https://founders.archives.gov.

10. Vickery, *Behind Closed Doors*. Vickery, in her extensive study of eighteenth-century account books, daybooks, and diaries, focuses on three families in her chapter entitled "His and Hers: Accounting for the Household." This is illuminating and a key to understanding the division of expenses in wealthy English households, a similarity seen in that of the Washingtons. Of particular interest were the Ardernes of Cheshire, 116–126.

11. Electronic correspondence with the author, 19 January 2016. The author extends her appreciation to D. A. Saguto, master boot- and shoemaker (emeritus), Colonial Williamsburg Foundation, and consulting curator for archaeological footwear, Historic Jamestowne, and apprentice shoemaker Rob Welch, also of Colonial Williamsburg, for their insights into Washington's shoe selections and information on the size of Colonel Baylor's lasts (US size 9–9.5), on which Washington asked Didsbury to base his shoes.

12. Harold B. Gill Jr., "Leather Workers in Colonial Virginia," August 1966, 52, Colonial Williamsburg Foundation Library Research Report Series 0107, Colonial Williamsburg Foundation Library, http://research.history.org/DigitalLibrary/.

13. The author is indebted to Gillian Cusack for her transcription of Didsbury's probate inventory, in which he is listed simply as John Didsbury, cordwainer of Pall Mall, St. James, Westminster, Middlesex. Didsbury died in 1803, predeceased by his wife Mary.

14. Author's electronic correspondence with Rebecca Shawcross, shoe operations manager at the Northampton Shoe Museum, United Kingdom, indicates that this collection does not have any material related to John Didsbury.

15. Letter from George Washington to John Didsbury, 27 September 1763, *Founders Online*, National Archives, https://founders.archives.gov.

16. Letter from George Washington to John Didsbury, 10 August 1764, *Founders Online*, National Archives, https://founders.archives.gov. It appears that Washington's shoe orders to Didsbury followed the cycle of tobacco culture—his shoe orders for example, appear to be primarily from June to September, with one in October. See Breen, *Tobacco Culture*.

17. Washington switched from his previous factors to Cary & Company when he and Martha wed. They had been engaged by her former husband, Daniel Custis. Retaining the factors from her previous marriage made sense in terms of streamlining the large accounts and purchasing needs of the couple's plantations. Washington may have kept Didsbury on as

the family's provider of footwear because of this earlier relationship. See various documents between Washington and Didsbury at *Founders Online*, National Archives, https://founders. archives.gov.

18. Letter from George Washington to John Didsbury, 27 September 1763, *Founders Online*, National Archives, https://founders.archives.gov.

19. Letter from George Washington to John Didsbury, 20 June 1768, *Founders Online*, National Archives, https://founders.archives.gov.

20. Letter from George Washington to Richard Washington, 5 April 1758, *Founders Online*, National Archives, https://founders.archives.gov.

21. Letter from George Washington to Robert Cary & Co., 1 May 1759, *Founders Online*, National Archives, https://founders.archives.gov.

22. Letter from George Washington to John Didsbury, 30 November 1759, *Founders Online*, National Archives, https://founders.archives.gov. When Washington cautioned Didsbury to "never more make any of Dog leather except one pair of Pumps in a Cargo," he was probably referring to a very thin but tough form of leather that served well for gloves. "Dog leather" gloves actually were often made of lambskin. Washington most likely was referring to the quality of the leather rather than to the actual animal from which it came, as he made it clear that the material did not hold up well. He wanted better leather—"the two pair of Shoes scarcely last me twice as many days and had a fair wearing"—as the leather that had been used obviously was not strong enough to satisfy his needs. Master boot- and shoemaker D. A. Saguto of the Colonial Williamsburg Foundation and Historic Jamestowne (quoted in "Revisited Myth #17: The Most Stylish Shoes Were Made of Dogskin, Hence the Expression 'Puttin' on the Dog,'" History Myths Debunked, https://historymyths.wordpress.com), notes that he has not found evidence of American shoes being made of dog leather. For the use of dogskin for gloves, see Yvette Mahe, "History of Gloves and Their Significance," 12 November 2013, *Fashion in Time*, www.fashionintime.org/history-gloves-significance/.

23. Author's electronic correspondence with D. A. Saguto, Colonial Williamsburg Foundation and Historic Jamestowne, 30 December 2015. He notes that, based on his extensive research, the heels were most likely five-eighths of an inch high. He has also shared the information that George Washington repeatedly told his tailors that he was six feet tall.

24. Donning high heels served to place one above the public gaze. From this lofty perch, the so-called noble classes perceived themselves as being figuratively as well as literally above everyone else. High hairstyles, and tall hats for men and women, also helped to achieve this effect. Thus stately fashions served as symbols of power and elevated status. See McNeil and Riello, "Art and Science of Walking"; Riberio, *Art of Dress*.

25. Letter from George Washington to John Didsbury, 10 July 1773, *Founders Online*, National Archives, https://founders.archives.gov.

7 • BOSTON'S CORDWAINERS GREET PRESIDENT WASHINGTON, 1789

1. Letter from George Washington to Henry Knox, 29 January 1789, *Founders Online*, National Archives, https://founders.archives.gov.

2. "George Washington," by Gilbert Stuart, oil on canvas, 1796, National Portrait Gallery, Smithsonian Institution, www.georgewashington.si.edu/portrait/dress.html.

3. There are numerous excellent accounts available online that discuss President Washington's visit to Boston, the procession, John Hancock's "power play," and so forth. See, for example, the websites *Boston 1775*, www.Boston1775.blogspot.com; Walking Boston: Walking Tours of Historic Boston, www.walkingboston.com; The American Revolution, www.theamericanrevolution.org.

4. "Procession, October 19, 1789, for the visit of President Washington," Bostonian Society, www.bostonhistory.org.

5. For an account of the Boston Tea Party by participant shoemaker Robert Twelves Hewes, see Young, *Shoemaker and the Tea Party*. For recent scholarship on the Boston Tea Party, see B. Carp, *Defiance of the Patriots*; Frank, *Objectifying China, Imagining America*, esp. chapter 5. For a list of Tea Party participants, their ages, and professions, see "Historic Accounts," Boston Tea Party Historical Society, www.boston-tea-party.org/accounts.html.

6. "Cordwainers Washington Procession Banner," catalog number 1910.0033, Bostonian Society, and the Worshipful Company of Cordwainers' coat of arms, with the motto "Corio et Arte [Leather and Art]," are both depicted in Kimberly Alexander, "Boston's Cordwainers Greet President Washington, 1789," 3 August 2013, Silk Damask, www.silkdamask.org/2013/08/. In addition to the Boston banner, a broadside in the Bostonian Society's collection, dated 19 October 1789, lists the requirements for the banners and the order of participants in the procession.

7. On the cordwainers' connection with St. Crispin, see "St. Crispin," Honorable Cordwainer's Company, www.thehcc.org/framelss.htm#crispin.

8. Hannah Loring's family-register sampler, 1812, is pictured in "Boston's Cordwainers Greet President Washington, 1789," 3 August 2013, Silk Damask, www.silkdamask.org/2013/08/.

9. The preservation of these examples of what were most likely intended to be short-lived pieces of ephemera is a credit to the families involved and to the Bostonian Society for maintaining them over the past century.

10. George Washington's diary, entry for 2 November 1789, *Founders Online*, National Archives, https://founders.archives.gov.

11. Royall Tyler, *The Contrast* (New York, 1787).

12. Crèvecoeur, *More Letters*, 29. Crèvecoeur also complained about the poor quality of postwar English goods: "Another [reason for American indebtedness] is that most of the articles they send us from England are extremely bad. What is intended for exportation is good enough when there are no rival merchants. Their linens and their duffle and their wool cards are much worse now than they were ten years ago."

13. Letter from Abigail Adams to John Adams, 16 July 1775, "Letters between John and Abigail," Massachusetts Historical Society, *Adams Family Papers: An Electronic Archive*, www.masshist.org/digitaladams/archive/browse/.

14. Letter to Thomas Jefferson from Abigail Adams, 12 August 1785, *Founders Online*, National Archives, https://founders.archives.gov.

15. Letter from Abigail Adams to John Adams, 1 May 1780, *Adams Family Papers: An Electronic Archive*, Massachusetts Historical Society, www.masshist.org/digitaladams/archive/browse/.

16. Ames, "Eulogy of Washington."

17. Letter from Abigail Adams to John Adams, 26 March 1794, *Adams Family Papers: An Electronic Archive*, Massachusetts Historical Society, www.masshist.org/digitaladams /archive/browse/.

18. Letter from Abigail Adams to Mary Smith Cranch, 21 March 1790, Adams Family Correspondence, vol. 9, *The Adams Papers: Digital Edition*, Massachusetts Historical Society, https://www.masshist.org/publications/apde2/browse-volumes/.

19. For additional information, see "Abigail Adams's Yellow Slippers," in First Ladies at the Smithsonian: First Ladies' Fashions, 5, National Museum of American History, http: //americanhistory.si.edu/first-ladies/first-ladies-fashions/.

CONCLUSION

1. Zerubbabel Porter account book, 1809–1833, Danvers, Massachusetts, MSS 1337.6, Phillips Library, Peabody Essex Museum.

2. Silk shoes, object number 1843.13.0a,b, Connecticut Historical Society.

3. While the assumption, based on family tradition, has been that the shoes were fabricated from an American flag or standard, it is not impossible that they were created from a captured British standard or banner. At present, the flag or banner has not been identified. Costume historian and shoemaker Nicole Rudolph is researching these shoes.

4. Blue-green silk shoes, accession number PC S 19a,b (238), Currier Museum of Art, Manchester, New Hampshire.

5. The handwritten label that accompanies the shoes reads: "Leonard Phillips April 1792–July 1832 Married Sally Head 1796–1881 Children John Henry 1820–1831 Sarah Almira 1823–1913 Sarah married Charles Henry Brown—lived at 111 Keeley Street. Their son John Henry—our grandfather—hence Leonard Phillips maker of the shoes—our great, great grandfather—Beatrice & Rosalie Keene, Kathleen K. Babb."

6. For more about the collection, see the Buttonwoods Museum, Haverhill, Massachusetts, www.haverhillhistory.org/collections.html.

7. Given the attention paid to the soles, one wonders about the religious background of the couple. Were the soles visible while kneeling for wedding rites or communion? It is not known whether the ornament included on the shoes was part of a European tradition that was familiar to the maker or his bride-to-be. There are examples—such as a pair of nineteenth-century French wedding clogs in the Musée des Arts Populaires in Laduz, France—that hold some similarity of purpose and motif and may be found in scattered worldwide collections. These items often escape notice by costume historians, as they are frequently found in ethnographical or anthropological collections.

Bibliography

BOOKS

Anderson, Jennifer L. *Mahogany: The Costs of Luxury in Early America*. Cambridge, MA: Harvard University Press, 2012.

Anishanslin, Zara. *Portrait of a Woman in Silk: Hidden Histories of the British Atlantic World*. New Haven, CT: Yale University Press, 2016.

Anonymous. *Shoepedia*. Osgood, IN: Amazon Drygoods, 1980.

Ashby, Ruth. *George & Martha Washington*. Milwaukee: World Almanac Library, 2005.

Baumgarten, Linda. *What Clothes Reveal: The Language of Clothing in Colonial and Federal America*. New Haven, CT: Yale University Press, 2012.

Blanco F., José, Mary D. Doering, Patricia Hunt-Hurst, and Heather Vaughan Lee. *Clothing and Fashion: American Fashion from Head to Toe*, 4 vols. Santa Barbara, CA: ABC-CLIO, 2016.

Bossan, Marie-Josèphe. *The Art of the Shoe*. New York: Parkstone, 2004.

Breen, T. H. *The Marketplace of Revolution: How Consumer Politics Shaped American Independence*. New York: Oxford University Press, 2005.

Breen, T. H. *Tobacco Culture: The Mentality of the Great Tidewater Planters on the Eve of Revolution*. Princeton, NJ: Princeton University Press, 1985.

Brook, Timothy. *Vermeer's Hat: The Seventeenth Century and the Dawn of the Global World*. London: Profile, 2009.

Brown, Jerald E. *The Years of the Life of Samuel Lane, 1718–1806: A New Hampshire Man and His World*. Edited by Donna-Belle Garvin. Hanover, NH: University Press of New England, 2000.

Campbell, Robert. *The London Tradesman*. 1747. Reprint Newton Abbot, Devon, UK: David & Charles, 1969.

Carp, Benjamin L. *Defiance of the Patriots: The Boston Tea Party and the Making of America*. New Haven, CT: Yale University Press, 2011.

Cleary, Patricia. *Elizabeth Murray: A Woman's Pursuit of Independence in Eighteenth-Century America*. Amherst: University of Massachusetts Press, 2000.

Committee of Finance, United States Senate. *Comparison of Customs Tariff Laws 1789 to 1909 Inclusive, and Intermediate Legislation Thereon*. Washington, DC: Government Printing Office, 1911.

Corrigan, Karina, Jan van Campen, and Femke Diercks, eds., with Janet C. Blyberg. *Asia in Amsterdam: The Culture of Luxury in the Golden Age*. Salem, MA: Peabody Essex Museum, 2015.

Crèvecoeur, J. Hector St. John de. *More Letters from the American Farmer: An Edition of the Essays in English Left Unpublished by Crèvecoeur*. Edited by Dennis D. Moore. Athens: University of Georgia Press, 1995.

Davis, Natalie Zemon. *The Return of Martin Guerre*. Cambridge, MA: Harvard University Press, 1983.

Dawley, Alan. *Class and Community: The Industrial Revolution in Lynn*. Cambridge, MA: Harvard University Press, 1976.

Deetz, James. *In Small Things Forgotten: An Archaeology of Early American Life*. New York: Anchor Books, 1977.

Diderot, Denis. *Encyclopédie, ou dictionnaire raisonné des sciences, des arts et des métiers*. 3 vols. Paris: Brisson, 1763.

Drinker, Elizabeth Sandwith. *The Diary of Elizabeth Drinker: The Life Cycle of an Eighteenth-Century Woman*. Edited by Elaine Forman Crane. Boston: Northeastern University Press, 1994.

DuPlessis, Robert S. *The Material Atlantic: Clothing, Commerce, and Colonization in the Atlantic World, 1650–1800*. Cambridge: Cambridge University Press, 2015.

Eaton, Arthur Wentworth Hamilton. *The Famous Mather Byles: The Noted Boston Tory Preacher, Poet, and Wit, 1707–1788*. Boston: W. A. Butterfield, 1914.

Fea, John. *The Way of Improvement Leads Home: Philip Vickers Fithian and the Rural Enlightenment in Early America*. Philadelphia: University of Pennsylvania Press, 2008.

Ferling, John. *John Adams: A Life*. New York: Oxford University Press, 2010.

Fields, Joseph E. *A Worthy Partner: The Papers of Martha Washington*. Westport, CT: Greenwood Press, 1994.

Foote, Henry Wilder. *Annals of King's Chapel from the Puritan Age of New England to the Present Day*, vol. 1. Boston: Little, Brown, 1882.

Fowler, William M. *The Baron of Beacon Hill: A Biography of John Hancock*. Boston: Houghton Mifflin, 1980.

Frank, Caroline. *Objectifying China, Imagining America: Chinese Commodities in Early America*. Chicago: University of Chicago Press, 2011.

Gallup-Diaz, Ignacio, Andrew Shankman, and David J. Silverman. *Anglicizing America: Empire, Revolution, Republic*. Philadelphia: University of Pennsylvania Press, 2015.

Gannon, Fred. *A Short History of American Shoemaking*. Salem, MA: Newcomb & Gauss, 1912.

Gerritsen, Anne, and Giorgio Riello. *The Global Lives of Things: The Material Culture of Connections in the Early Modern World*. New York: Routledge, 2015.

Ginzburg, Carlo, and John Tedeschi. *The Cheese and the Worms: The Cosmos of a Sixteenth-Century Miller*. Baltimore: Johns Hopkins University Press, 1992.

Goldthwaite, Charlotte. *Boardman Genealogy, 1525–1895*. Hartford, CT: William F. J. Boardman, 1895.

Golinski, Jan. *British Weather and the Climate of the Enlightenment*. Chicago: University of Chicago Press, 2007.

Goodwin, Lorinda B. R. *An Archaeology of Manners: The Polite World of the Merchant Elite of Colonial Massachusetts*. Boston: Springer, 1999.

Graddy, Lisa Kathleen, and Amy Pastan. *The Smithsonian First Ladies' Collection*. Washington, DC: Smithsonian Books, 2014.

Gray, Edward. *William Gray of Lynn Massachusetts and Some of His Descendants*. Salem, MA: Essex Institute, 1916.

Greenfield, Amy Butler. *A Perfect Red: Empire, Espionage, and the Quest for the Color of Desire*. New York: Harper Perennial, 2006.

Hartigan-O'Connor, Ellen. *The Ties That Buy: Women and Commerce in Revolutionary America*. Philadelphia: University of Philadelphia Press, 2009.

Haulman, Kate. *The Politics of Fashion in Eighteenth-Century America*. Durham: University of North Carolina Press, 2011.

Hill, Don Gleason, ed. *The Record of Births, Marriages and Deaths, and Intentions of Marriage, in the Town of Dedham, 1635–1845*, 2 vols. 1888. Reprint Boston: New England Historic Genealogical Society, 1996.

Hopkins, Alan, and Vanessa Hopkins. *Footwear: Shoes and Boots from the Hopkins Collection, c. 1730–1950*. London: School of Historical Dress, 2015.

Jabour, Anya. *Marriage in the Early Republic: Elizabeth and William Wirt and the Companionate Ideal*. Baltimore: Johns Hopkins University Press, 1998.

Jaffee, David. *A New Nation of Goods: The Material Culture of Early America*. Philadelphia: University of Pennsylvania Press, 2011.

Johnson, Barbara, and Natalie Rothstein. *A Lady of Fashion: Barbara Johnson's Album of Styles and Fabrics*. New York: W. W. Norton, 1987.

Johnston, Lucy, and Linda Woolley. *Shoes: A Brief History*. London: V&A, 2015.

Kamensky, Jane. *A Revolution in Color: The World of John Singleton Copley*. New York: W. W. Norton, 2016.

Kelly, Catherine E. *Republic of Taste: Art, Politics, and Everyday Life in Early America*. Philadelphia: University of Pennsylvania Press, 2016.

Kenslea, Timothy. *The Sedgwicks in Love: Courtship, Engagement, and Marriage in the Early Republic.* Boston: Northeastern University Press, 2006.

Kidwell, Claudia, and Margaret C. Christman. *Suiting Everyone: The Democratization of Clothing in America.* Washington, DC: Smithsonian Institution Press, 1974.

Knight, Sarah Kemble. *The Journal of Madame Knight.* Edited by Perry Miller and Thomas H. Johnson. New York: American Book, 1938.

Koda, Harold, and Andrew Bolton. *Dangerous Liaisons: Fashion and Furniture in the Eighteenth Century.* New York: Metropolitan Museum of Art, 2013.

Kuechler, Suzanna, and Daniel Miller, eds. *Clothing as Material Culture.* Oxford: Berg, 2005.

Lewis, Alonzo. *The History of Lynn.* Boston: J. H. Eastburn, 1829.

Lockridge, Kenneth A. *A New England Town: The First Hundred Years, Dedham, Massachusetts, 1636–1736.* New York: W. W. Norton, 1980.

Mackenzie, Althea. *Shoes and Slippers.* London: National Trust, 2004.

Mackie, Erin, ed. *The Commerce of Everyday Life: Selections from the* Tatler *and the* Spectator. New York: Bedford / St. Martin's, 1998.

Maier, Pauline. *The Old Revolutionaries: Political Lives in the Age of Samuel Adams.* New York: W. W. Norton, 1990.

Metzger, Barbara. *Wedded Bliss.* [San Francisco]: Untreed Reads, 2012.

Miller, Lesley Ellis. *Selling Silks: A Merchant's Sample Book, 1764.* London: V&A, 2014.

Miller, Marla. *The Needle's Eye: Women and Work in the Age of Revolution.* Amherst: University of Massachusetts Press, 2006.

Nylander, Jane. *Our Own Snug Fireside: Images of the New England Home, 1760–1860.* New York: Alfred A. Knopf, 1993.

Padilla, Carmella, and Barbara Anderson, eds. *A Red Like No Other: How Cochineal Colored the World.* New York: Skira/Rizzoli, 2015.

Peck, Amelia, and Amy Elizabeth Bogansky. *Interwoven Globe: The Worldwide Textile Trade, 1500–1800.* New York: Metropolitan Museum of Art, 2013.

Pinckney, Elise, ed. *The Letterbook of Eliza Lucas Pinckney, 1739–1762.* Charleston: University of South Carolina Press, 1997.

Raiselis, Tara Vose. *From the Elegant to the Everyday: 200 Years of Fashion in Northern New England.* Saco, ME: Saco Museum, 2014.

Rexford, Nancy. *Women's Shoes in America, 1795–1930.* Kent, OH: Kent State University Press, 2000.

Riberio, Aileen. *The Art of Dress: Fashion in England and France, 1750–1820.* New Haven, CT: Yale University Press, 1995.

Richter, Paula Bradstreet. *Painted with Thread: The Art of American Embroidery.* Salem, MA: Peabody Essex Museum, 2002.

Richter, Paula Bradstreet, Jeffrey A. Butterworth, Nancy Rexford, and Essex Institute. *Step Forward, Step Back: Three Centuries of American Footwear.* Essex Institute Historical Collections Series, vol. 127, no. 2. Salem, MA: Essex Institute, April 1991.

Riello, Giorgio. *A Foot in the Past: Consumers, Producers, and Footwear in the Long Eighteenth Century*. New York: Oxford University Press, 2006.

Roosevelt, Theodore. *The Winning of the West*, vol. 2, *From the Alleghenies to the Mississippi, 1777–1783*. New York: Charles Scribner, 1906.

Rudolph, Nicole. *18th Century Turn Shoe Construction*. San Francisco: Blurb, 2014.

Saguto, D. A. *M. de Garsault's 1767 Art of the Shoemaker: An Annotated Translation*. Lubbock: Texas Tech University Press, 2009.

Schoelwer, Susan P. *Connecticut Needlework: Women, Art, and Family, 1740–1840*. Hartford: Connecticut Historical Society, 2010.

Secretary of the Commonwealth. *Massachusetts Soldiers and Sailors of the Revolutionary War*, 17 vols. Boston: Wright & Potter, 1896–1908.

Shephard, Norma. *In Step with Fashion: 200 Years of Shoe Styles*. Atglen, PA: Schiffer, 2008.

Smith, John. *Generall Historie of Virginia*. London: printed by I. D. and I. H. for M. Sparkes, 1624.

Strype, John. *A Survey of the Cities of London and Westminster*. London: 1720.

Styles, John. *The Dress of the People: Everyday Fashion in Eighteenth-Century England*. New Haven, CT: Yale University Press, 2007.

Swann, June. *Shoes*. London: B. T. Batsford, 1983.

Sydnor, Charles S. *American Revolutionaries in the Making: Political Practices in Washington's Virginia*. New York: Free Press, 1952.

Tyler, Royall. *The Contrast*. New York, 1787.

Ulrich, Laurel Thatcher. *The Age of Homespun: Objects and Stories in the Creation of an American Myth*. New York: Vintage, 2002.

Ulrich, Laurel Thatcher. *A Midwife's Tale: The Life of Martha Ballard, Based on Her Diary, 1785–1812*. New York: Knopf, distributed by Random House, 1990.

Unger, Harlow G. *John Hancock: Merchant King and American Patriot*. New York: John Wiley & Sons, 2000.

Vickery, Amanda. *Behind Closed Doors: At Home in Georgian England*. New Haven, CT: Yale University Press, 2010.

Vickery, Amanda. *The Gentleman's Daughter: Women's Lives in Georgian England*. New Haven, CT: Yale University Press, 2003.

Von La Roche, Sophie. *Sophie in London, 1786: Being the Diary of Sophie v. la Roche*. London: Jonathan Cape, 1933.

Walford, Jonathan. *The Seductive Shoe: Four Centuries of Fashion Footwear*. New York: Stewart, Tabori & Chang, 2007.

Washington, George. *The Writings of George Washington*, vol. 11, *1785–1790*. Edited by Worthington Chauncey Ford. New York: G. P. Putnam's Sons, 1891.

Waters, Thomas Franklin. *Ipswich in the Massachusetts Bay Colony*, 2 vols. Ipswich, MA: Ipswich Historical Society, 1905–1917.

Willcocks, Clive. *Cordwainers: Shoemakers of the City of London*. London: Worth, 2009.

Wood, Gordon. *The Radicalism of the American Revolution.* New York: Vintage, 1993.

Wood, William. *New England's Prospect.* 1634. Reprint Boston: Prince Society, 1865.

Woodbury, Ellen C. D. Q. *Dorothy Quincy, Wife of John Hancock.* Washington, DC: Neale, 1905.

Young, Alfred F. *The Shoemaker and the Tea Party: Memory and the American Revolution.* Boston: Beacon Press, 2001.

THESES AND DISSERTATIONS

Farrell, William. "Silk and Globalisation in Eighteenth-Century London: Commodities, People and Connections, c.1720–1800." PhD diss., Birkbeck, University of London, 2014.

Hoffman, Susan A. "Consuming Women: Gender, Ideology, and the Consumer Revolution in Pennsylvania and New Jersey, 1740–1800." Master's thesis, Leigh University, 1999.

Murrin, John H. "Anglicizing an American Colony: The Transformation of Provincial Massachusetts." PhD diss., Yale University, 1966.

Reddick, Meaghan M. "An American Identity: Shoemaker's Labels in Colonial, Revolutionary and Federal America, 1760–1820." Master's thesis, George Mason University, 2014.

Walsh, Claire. "Shop Design and the Display of Goods." Master's thesis, Royal College of Art, 1993.

ARTICLES

Alexander, Kimberly, "Footwear, Men's, 1715–1785." Pp. 109–110 in *Clothing and Fashion,* vol. 1. Edited by Blanco F. et al.

Alexander, Kimberly, "Second Hand Clothing, 1715–1785." Pp. 248–249 in *Clothing and Fashion,* vol. 1. Edited by Blanco F. et al.

Ames, Fisher. "Eulogy of Washington," 8 February 1800. P. 523 in *Works of Fisher Ames,* vol. 1. Edited by W. B. Allen. Indianapolis: Liberty Fund, 1983.

Blewett, Mary H. "Work, Gender and the Artisan Tradition in New England Shoemaking, 1780–1960." *Journal of Social History* 17, no. 2 (Winter 1983): 221–248.

Breen, T. H. "Back to Sweat and Toil: Suggestions for the Study of Agricultural Work in Early America." *Pennsylvania History: A Journal of Mid-Atlantic Studies* 49, no. 4 (October 1982): 241–258.

Breen, T. H. "An Empire of Goods: The Anglicization of Colonial America, 1690–1776." In "Re-Viewing the Eighteenth Century," special issue, *Journal of British Studies* 25, no. 4 (October 1986): 467–499.

Carr, Jacqueline Barbara. "Marketing Gentility: Boston's Businesswomen, 1780–1830." *New England Quarterly* 82, no. 1 (March 2009): 25–55.

Carp, E. Wayne. "Early American Military History: A Review of Recent Work." In "Virginians at War, 1607–1865," special issue, *Virginia Magazine of History and Biography* 94, no. 3 (July 1986): 259–284.

Eacott, Jonathan P. "Making an Imperial Compromise: The Calico Acts, the Atlantic Colonies, and the Structure of the British Empire." *William and Mary Quarterly* 69, no. 4 (October 2012): 731–762.

Gould, Eliga H. "A Virtual Nation: Greater Britain and the Imperial Legacy of the American Revolution." *American Historical Review* 104, no. 2 (April 1999): 476–489.

Green, Stuart A. "Repeal of the Stamp Act: The Merchants' and Manufacturers' Testimonies." *Pennsylvania Magazine of History and Biography* 128, no. 2 (April 2004): 179–197.

Henretta, James A. "Families and Farms: Mentalité in Pre-Industrial America." *William and Mary Quarterly* 35, no. 1 (January 1978): 3–32.

Henretta, James A. "'Families and Farms: Mentalité in Pre-Industrial America'; Reply," *William and Mary Quarterly* 37, no. 4 (October 1980): 696–700.

Hill, William. "Colonial Tariffs." *Quarterly Journal of Economics* 7, no. 1 (October 1892): 78–100.

Lazaro, David E. "Fashion and Frugality: English Patterned Silks in Connecticut River Valley Women's Dress, 1660–1800." *Dress: The Journal of the Costume Society of America* 33, no. 1 (2006): 57–77.

Lemire, Beverly, "Consumerism in Preindustrial and Early Industrial England: The Trade in Secondhand Clothes." *Journal of British Studies* 27, no. 1 (January 1988): 1–24.

Lemon, James T. "Comment on James A. Henretta's 'Families and Farms: Mentalité in Pre-Industrial America.'" *William and Mary Quarterly* 37, no. 4 (October 1980): 688–696.

Marsh, Ben. "'One Man Might Bring it to Perfection': Rev. Ezra Stiles and the Quest for New England Silk." 2014. Kent Academic Repository, https://kar.kent.ac.uk/51923/1/BJM%20Stiles%20TEXT%20Article.pdf.

McNeil, Peter, and Giorgio Riello. "The Art and Science of Walking: Gender, Space, and the Fashionable Body in the Long Eighteenth Century." *Fashion Theory* 9, no. 2 (2005): 175–204.

Merrill, Michael. "Putting 'Capitalism' in Its Place: A Review of Recent Literature." *William and Mary Quarterly* 52, no. 2 (April 1995): 315–326.

Moran, Donald M. "George Washington and Martha Custis: Unpublished Letter on Their Courtship." *Liberty Tree Newsletter*, December 2001.

Murrin, John H. "The Legal Transformation: The Bench and Bar of Eighteenth-Century Massachusetts." Pp. 540–572 in *Colonial America: Essays in Politics and Social Development*, 3rd ed. Edited by Stanley N. Katz and John M. Murrin. New York: Alfred A. Knopf, 1983.

Myers, Kenneth John. "Reinventing the American Wing: The Detroit Institute of Arts." *American Art* 24, no. 2 (Summer 2010): 18–20.

Reddick, Meaghan M. "Footwear Industry in Early America, 1715–1785." Pp. 118–119 in *Clothing and Fashion*, vol. 1. Edited by Blanco F. et al.

Thompson, Todd. "'Invectives . . . Against the Americans': Benjamin Franklin's Satiric Nationalism in the Stamp Act Crisis." *Journal of the Midwest Modern Language Association* 40, no. 1 (Spring 2007): 25–36.

Timm, Chad William. "Hunting for the Market Economy: Using Historiographical Debates to Critique the Evolution of the Market Economy and Capitalism." *Radical Teacher* 79, miscellany (Fall 2007): 13–18.

Wheeler, Robert G. "The Albany of Magdalena Douw." *Winterthur Portfolio* 4 (1968), 63–74.

Index

Act Laying Duties on Imports, 207-8n6

Adams, Abigail, 3, 4, 5, 36, 72, 109, 123-24, 142, 147, 166–69, 193n33

Adams, John, 36, 72, 123-24, 132, 142, 147, 166-67, 168, 169, 192n26, 193n33

Adams, John, Sr., 36, 192n26, 193n33

Adams, Samuel, 46, 118, 128

Adams family, 136

advertisements, 10, 112; in American newspapers, 84; for calamancos, 113-14, 115; for calamancos vs. silk shoes, 110-11; and Didsbury, 152, 153; for John Hose, 135, 136; and labels, 88, 93; for shoes made in Lynn, 86; for John Welsh, 121

African Americans, 159. *See also* slaves

Albert, Prince, 71

Allen family, 38

Allestree, Richard, *The Ladies' Calling,* 47

American Exchange Tavern, Boston, 103

American Revolution, 9, 31, 83, 120, 131, 133, 159, 172, 179; eve of, 112; fashion after, 164, 166; and Hancock family, 67, 68; imports after, 166; imports during, 87; and S. Lane, 37; non-intercourse agreements before, 23-24; period after, 28, 38, 87, 130, 136; period before, 85, 93, 102, 104-5; and politics, 44

Ames, Fisher, 167–68

Andrews, Ebenezer, 161

anglicization, 11, 13, 82

apprentices, 27, 29, 32-33, 36, 192n26

Ashby, Ruth, 63

auctions, 84, 125

Ballard, Martha, 36

banner, cordwainers', 162

Bardwell, Elias, 116

Bardwell, Gideon Peck, 116

Bardwell, Robert, 116

Bardwell, Wealthy Peck, 116, 117

Barker, Ezra, 14

baroque style, 44

Bartlitt, William, 84

Bassett, Isaac, 120

Bata Shoe Museum, 76

Baumgarten, Linda, *What Clothes Reveal,* 123

Baylor, John, 151, 156

Behind Closed Doors (Vickery), 151

Bell, John, 132, 195n5

Bernard, Francis, 46
Bierton, Mr., 14
Billings, William, 120
Blanchard, Caleb, 136
Blythe, Benjamin, portrait of Abigail
    Adams, 4
Bosse, Abraham, "The Shoemaker," 82
Boston, MA, 10, 24, 32, 105; advertise-
    ments for calamancos in, 115; antitax
    sentiment in, 56; auction houses in, 84;
    and H. Caine, 85; Cornfields in, 101–2;
    dyers in, 72; guilds in, 106; non-
    importation picketing in, 112–13; and
    non-intercourse acts, 87; and Tailer
    family, 53; G. Washington's visit to,
    160–64, 171, 172
Boston Evening-Post, 137, 139
Boston Harbor, 87, 131, 143
Bostonian Society, 50, 67, 119, 160–61, 168
Boston Massacre, 46, 136
Boston Port Act, 142
Boston Post-Boy, 84
Boston Tea Party, 128, 142, 163, 164
Bott, James, 83
Bowditch, Hubbakuk, 83
Bowen, Emanuel, "A New Chart of the
    Vast Atlantic Ocean," 6–7
Bragg & Luckin, 119
Braintree, MA, 36
Brathwaite, Richard, *The English Gentle-
    woman,* 47
Breed, Ebenezer, 121
Breed, Hiram N., 37
Breen, T. H., 13, 50, 112, 133, 136
Brewster, William, 164, 165
Brewster's Tavern, 164
Bristol, England, 83, 115
British America, 39; cordwainers in, 24–38;
    cultural identity of, 84; economy of, 25;
    fashion in, 82; gentility of, 5; and im-
    ports from Britain, 22, 40, 81–108; travel
    in, 25; weddings in, 42
broadcloth, 113
brocade, 22–23, 44. *See also* silk brocade

buckle shoes; silk brocade shoes; wool
    shoes: brocade
Brockton, MA, 171
buckles, 43, 44, 45, 98, 105, 118, 131
buckle shoes, 108, 113; by W. Chamberlain,
    100; of M. D. Gansevoort, 73, 75; of
    C. D. Haven, 76; by J. Hose, 39, 40; by
    John Hose & Son, 11, 23, 24; of E. L.
    Pinckney, by T. Hose, 94–95, 97–98; red
    broadcloth, English, 75; red wool, from
    British America, 79; by Ridout & Davis,
    93, 94
Bull, Hannah, 56
Burford, William, 40
Burr, Aaron, 52
Bute, John Stuart, 132
Butler, Gilliam, 130
Buttonwoods Museum, Haverhill, MA,
    173
Byles, Mather, 53, 54, 55, 56, 77
Byles, Mather, Jr., 56
Byles, Rebecca Tailer, 44, 51, 53–56, 72,
    73, 77
Byles family, 197n26

Caine, Henrietta Maria East, 85
Caine, Hugh, 85
calamanco shoes, 10, 105, 108, 109–10;
    and A. Adams, 167; advertisements for,
    113–14, 115; brocaded, 110; colors of, 110,
    115; cost of, 114; damasked, 110; and
    J. and D. Hancock, 8, 118–21; high qual-
    ity, 76–77; imports of, 111, 112, 114, 115,
    125; in Irma Bowen Collection, 117–18,
    119; from Lynn, 130; from Norwich, 23;
    and patriotism, 107; and politics, 112;
    popularity of, 86; and rural southern
    planters, 86; silk shoes vs., 114; of M. F.
    Spofford, 77, 116; ubiquity of, 111; for
    M. Washington, 145; as wedding shoes,
    44, 46
Camper, Petrus, "On the Best Form of
    Shoe," 107
Capen, Hopestill, 102

Carp, Benjamin, 139

Cary & Company, 153, 210n17

Chamberlain, Charlotte, 57–58

Chamberlain, William, 17, 99, 100, 101, 190–91n5

Chamberlain & Son, 98

Chamberlain & Sons, 10, 99, 100, 101

Charleston, SC, 24, 32, 83

Charleston Gazette, 84

Charleston Museum, 131

children, 23, 36; clothing for, 65; shoes for, 29, 38, 39, 116, 117

chinoiserie, 22

Church, Benjamin, 119

class: lower, 13; middling, 13, 46, 84, 105, 111, 159; upper, 84; working, 111, 159

Clements, John, 40

cobblers, 11, 106

cochineal, 22, 71–72

Coercive Acts, 136

Collins, Steven, 121

Colonial Williamsburg, 62–63, 86, 91, 93, 94, 131

Colonial Williamsburg Foundation, 125

Committees of Safety, 87

Concord, battle of, 118

Congress, US, 130

Connecticut Historical Society, 52, 91, 94, 131, 142, 172

consumers, 9, 13, 39, 50, 84, 85, 113–14, 124–25, 139

Continental Army, 103, 121, 159

Continental Congress, 68, 109; Second, 8, 67, 118

Contrast, The (Tyler), 166

Copley, John Singleton, portrait of Dorothy Quincy Hancock, 67

"Cordonnier" (drawing), 17

cordwainers, American, 5, 11, 87; career of, 32–33; diversification and specialization by, 30; and farming, 30–31; and home-shop system, 171; journeymen, 32; as semi-itinerant artisans, 30; shops/sheds of (*see* ten-footers); skills of, 29;

traveling, 106; and G. Washington's visit to Boston, 161–63

cordwainers, British, 5, 161–63, 178–79; and American consumers, 9, 10; and fashion, 20; London businesses of, 17–24; materials used by, 20, 22; records of, 15; and theft and shoplifting, 20–21, 23

cordwainers, definition of, 189–90n3

Cranch, Mary Smith, 3, 168

crewel-on-linen dress fragment, 51–52

Crispin, Saint, 162

Cundry & Sons, 71

Currier Museum of Art, Manchester, NH, 172

Custis, Daniel Parke, 57, 210n17

Custis, Eleanor Parke, 144

Custis, George Washington Parke, 144

Custis, John Parke (Jacky), 116, 149, 150–51, 153

Custis, Martha Parke (Patsy), 115, 116, 153

Dandridge, Frances Jones, 115, 116

Danvers, MA, 27, 77, 116

DAR Museum, Washington, DC, 131

Dasson (Basson), Robert, 56, 197n27

Davis, James, 10, 15, 61–62, 89, 91, 93, 94, 95, 106, 107. *See also* Ridout & Davis

Deaggeor, John Adam, 123

Deall, Samuel, 135

Deerfield, MA, 38–39, 113

Dexter, Samuel, 75, 76

Diderot, Denis, *Encyclopédie,* 17

Didsbury, John, 210–11n17, 211n22; and black calamanco shoes, 115; business of, 151–53; and Washington family, 29, 61, 113, 115–16, 145, 146, 150, 153–57; and G. Washington, 61; and G. Washington's ideas of gentility, 147; G. Washington's shoe order to, 146; and M. Washington, 113

Dinah (slave), 41

Douw family, 73

Downman, Rawleigh, 123

Dunston, John, 152

Dwight, Timothy, 52
dyes, 22, 71–72, 95, 110, 160

Edwards, Hannah, 46, 50–53, 196n18
Edwards, Jonathan, 52; "Sinners in the
    Hands of an Angry God," 113
Edwards, Mary (Molly), 50, 52, 196n18
Edwards, Timothy, 51
Eliot, Jared, 23
Eliot, John, 56
elites, 9, 93, 129, 130, 197n26; and calamanco,
    111; and Camper, 107; and Didsbury, 61,
    145, 147, 154; and education, 51, 52; and
    Gray, 102; and Gresham, 61; and luxury
    British shoes, 26–27; and Lynn, 105; and
    naturalistic motifs, 44; and secondhand
    goods, 85; and Tailer family, 53, 54; and
    ties to England, 84, 179; and weddings, 46
Elwell, Henry, 25
embroidery, 29, 60, 63, 85, 91, 122, 124, 172,
    173, 190n2; and education, 46; and
    H. Edwards, 50–51, 52, 196n18; home,
    105; and H. Loring, 163, 164; and
    patriotism, 140; as piecework, 28; by
    E. B. Price, 47, 49, 50, 195n11; supplied
    by wearer, 10, 11, 44; and Tailer, 54,
    196n23; and M. Washington's wedding
    shoes, 58
Engelbrecht, Martin, *The Shoe Seller*, 2
English Gentlewoman, The (Brathwaite), 47
Enlightenment, 37
Erasmus, Desiderius, 47
Evening-Post, 136
Exeter, NH, 26, 35, 99
Exeter Packet, 83

Fairfax, George William, 147
Farley, Daniel, 64
Farley, Elizabeth Cogswell, 64
Farley, Mary Wise, 64–65
Farley, Nathaniel, 64
Farley, Nathaniel (son), 64
fashions, 3, 10, 83, 101, 118, 119, 130, 138,
    147; and A. Adams, 167, 169; and angli-
cization, 13, 82; Atlantic community of,
    5, 9; and R. T. Byles, 55–56; and
    H. Caine, 85; and calamanco, 110, 111,
    112; changes in, 22; and colonial con-
    nections with Britain, 84, 139; constant
    changes in, 87; and cordwainers, 20, 179;
    criticism of, 107; desire for latest, 39;
    and Hancock family, 68–69, 120; and
    J. Hancock, 173; and C. D. Haven, 76;
    and labels, 88; and patriotism, 140, 142;
    and E. B. Price, 47; and M. S. Rand,
    128; after Revolutionary War, 164, 166;
    and Ridout & Davis, 93; and slap-sole
    construction, 65; and taxes, 125; and
    G. Washington, 115, 148, 149–51, 153–54,
    159–60; and M. Washington, 57, 58, 63,
    115; and weddings, 43, 44
Ferling, John, 36
Fitch, Mrs. Horatio, 172
Flint, Elisha, 77
Flint, Mirriam Putnam, 77
floral patterns, 11, 44, 71, 91, 97, 101, 102,
    172, 201n13; of R. T. Byles's shoes, 55;
    and H. Edwards's wedding shoes, 52;
    and E. B. Price, 49; on D. T. Todd's
    wedding shoes, 66; and M. Washington's
    wedding shoes, 58
Foster, Samuel, 121
France, 87, 179, 208–9n17
Francis Lewis & Son, 136
Franklin, Benjamin, 8, 31, 107, 133, 134, 142,
    194n36; "The Way to Wealth," 37
Freemasons, 102, 103
French and Indian War, 46, 147–48
French heels, 11, 39, 55, 59, 73, 75, 76, 93,
    97, 113, 140

Gage, Thomas, 118, 124, 159
Gansevoort, Harman, 73, 75
Gansevoort, Magdalena Douw, 73–75;
    portrait of, 73, 74, 75
Gaspee Affair, 104
General Advertiser, 136
Generall Historie of Virginia (Smith), 25

gentility, 9, 10, 93, 101
George III (king), 132, 137, 179
Gerrish, John, 84
Gerrish, Sally Brewster, 8, 98, 164, 165, 178
Gill, Harold, 152
Gilman, Trueworthy, 101
gold damask, 59, 63
gold lace, 21, 22
gold thread, 52, 101, 102
Gonsolve, John, 104
Gray, William, 103
Gray, Winthrop, 31, 101–4, 105, 202n29
Great Britain: and American market, 9; calamancos from, 114, 115, 125; circumvented duties in, 125; colonial alternatives to goods from, 50, 51, 121–23; and export revenues, 22; fashion from, 58; imports from, 9; lace industry in, 71; manufactories in, 9, 67. *See also* imports
Green, Edward, 76
green color, 55, 71, 110, 196–97n25
Greenland, NH, 26
Gresham, John, 61, 119
guilds, 106

Hamilton, Alexander, 130
Hampton, NH, 25
Hancock, Dorothy Quincy, 67–71, 118–21; and calamancos, 109, 123; portraits of, 67; wedding shoes of, 47, 67–68, 69
Hancock, John, 24, 67, 68–71, 118–21, 166, 173; and calamancos, 109, 110; civility of, 206n39; crimson coat of, 46–47; servant of, 120; and silk and calamanco shoes, 8
Hancock, John George Washington, 68
Hancock, Lydia Henchman (aunt), 68, 118
Hancock, Lydia Henchman (daughter), 68
Hancock, Thomas, 50, 67
Hancock family, 68, 136, 168–69
Hartford, CT, 106
Haven, Catherine Dexter, 72, 75–77
Haven, Jason, 75–76
Haven, Moses, 75
Haverhill, MA, 171

Haverhill, NH, 105, 106, 116, 131
Heaton, John, portrait of Magdalena Douw Gansevoort, 73, 74, 75
heels, 87, 101, 172, 204n15; of W. P. Bardwell's shoes, 117; of R. T. Byles shoes, 55; and calamancos in Irma Bowen Collection, 118, 119; carved, 19, 28; criticism of, 107; French, 11, 39, 55, 59, 73, 75, 76, 93, 97, 113, 140; of M. R. Rogers's shoe, 106; updating of, 11; and G. Washington, 157; of M. Washington's wedding shoes, 58; wooden, 93, 94
Hewe family, 27
Hewes, Robert Twelves, 120, 164
Hill, Samuel, "View of the triumphal ARCH and COLONNADE," 161
Historical Society of Pennsylvania, Philadelphia, 85
Historic Deerfield, MA, 38–39, 67, 78, 113, 116, 131; Flynt Center of Early New England Life, 38–39
Historic New England, 101, 131
History of Lynn (Lewis), 123
Hogarth, William, *The Wedding of Stephen Beckingham and Mary Cox,* 42
Hollis Street Congregational Church, Boston, 56
Hoppe & Heath, 168–69
horsewhips, 29
Hose, Elizabeth Collver, 190–91n5
Hose, John, 10, 15, 17–24, 131, 179; advertisements for, 135, 136; American disdain for, 122, 133, 135; and W. Chamberlain, 99, 100; colonial contacts of, 94–95; and colonial elite, 130; contemporaries of, 91; daughter of, 40–41; death of, 89, 94, 141–42; labels of, 10, 22, 39, 88, 136; and S. Lane, 30, 35, 40, 83; last will of, 40–41; life of, 190–91n5; Milk St. property, home, and business of, 41; and morality, 137, 138; reputation of, 128; son of, 40, 41, 89; and Stamp Act, 107, 132, 133, 135, 141, 142; and support for colonial products, 140; testimony before Parliament, 8, 20, 133;

Hose, John (*continued*)
  wool buckle shoes by, 39, 40; workers
    employed by, 20, 83, 133. *See also* John
    Hose & Son
Hose, Thomas, 17, 19, 22, 41, 89, 91, 94–95,
    97–98, 99, 101, 131, 190–91n5
Hose, Thomas, Jr., 22
House, George, 114
Howe, William, 56
Hutchinson, Thomas, 46, 132

imports, 44, 47, 121–23; and anglicization,
    13, 81–82; of calamanco, 111, 112, 114, 115,
    125; colonial alternatives to, 50–51, 105;
    customs duty on, 130; and labels, 88–94;
    from London, 9–10, 55–56, 83–84, 88–89,
    91, 135–41; and morality, 112–13, 122,
    135–41, 166–67; and non-intercourse
    agreements, 87, 122, 127, 131, 133, 179;
    after Revolution, 166; and Revolution,
    87, 112; tracing of, 83–87; urban residen-
    tial areas with access to, 191n13. *See also*
    Great Britain; Stamp Act
Independent Chronicle, 84
indigo, 95, 98
Intolerable Acts, 142
Ipswich Museum, Ipswich, MA, 37, 64
Irma Bowen Collection, 117–18, 119
ironworkers, 105
Isles of Shoals, 26

Jackson's Oxford Journal, 85
Jacobean designs, 47
Jamestown, VA, 25
Jefferson, Thomas, 50, 166, 167, 169
Joanna (ship), 84
John Hose & Son, 40, 132; brocaded silk
    buckle shoes by, 11, 23, 24; labels of, 10,
    24, 88, 89, 113; and M. S. Rand's shoes,
    127–30. *See also* Hose, John; Hose,
    Thomas
Johnston, Lucy, 89
Jones, John, 31
Jones, Timothy, 34

Julius (slave), 150, 153

King's Chapel, Boston, 50
Kirkland, Philip, 25
Knox, Henry, 160

labels, 39, 88–91, 93, 131–32; of Chamber-
    lain & Sons, 10, 100; characteristics of,
    88, 89; of Davis, 107; and Didsbury, 61,
    145, 153; of Gonsolve, 104; of Winthrop
    Gray, 101, 102, 103; of Gresham, 61; of
    J. Hose, 10, 22, 39, 88, 136; of J. Hose &
    Son, 10, 24, 88, 89, 113; as pasted onto
    footbed, 56; of Ridout & Davis, 88, 177;
    tracing through, 10
lace industry, 71
Ladd, Phebe, 105
Ladd family, 105, 106–7
Ladies' Calling, The (Allestree), 47
Lady's New-Years Book, A (Savile), 47
Lafayette, Marquis de, 52
Lane, Ebenezer, 14, 35, 38, 39
Lane, Huldah, 38, 39
Lane, Jabez, 29, 41
Lane, Joshua (father of Samuel Lane), 35,
    38
Lane, Joshua (son of Samuel Lane), 26, 41
Lane, Rachel, 41
Lane, Samuel, 20, 25–37, 39, 83, 132, 136,
    179, 192n26, 194n36; almanac of, 14, 15,
    25; apprenticeship of, 32; barkhouse of,
    33, 35; as church deacon, 37; and En-
    lightenment, 37; and Exeter, 35; family
    of, 41; farming by, 30–31; in Hampton,
    34; and J. Hose, 40; and "Jacob Sheafe"
    invoice, 26; leather money case made
    by, 31; legal knowledge of, 31; marriage
    of, 33–34; and Newmarket, 35; and
    Portsmouth, NH, 33, 35; reading by,
    37; and shoes as payment for services,
    34–35; shop of, 35, 36; in Stratham, 16,
    34, 35, 41; and surveying, 31, 35; wife and
    daughters of, 35; wills of, 41; and winter
    weather, 35–36

Lane, Samuel, Jr., 41
Lane family, 25, 36, 39; barkhouse of, 41; and connections with neighbors, 36; daughters of, 41; and S. Lane's will, 41; in Stratham, 30
Lang, William, 84
Larkin, Samuel, 84
La Roche, Sophie von, 81, 83
Law, Elizabeth "Eliza" Parke Custis, 154, 155
Lawrence, Isaac, 72
leather, 10, 29, 44, 46, 79, 130; and colonial cordwainers, 28; from Cordoba, 22; dog, 29; and Lane, 34–35; of money case by S. Lane, 31; Morocco, 44; Spanish, 44; and M. Washington's wedding shoes, 58
leather shoes, 38, 39, 86, 105, 110; by Davis, 94, 95; by Hoppe & Heath, 168–69; worn by L. Phillips, 173–75
leatherworkers, 105
Lee, William, 144
Lewis, Alonzo, *History of Lynn*, 123
Lexington, battle of, 118
linen, 40, 46, 51, 52, 58, 75, 79, 95, 104, 117, 141, 151, 168, 172, 196n18
Little Ice Age, 35, 193n29
London, 127, 130; and American identity, 178–79; calamancos from, 115; cleaning in, 85–86; cordwainers in, 9, 10, 15, 17–24, 28, 104, 129; fashions from, 5, 43, 76, 83; import of shoes made in, 9–10, 83–84; labeled shoes from, 88–89, 91; and La Roche, 81, 83; morality of luxuries from, 112–13, 122, 135–41, 166; and E. L. Pinckney, 95, 97, 98; and purchase through factors or brokers, 86–87; recycling in, 85; and Revolution, 131; ships from, 83; shoe-cleaning in, 85–86; and Vincent, 72; Ward of the Cordwainer, 18, 83, 89; wedding shoes from, 55–56
Lord, Elizabeth, 23
Loring, Hannah, 163–64
Loring, Matthew, 163–64
Loring, Sarah, 163

lower classes, 13
Lye Shoe Shop, 28
Lye-Tapley Shoe Shop, 37, 194n35
Lynn, MA, 25, 83, 102, 103, 104, 105, 121, 130; advertisements for, 86; calamancos manufactured in, 112, 115, 116; factories in, 27; ladies' shoes in, 27; mechanization in, 171; numbers of shoes produced in, 122–23; and Revolution, 112–13; shoemakers in, 37; shoes made in, 86
Lynnfield, MA, 27
Lynn Museum, Lynn, MA, 37

MacMaster, John, 130
Maine Historical Society, 65, 66
Mandeville, Bernard, "The Vanity of Men and Women," 72
maps, 6–7, 16, 18, 19
Mason, Davis, 34–35
Mason, George, 147
Masonic compass symbol, 102, 103
Massachusetts Bay Colony, 25
Massachusetts Historical Society, 83, 118, 147
Mather, Catherine, 56
Mather, Cotton, 136; *Ornaments for the Daughters of Zion*, 47
Mather, Mary, 56
Matthews, John, 85
McEvers, James, 135
Mears, Catherina, 75
Mease & Miller, 136
mechanization, 171, 172
mending, 29
Merrill, Phinehas, "Plan of the Town of Stratham," 16
Meserve, George, 132
metallic braid, 75, 76, 79, 97
metallic lace, 58, 62, 75, 76, 111
metallic thread, 44, 52, 54, 101, 102, 129, 196n18
Metropolitan Museum of Art, 91; Brooklyn Museum Costume Collection, 122

middle class, 13
middling sorts, 13, 46, 84, 105, 111, 159
Miss Perkin's Academy, Boston, 163
Moll (slave), 153
Montgomery, John, 105
Moody, Eliezer, *The School of Good Manners,* 47
Morden College, Blackheath, 22, 131
Moroccan leather, 105, 114
Murrin, John H., 11–12

National Archives, US, 83
needlework, 46, 50, 51–52, 105, 164, 197n26
Newburyport, MA, 105
"New Chart of the Vast Atlantic Ocean, A" (map), 6–7
New England, 38, 86; agriculture in, 28; auction houses in, 84; cordwainers in, 11; home-shop system in, 28; mechanization in, 28, 171; payment for labor in, 130; piecework in, 28; shoe shops in, 27, 28
New England Prospect (Wood), 25
New Hampshire Historical Society, Concord, NH, 38
Newmarket, NH, 35
Newport, RI, 112, 122, 138
Newport Mercury, 122, 136, 138, 139
New York (city), 87
New-York Gazette, 135
New-York Mercury, 135, 139
non-intercourse agreements, 87, 122, 127, 131, 133, 179. *See also* imports
Norfolk, VA, 24
Norwich, England, 112, 115

Old State House, Boston, 46
"On the Best Form of Shoe" (Camper), 107
Ornaments for the Daughters of Zion (Mather), 47

Pamela (Richardson), 43
Parker, Nathaniel, 101

Parliament, UK, 8, 132–33, 135, 137, 141, 142, 179
pattens (clogs), 10, 89, 91, 92, 201n14
Peabody Essex Museum, Salem, MA, 37, 83, 91, 93
Peck, Gideon, 116
Peck, Irene, 116
Penhallow, Samuel, 130
Pennsylvania Gazette, 136
Pepys, Samuel, 45, 89, 91
Perkins, Moses, 27
Perrigo, Robert, 136
petticoats, 45, 47, 49, 59, 63, 65, 96, 110, 111, 140
Philadelphia, PA, 10, 24, 32, 84, 87, 105, 106, 114, 121
Phillips, Leonard, 173–75
Phillips, Sarah Head, 173
piecework, 23, 28, 105
Pinckney, Charles, 95, 98
Pinckney, Eliza Lucas, 61, 94–95, 96, 97–98
Pingree, Francis, 27
Plaistow, NH, 27, 116
"Plan of the Town of Stratham" (map), 16
Plymouth, England, 83
Pope, Eleazar, 27
Porter, Zerubbabel, 171–72
portraits: of A. Adams (Blythe), 4; of M. D. Gansevoort (Heaton), 73, 74, 75; of D. Q. Hancock (Copley), 67; of D. Q. Hancock (Savage), 67; of G. Washington (Stuart), 160; of M. C. Washington (Wollaston), 59
Portsmouth, NH, 24, 26, 30, 33, 35, 93, 121, 130; advertisements for calamancos in, 115; auction houses in, 84; population of, 207n56; and Stamp Act, 132
Portsmouth Historical Society, NH, 99, 164
Price, Elizabeth Bull, 42, 46–50, 52, 56, 72, 73, 75, 77, 195n11
Price, Roger, 42, 49, 50, 77
prices of boots and shoes, 126

Providence Gazette and Country Journal, 136

Puritans, 25

purple color, 58, 59, 60, 61, 62, 63, 197–98n35, 198n43

Putnam, Daniel, 32–33, 192n25

Putnam family, 27, 192n26

Quakers, 121

quilt, calamanco, 110

Quincy, Edmund, 67

rand, 79, 94, 101, 104, 202n28; of R. T. Byles's shoes, 55, 56; of C. D. Haven's shoes, 76; and M. Washington's shoes, 58, 59

Rand, Mary Simpkins, 88, 127–30, 131, 132, 136, 137, 141, 142, 143

Rand, Robert, 127–30, 132, 137

Rasielis family, 192n26

rebinding, 11, 29

recycling, 11

red color, 44, 52, 94, 114, 116, 124, 172, 174, 175, 198n43; dye for, 22, 71–72; and wedding shoes, 71–79

Reddick, Meaghan, 122

resoling, 11, 29

Revenue Act (Sugar Act), 137, 140

Revere, Paul, 103

Rhode Island, 136

Richardson, Samuel, *Pamela,* 43

Richmond, VA, 83

Ridout, Thomas, 10, 15, 62, 89, 91, 93, 95

Ridout, Thomas (son), 91

Ridout & Davis, 10, 18, 88, 89, 91, 93, 94, 177. *See also* Davis, James

Riello, Giorgio, 130

Robert Cary & Company, 57, 94, 115, 156, 157

rococo style, 44, 47, 52, 66, 93, 113, 157

Rogers, Daniel, 99, 106

Rogers, Martha (Patty), 98, 99, 101

Rogers, Mehitable Rindge, 93, 106

Rogers, William, 136

Roosevelt, Theodore, *The Winning of the West,* 109

Root family, 116

Rowley, MA, 27, 116

Rowson, Susanna, 47

Royal Navy, 142–43

Royal Ontario Museum, 91

"Rules of Civility and Decent Behavior" (G. Washington), 145, 147, 148, 149

rural areas, 86–87, 105

russell, 76, 105, 113, 114

Rutherford, Alexander, 121

Saguto, D. A., 18, 29, 59, 151–52

Salem, MA, 27, 83, 84, 93, 103, 115, 116

Salem Village, Danvers, MA, 77

samplers, 46

Sandwith, Elizabeth, 121

Sargent, Francis, 147

satin shoes, 86; by W. Chamberlain, 100; by Cundry & Sons, 71; from France, 208–9n17; for D. Hancock, 119; for J. Hancock, 119; and J. Hose, 135; and Lynn manufacturers, 123; of M. Washington, 59, 62–63, 94

Savage, Edward: portrait of D. Q. Hancock, 67; "Washington's Family," 144

Schoelwer, Susan, 52

School of Good Manners, The (Moody), 47

Scott, James, 71

Seven Years' War, 132, 137

Sewall, Reverend, 53

Sheafe, Jacob, 26

Sheafe family, 34

Sheels, Christopher, 144

Shelbourne, Frances, 57

Sherburne, Dorothy, 92

Sherman, Roger, 31

Shippen, Edward, 151, 152

"Shoemaker, The" (etching), 82

Shoe Seller, The (engraving), 2

Shoomakers of Boston, 25

silk, 44, 79, 196n18; brocaded, 128, 129; celadon green, 49; from China, 23, 44, 47; of H. Edwards's wedding shoes, 52; and embroidery from Rowson's Female Academy, 47; of C. D. Haven, 76; of E. B. Price's wedding dress, 47; in taffeta robe, 12; and Tailer's waistcoat, 54
silk brocade buckle shoes: by John Hose & Son, 11, 23, 24; by Ridout & Davis, 93, 94
silk brocade shoes, 10, 110; calamancos vs., 111; of M. W. Farley, 64; of S. B. Gerrish, 8, 164, 165; by Winthrop Gray, 101–2, 105; of M. S. Rand, 127–30, 141; by Ridout & Davis, 91, 93; of D. T. Todd, 66, 67; and M. Washington, 58, 59
silk damask, 10, 44, 93, 110, 111, 128, 129; of R. T. Byles's wedding dress, 53, 54; of R. T. Byles's wedding shoes, 55; by Gonsolve, 104; green, 73
silk dress, of M. Washington: lampas, 156; satin, 155
silk satin shoes, 60; by Chamberlain & Son, 98; by Chamberlain & Sons, 99; with metallic silver lace and leather, 61, 62; of M. R. Rogers, 107
silk shoes, 86, 105, 110–11, 114; blue-green and matching patten, 92; calamanco shoes vs., 114; by Davis, 106; European, 1760s, 60; fabricated from banner, flag, or standard, 170, 172; from France, 208–9n17; of M. D. Gansevoort, 75; and J. Hancock, 8; made from embroidered silk waistcoat, 172–73; by Ridout & Davis, 177; with silver lace and braid embellishments, 63
silk thread, 47, 129, 196n18; of H. Edwards's wedding shoes, 52; and E. B. Price's wedding dress, 49; and Tailer's waistcoat, 54
silver lace, 22, 62
silver thread, 101, 102
Simpkins, William, 127

"Sinners in the Hands of an Angry God" (Edwards), 113
slap-sole construction, 65
slaves, 27, 116, 171–72. See also African Americans
slippers, 10, 29, 95, 105, 130; of A. Adams, 5; French, 87; by J. Hose, 135; and G. Washington, 145, 149, 153
Smith, Charles, 147–48
Smith, Fanny, 104
Smith, James, 104
Smith, John, Generall Historie of Virginia, 25
Smith, Phebe Wardell, 104
Smith Shoe Shop, Reading, MA, 27
Society for the Promotion of Arts, Agriculture, and Economy, 140–41
"South part of New England, The" (map), 8
Spitalfields, London, 23, 53, 54, 73, 113
Spofford, Eleazer, 78
Spofford, Isaac, 78
Spofford, Mary Flint, 77–79, 116, 123
Stages of Man (watercolor), 45
Stamp Act, 22, 105, 107, 132–36, 141, 142, 195n5
Stamp Act Resolves, 132
Stebbins, Asa, 38
St. Jean de Crévecoeur, J. Hector, 166, 168
Stoughton family, 53
Stratham, NH, 15, 25, 26, 30, 116
Strawbery Banke Museum, Portsmouth, NH, 89, 91
Strype, John: A Survey of the Cities of London and Westminster, 18; "Walbrook Ward and Dowgate Ward," 18, 19
Stuart, Gilbert, portrait of G. Washington, 160
Survey of the Cities of London and Westminster, A (Strype), 18
Swan, Phineas, 105
Swann, June, 5

Tailer, William, 53, 54
tanning, 25, 29, 33, 35, 105, 107
tariffs, 93, 130

taxes, 8
Tea Act, 127
ten-footers, 27, 36–37, 81, 192n20,
    193–94nn34–35
theft, 20–21, 23, 53, 72
Thomas, Isaiah, 161
Thrifty, Sophia, 122, 137, 139, 140
Tilton, Catherine, 101
Todd, Deborah Thaxter, 65–67
Todd, James, 65, 66
Trail, Robert, 130
Trecothick, Allen, 133
Trecothick, Barlow, 22, 133
turquoiserie, 22
Tyler, Royall, *The Contrast*, 166

upper classes, 84

Vamp Building, 193–94n34
"Vanity of Men and Women, The"
    (Mandeville), 72
Verry, Joseph, 32–33, 192n25
Verry family, 192n26
Vibird, Isaac, 112–13
Vibird, Mary, 112–13
Vickery, Amanda, *Behind Closed Doors*, 151
Victoria, Queen, 71
"View of the triumphal ARCH and
    COLONNADE" (engraving), 161
Vincent, James, 72
Virginia, 25, 115; House of Burgesses, 132,
    147, 148
Virginia Gazette, 153

"Walbrook Ward and Dowgate Ward"
    (map), 18, 19
Waldron, Thomas, 20–21
Walker, Brett, 38
Walker, John, 151
wallets, 29, 99, 101, 202n26
Warner House, Portsmouth, NH, 91, 93
Washington, George, 29, 43, 50, 57–58, 63,
    113, 122–23, 144; and J. Adams, 166; and
    agents, 154; appearance of, 147, 148–49;

blue wool coat of, 154; Boston visit of,
    172; and S. Brewster, 165; brown broad-
    cloth suit of, 158; and calamancos, 109,
    115–16; and Cary & Company, 210n17;
    and Continental Army, 121; and Dids-
    bury, 145, 146, 150, 153–57, 210–11n17,
    211n22; and French and Indian War,
    147–48; and Gerrish, 8; inauguration of,
    160; and Knox, 160; as leader in Fairfax
    County, 147–48; "Rules of Civility and
    Decent Behavior," 145, 147, 148, 149; and
    Stamp Act, 132; Stuart portrait of, 160;
    and tariff laws, 130; traveling in 1789,
    160, 164; visiting Boston, 159, 160–64,
    171
Washington, George Steptoe, 149
Washington, Martha Dandridge Custis,
    43, 57–63, 86, 94, 95, 113, 144, 149, 154;
    brown silk dress of, 155; and calamancos,
    109, 110, 115–16, 123, 145; and Didsbury,
    145, 146, 154–55; and Gresham, 119; por-
    trait by Wollaston, 59; wedding clothing
    of, 197–98n35; wedding dress of, 59, 63;
    wedding shoes of, 58, 59; yellow-gold silk
    dress of, 156
Washington, Richard, 155
"Washington's Family" (painting), 144
"Way to Wealth, The" (Franklin), 37
wedding dresses, 43; of R. T. Byles, 53, 54,
    73; colors for, 71; of M. D. Gansevoort,
    73, 75; of D. Q. Hancock, 67; of E. B.
    Price, 46–50; of M. Washington, 59, 63
*Wedding of Stephen Beckingham and Mary
    Cox, The* (painting), 42
weddings, 42, 43–44, 71
wedding shoes, 43–79; of R. T. Byles,
    53, 55–56; colors for, 71; by Davis, 95;
    of H. Edwards, 50–53; of M. W. Farley,
    64–65; of M. D. Gansevoort, 73, 75;
    of D. Q. Hancock, 67–68, 69; of C. D.
    Haven, 76; by T. Hose, 94–95;
    London-made, 55–56; of L. Phillips,
    173–75; of E. L. Pinckney, 94–95, 97–98;
    preservation of, 46; of E. B. Price, 50;

wedding shoes (*continued*)
of Queen Victoria, 71; of M. S. Rand,
127–30, 131, 132, 141, 142; red, 71–79; of
M. R. Rogers, 106; of P. Smith, 104; of
M. F. Spofford, 77, 116; of D. T. Todd,
65–67; of M. Washington, 57–63; of P. P.
Winslow, 195n6
Welch, Joseph, 27, 29, 31, 116, 192nn19–20
Welch, Rob, 86, 152
Welsh, John, 121
Wentworth, John, 125
West Indies, 22
Wetmore, Seth, 50, 53
Wetmore family, 52
Wetmore house, 52–53
What Clothes Reveal (Baumgarten), 123
Whately, MA, 116
white work, 46
Williams, Anna, 38
Williams, Ebenezer, 38
Williams, Sarah, 113
Williams, Thomas, 121
Williamsburg, VA, 24, 87
Willing, Nancy, 85–86
Willing, Thomas, 85
Willing family papers, 85–86
Wilson, George, 86
Winning of the West, The (Roosevelt),
109
Winslow, Josiah, 195n6

Winslow, Penelope Pelham, 195n6
Wollaston, John, portrait of M. C. Washington, 59
women, 61, 159; and A. Adams, 169;
and calamancos, 109, 113, 114, 115, 118,
121, 123; in clerical families, 52; and
cordwainers, 11; education of, 46, 51, 52;
and high heels, 107; and Hose family,
127, 130, 135, 136; and Ladd family, 105;
lives and stories of, 9, 10; and needlework, 197n26; and patriotism, 139–41;
and piecework, 23; and Revolution, 87,
131; and Ridout & Davis, 91; and rococo
style, 157; and slap-sole construction,
65; textiles produced by, 36; and
G. Washington, 164
Wood, William: *New England Prospect*, 25;
"The South part of New England," 8
wool, 79, 86, 108, 109–10
Woolley, Anne, 40–41
Woolley, Linda, 89
wool shoes, 111; with bargello, or flame
stitch, 122; brocade, 39, 113; green and
teal, 125. *See also* calamanco shoes
wool shoes, buckle, 108; by John Hose,
39, 40; red, 79; red broadcloth, English,
75
working class, 111, 159
Worshipful Company of Cordwainers, 15,
18, 19, 21, 22, 91, 161–63